CU00944201

Breaking Into UK Film & TV Drama

A comprehensive guide to finding work in UK Film and TV Drama for new entrants and graduates.

By Matt Gallagher

Gravity to *Game of Thrones, This is England* to *Downton Abbey, Sherlock* to *Bond*. You will find this book packed with authoritative insider knowledge from some of the very best in the business.

Copyright © 2016 by Matt Gallagher

The moral right of the author of this book has been asserted

This book contains information on

- **How to get your first job in film and TV drama**
- **What it means to be a runner**
- **How prep, production and post really work**
- **The UK job market and production companies**
- **How to write a brilliant CV and cover letter**
- **Networking, finding jobs and building a career**

Plus!

- **10+ industry interviews, including Oscar- and BAFTA-winning crew**
- **50 'pearls of wisdom' from the best in the business**
- **100+ job titles and departments explained**
- **200+ industry terms explained in the glossary**
- **250+ useful links and leads**

Contents

Introduction

'How do I get a job in film and TV drama?'

It's the most common question that film and TV professionals are asked, and one of the hardest to answer. There is not one set way to get your foot in the door and there are tens of thousands of people trying to do exactly the same thing: find an opening in a relatively small industry amongst a lot of competition, nepotism, geographical isolation and lack of appropriate training. Just where do you start?

Indeed, there is a lot of concern within the film and TV industry that we will face a significant skills' gap in the next few years. In a speech to the CBI in 2014, Ivan Dunleavy, Chief Executive of Pinewood Studios Group, said:

'The UK film industry is a thriving part of a thriving sector, delivering jobs, exports, a platform to promote Britain abroad - and a large flow of inward investment and revenue to the Exchequer... We mustn't let this success be put at risk by failing to look ahead and seeing the dangers on the horizon from a skills shortage or in missed opportunities for our exports.'

Back in 2010, a government select committee spoke to a number of industry professionals about their concerns, including inadequate training. The resulting report, entitled *The British Film and Television Industries – Decline or Opportunity*, stated that 'even graduates with a vocational element in their media studies degree, still require another one or two years of training once they enter the industry'. The report quotes Sophie Turner Laing of BskyB lamenting the fact that students 'are not particularly brilliantly taught and then we have to retrain them as soon as they come out'.

The problem has also been highlighted elsewhere. Speaking to *Screen International*'s World of Locations: United Kingdom in May 2015, Jerry Ketcham, senior vice president of physical production for Disney – a company that has brought over £1bn of film production to the UK – suggested that it would be 'helpful' to have 'more crew trained'. The UK Commission for Employment and Skills (UKCES) stated in their June 2015 report *Sector insights: skills and performance challenges in the digital and creative sector*, that 'Graduate recruitment is an important source of workers for the sector, but there are concerns that many graduates leave university without up-to-date technical skills, or the softer skills required to be effective in the workplace'.

While the industry does need more fresh talent to service the increasing volume of production in the UK, it also has a desire to keep standards as high as possible at every level and on every production. Crew in the UK are considered to be among the very best in the world; a hard-earned reputation it does not want to lose.

This book will guide you through this demanding industry and help you kick-start your career in film and TV drama. It will give you an honest insight into the professional side of the business, including the realities of the production process, how to craft a killer CV and the importance of set etiquette, so you can significantly increase your chances of finding work and building a successful career.

As the author of this extensive and useable guide to the industry, I bring over 15 years of experience to its pages. I've worked in various production roles, from runner and researcher to playback operator and production manager; across myriad platforms including commercials, music videos, party political broadcasts, TV comedy and drama and, of course, feature films, with budgets ranging from micro to blockbuster.

Five years ago, I established a website called *thecallsheet.co.uk*, a professional network of film and TV crew with several thousand members, including Oscar- and BAFTA-winning talent. Through the website, I've helped hundreds of film and TV drama productions find crew, for companies including Universal, Working Title, Disney, BBC, ITV, Channel 4, Lionsgate, Sony Pictures, Sky Atlantic, Twentieth Century Fox, the Weinstein Company and more. I've also read thousands of CVs and job applications, and helped many talented young people get their first job in the business.

Along the way, I've met a lot of people and learned a lot of things, and this book draws on that first-hand experience and knowledge. It also features the wisdom of over 50 friends, colleagues and industry leaders who have between them worked on most of the major feature films and TV dramas made in the UK over recent years, from *Gravity* to *Game of Thrones*, *This is England* to *Downton Abbey*, *Sherlock* to *Bond*. Their exclusive input is forged from years of hard work covering all sectors of the industry and, as professional advice goes, it is pure gold.

We all, without exception, stress the importance of understanding the industry in order to progress. Our aim is to encourage you to see the wider perspective of the sector, which will, hopefully, inform your approach to getting into the business. So before we even think about constructing CVs and applying for jobs, we will look at the industry as a whole and the landscape of the job market.

One of the complaints that I have heard from many department heads is the lack of understanding that newcomers have about the business, and the lack of desire to learn more about it, so this basic industry knowledge will give you a genuine advantage in your career. You will probably be entering the industry as a runner or trainee, and if you are passive or disinterested you will find it hard to progress. It's great if you can talk about character arcs, dialogue or even the use of a Dutch tilt, but that will not be much use when you need to find a unit base, lock-off a location or distribute radios.

A passion for movies and working on a job are two very different things. This book will not describe the difference between a three-act structure and a five-act structure, explain how to get your short film into festivals or shoot like Roger Deakins. It will however guide you through the inner workings of the industry, including its history and landscape, the job market, the production process, the paperwork involved and an introduction to the hundreds of different jobs and all the departments that are involved in making a film.

In terms of actually finding work, it will also help you craft a first-class CV, find and apply for jobs and give you the skills to network effectively. It will also give you the skills you need to keep your foot in the door, once you've got it there, from set etiquette and social media to the practicalities of bookings, tax and insurance, and changing career paths. There's also a wealth of additional resources, from magazines and books to courses and websites, which will help you find a place to start putting all of this valuable advice into practice.

I want this book to educate, inform and inspire you to build a career in film and TV drama, but it pulls no punches about how hard that journey will be. Do not expect overnight success or singular break-through, rather a series of little moments that will build a sustainable career. The information, advice and experience are all in these pages; what you do with it is up to you.

Matt Gallagher, London, July 2016.

Note: I wrote this book during a peak time for the UK creative industries. On the eve of publication, however, Britain voted to leave the European Union. As many British independent feature films receive funding, both directly and indirectly, from the EU's Media Program / Creative Europe, and as the EU also provides funds for training freelancers and sets laws around working time regulations and freedom of movement for workers, this decision will undoubtedly have an impact. As the time of writing it is impossible to know what this will be, so be sure to keep an eye on developments as they unfold.

CHAPTER 1

About The Industry

A Brief History of British Production

Film and TV drama production in the UK is currently enjoying its busiest period since World War II. Many big Hollywood blockbusters, including the new *Star Wars* sequels and *The Avengers,* are being filmed in studios like Pinewood and Shepperton, and the rise of high quality TV drama has pumped millions of pounds into the economy and created thousands of jobs. Not only are there more people employed, but there are more training opportunities available, thus feeding the pipeline of crew needed to make the shows.

It's not just film and TV drama production that is growing but, as the number of TV channels increases, so ever more commercials are being made to fill the advertising space. Big blue-chip companies have deep pockets for making glossy internal corporate communication, and advertising agencies are spending more on branded content following the rise of digital advertising. The industry is booming, and there are more jobs than ever before.

If the UK film and TV drama sector is almost at peak employment, then why is it still so difficult to get your first job? The key to answering that question is to look at the history of the business to reveal the reasons why it can be so difficult to get your foot in the door.

The UK film industry has survived several ups and downs since the Lumiere brothers screened their first film in 1896, of a train pulling into a station, at what is now Regent Street cinema. According to BFI's Screenonline guide to Britain's film and TV history, by 1909 over 650 films were being made in the UK. US cinema pioneers also invested heavily, and saw the potential for exporting to European markets. Of course, in the early 20th Century films were silent and of variable quality, but the appetite of audiences was evident from the start.

While the BBC began its first radio broadcast service in 1922, it wasn't until 1929 that sound and vision were merged for the first British 'talkie' film, Alfred Hitchcock's *Blackmail*. Technical innovations in sound and colour were pushing the industry forward; large-scale investments poured into the nascent world of film production, and distribution companies began to capitalise on the audiences' demands. American distributors had a bigger domestic market and vertically integrated companies, when many of the European content producers went bust and American films soon dominated the European box office.

The Government recognised this problem of getting UK products on screens and in 1927 the Cinematograph Films Act was passed, which legislated that a certain quota of films – initially 7.5%, rising to 20% in 1935 — screened by British exhibitors must have been domestically produced. The resulting movies were nicknamed the 'Quota Quickies' because they were hastily put together to meet the quota. While often of questionable quality, the Quota Quickies did give directors like Michael Powell and David Lean a chance to cut their teeth and, despite many companies going bankrupt from over-expansion, an infrastructure started to emerge.

In 1912 Dr Ralph Jupp bought an old ice rink in South West London and built Twickenham Studios in order to start making films to satisfy increasing audience demand. In the early 1930s, businessman Norman Loudon purchased an estate in South West London on which he built Shepperton Studios, and on a greenbelt plot on the western edge of London, Polish-born director Alexander Korda founded Denham Studios, which opened its doors in 1936.

Having bought Heatherden Hall Estate in Buckinghamshire in 1934, construction entrepreneur Charles Boot joined forces with flour mill industrialist J. Arthur Rank to turn the estate into a working film studio. A devout Methodist, Rank began making religious films, which he distributed to UK churches, so developing a keen understanding of the power of film and audience appetite for it. Heatherden Hall was soon renamed Pinewood Studios – so named to deliberately emulate Hollywood – and has been home to the production of many British films, right up to the present day.

In 1937 J. Arthur Rank set up the Rank Organisation, which brought together a number of industry businesses including Pinewood and the previously acquired Denham Studios. The following year he bought the Odeon cinema chains, so eliminating the costly middlemen of distribution and taking films produced at Pinewood Studios straight to market. Rank also bought Elstree and Ealing Studios as well as Deluxe Post Production, and created Rank Advertising. Eventually he owned the entire pipeline, from concept to delivery; a concept known as vertical integration.

During the Second World War, Pinewood and Shepperton were requisitioned by the armed forces, who also established the RAF Film Unit. The Unit included the famed cinematographer Jack Cardiff and a young Sir Richard Attenborough, who would photograph German military targets from the sky. Many of the unusual terms you might hear in the film industry, like 'recce' and 'movement order' are said to have originated from the armed forces, as the early production managers were former military personnel skilled in logistics and organising troops of people.

While the film industry was being established, John Logie Baird had invented an early form of television, which he first demonstrated in 1926. In November 1936, the BBC began broadcasting television as well as radio and, over the next 16 years, introduced a news service and live outside broadcasts for events like the 1948 London Olympics. It wasn't until the Queen's televised Coronation in 1953, however, that sales of TV sets rocketed, and in 1954 the Conservative Government's Television Act established a new commercial TV network. Made up of several companies, this network would broadcast regionally with local content, but also share some programming. This also opened up the airwaves to advertising, and on September 22, 1955, the first ever advert – for toothpaste – was broadcast on UK TV.

With increasing numbers of TV sets on the market and a large audience to satisfy, the BBC began work on building Television Centre in White City, London, less than 16 miles from Pinewood Studios. When TVC was officially opened on June 29, 1960, it meant that a large talent-pool of film and TV crew now lived and worked within a 20-mile radius encompassing TV Centre, Pinewood, Shepperton, Twickenham Studios, Ealing Studios, Teddington Studios, Broadcasting House in Central London, Elstree Studios, Denham Studios, Heathrow and Soho, where most of the UK film production and post-production companies are based. This geographical concentration of talent and facilities formed the close-knit roots of the film and TV industries.

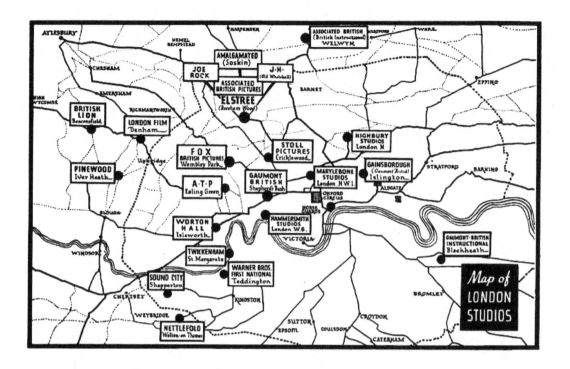

©THE MOTION PICTURE ALMANAC, Quigley Publishing Company, a division of QP Media, Inc.

However, the increasing popularity of TV and radio resulted in a dramatic decrease in cinema attendance. In response, the Eady Levy, which had been initially established in 1950, was made statutory in 1957, taxing box office receipts so that half the cost went to the exhibitors, and half back to the film-makers. In the 1960s, tax incentives encouraged US producers and directors like Stanley Kubrick to set up base in London and, spearheaded by James Bond and the Beatles, British culture was in global demand.

Another important TV landmark came in 1966 with the BBC broadcast of *Cathy Come Home,* directed by Ken Loach. Part of the Wednesday Play series, it broke the mould with its documentary-style camerawork and fearless examination of social issues such as homelessness, poverty and parental custody. Audiences had never seen anything remotely like it; BBC switchboards were jammed and the programme was discussed in Parliament. In that same year, BBC Two, which was launched in 1964, began broadcasting in colour in 1967.

The 1970s brought new challenges to the British film industry: US money dried up after Hollywood revised its own tax incentive to wrestle production back to California. (Like most industries, British film does rely heavily on incoming investment, predominantly from US studios, so this boom-and-bust financial cycle will inevitably happen again.)

While British screenwriter Colin Welland demonstrated admirable optimism when accepting his Academy Award for *Chariots of Fire* in 1982 – one of four bestowed on the film – exclaiming: 'The British are coming!', UK cinema audiences continued to decline, reaching an all-time low in 1984. And although the first *Star Wars* trilogy was largely filmed in the UK, the early 1980s saw a continued decrease in domestic British film production and employment. Margaret Thatcher's Government removed the Eady Levy, the Americans were leaving and Rank was in tatters after a number of flops. When Rank stopped funding features, and was later sold off in chunks, the UK lost its only domestic, vertically integrated company. The Cannon Group and Polygram both attempted to recreate Rank's success in the 1980s and 90s, but the former was sold to Pathé and the latter to Seagram (who also owned Universal Pictures at that time). Home video further battered the box office, with people waiting to see movies on VHS or Betamax, rather than go to the cinema.

The same year that *Chariots of Fire* swept the board at the Oscars, Channel 4 was launched. Initially backed by advertising money from ITV, it had a specific government remit to source much of its programming externally, effectively marking the start of the UK independent-television sector. Channel 4 needed programmes, and ex-BBC and ITV producers left their broadcasters to set up their own independent production companies. When Channel 4 began, it also launched Film Four (now known as Film4) which backed several low-budget British movies like Stephen Frears' *My Beautiful Laundrette*, starring Daniel Day Lewis, which went on to worldwide acclaim. This graph from the BFI displays just how popular the cinema was at its peak during the Second World War and the decline ever since. Today the UK box office averages around 160 million admissions a year.

Figure 1.2 Annual UK cinema admissions, 1935-2013

Admissions (million)

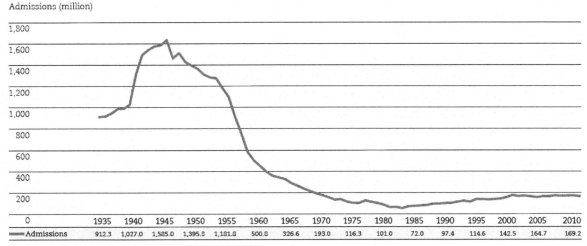

	1935	1940	1945	1950	1955	1960	1965	1970	1975	1980	1985	1990	1995	2000	2005	2010
Admissions	912.3	1,027.0	1,585.0	1,395.8	1,181.8	500.8	326.6	193.0	116.3	101.0	72.0	97.4	114.6	142.5	164.7	169.2

Source: BFI, CAA, Rentrak

Today people consume media, entertainment and all manner of content on their phones, laptops, tablets and home cinema systems, as well as at their local cinema and, of course, on their TV. It's therefore difficult to imagine what it was like to have only four TV channels – that all stopped broadcasting at midnight, with no catch-up, online, or on demand – and only a video shop or the cinema to get your fix. With far fewer outlets, there was less demand for programmes, which meant fewer people making them, meaning that there was only a need for a certain number of jobs.

This all began to change in the late 1980s when News Corporation boss Rupert Murdoch 'bet the house' on the success of Sky TV. The Australian tycoon was very keen to enter the world of TV in the UK, and form a powerful media triumvirate between his high-minded newspaper (*The Times*) and tabloid (*The Sun*), so invested heavily in new satellite technology and doubled the number of channels available in the UK to eight!

In the early days, Sky used movies to entice subscribers; it wasn't until Sky merged with BSB and set up the Premier League football deal in 1992 that advertisers began to show any real interest in the company. In 1989 the company was losing millions of pounds per week; today Sky has over 12 million customers in the UK and Ireland, employ over 22,000 people and make well over a billion pound in profit each year. Other media organisations are also thriving: the BBC employs around 17,000 people, ITV around 6,200 and Endemol Shine, the largest independent production company, employs around 5000 people through its subsidiary companies. And not forgetting the huge volume of freelancers they all engage.

Anyone entering the film or TV industries should understand that employment opportunities come in cycles, and job creation is inextricably linked to government legislation and market appetite. At the moment we are almost at peak employment, thanks to our generous tax credit system (which we will look at later), but nothing lasts forever. The job market is over-saturated at entry level, and almost at capacity everywhere else.

Of course creative talent will always be vital to the success of the industry. In employment terms, UK film success is directly influenced by our ability to attract producers to these shores, as well as make great domestic films and TV drama that can be sold and seen around the world. It's not about one or two films breaking box office records, although that helps, it's about building a wide-reaching, diverse and sustainable industry that can consistently compete on a global level. The Hollywood money being spent in the UK improves the overall infrastructure for domestic producers, but it comes at a price. Hollywood films have the marketing and distribution muscle to marginalise UK independent feature films and hoover up the best crew.

Despite that, UK production spend is increasing overall. According to their annual report, the BBC spent £2.4bn on TV content in 2014/2015. While figures on individual production spend are not published, outgoing BBC Head of Drama, Ben Stephenson told *The Hollywood Reporter* in February 2013 that 'the BBC makes 450 hours of drama a year on an annual budget of around £250m.' BBC Worldwide also sells the broadcaster's programmes and formats around the globe. According to the BBC website, BBCWW turnover was over £1bn for the year 2014/15 and returned £226.5m the corporation. In his MacTaggart lecture at the 2015 Edinburgh Television Festival, Armando Ianucci argued that the BBC should be more aggressive in selling content to international markets.

According to their annual reports, ITV spent just over £1bn on all of their content in 2015 and Channel 4 invested a record £629m (although only £455m of that was spent on original production). Sky has a total content budget of around £2.5bn a year, mainly spent on sporting and movie rights; around £600m of that is spent on original British drama, comedy and entertainment content. And while billions of pounds are invested in UK production by its own broadcasters, the tax credit initiative has also brought high-spending US companies, including Disney, Starz, Netflix, NBC, HBO, Amazon and AMC to produce on these shores.

On the big screen, British qualifying films made a combined $9.4bn at the international box office in 2015, and the previous year saw a record breaking £1.497bn spent on film production. Across both the TV and film industries, incoming and domestic production spend has doubled in the last eight years according to the BFI Statistical Yearbook.

All this additional investment has resulted in a buoyant industry and job market, the size, shape and history of which we are now going to explore...

Different Types Of UK Production

We've established that UK film and TV production is growing, and it's an industry that encompasses many different fields. Once an individual gets fully established in one of those fields, he or she may find it difficult to move between them. People often enter the industry with the ambition of becoming a director or cinematographer but, once they start feeling their way in the industry, their head is turned by another type of role that they never even considered or knew about. Or the available work takes them on a different route than originally planned. It's only once you start to explore the industry that you can make an informed and conscious decision about the direction you want to take.

In the early days of a career, however, it's good to get whatever experience you can and pay the bills whatever the genre. So let's examine the different types of UK production, the job opportunities that may be available and where they are. We'll also look at the overall job market and how it breaks down depending on your background and location; information that should prepare you to look for those first opportunities.

TV Drama

We'll start by looking at TV drama and the BBC, the cornerstone of the domestic UK television industry and our cultural flag bearer around the world.

Overall, the BBC produces around 450 hours of drama every year on a budget of around £250m, rising to around £280m now that £30m of BBC3's funds are transferred to drama after it is reduced in scale and sent online. There are different categories of drama within the BBC, and a variety of budget levels.

The BBC keeps the budget details of individual programmes under wraps, but examples include *Doctors* (category one) and *Doctor Who* (category seven). There are more hours produced at the lower end than there are in the expensive category seven, which are usually prime time shows like *Sherlock*. Productions within all categories require runners, but the lower budget productions of category one are more likely to employ brand new runners with less experience. Regardless of the category, the person booking you for the job will probably be a freelancer, more likely with the higher budget productions.

Category (BBC Drama)	Cost (per hour)
Daytime and Low Cost Drama	
Drama 1	Up to £375k
Drama 2	£375k to £500k
Lower to Mid Cost Drama	
Drama 3	£500k to £630k
Drama 4	£630k to £700k
High Cost Drama	
Drama 5	£700k to £790k
Drama 6	£800k to £900k
Premium Drama	
Drama 7	£900k +

Source: BBC (http://downloads.bbc.co.uk/commissioning/site/tariff_prices_for_independents.pdf)

In terms of crew pay rates, these vary slightly, depending on the type of production and the working hours, and are negotiated for each individual project. It's useful to visit the website of BECTU, the UK's media and entertainment union, to find out what the current payment guidelines are. At the time of writing, they are working on the first ever runners rate-card and they are offering a reduced membership rate for new entrants. Runners are usually given a flat daily or weekly rate. At the time of writing, the Assistant Directors Association (ADA) branch of BECTU's minimum recommended rate is £550 per week. Indeed, it's worth noting that if you are serious about joining the industry, you should seriously consider joining BECTU yourself, where you can view and download the terms, conditions and up-to-date rates mentioned above.

As well as content made by the main UK broadcasters (BBC, ITV, C4 and Sky) there is high-end TV drama produced in the UK that you might not even be aware of. The introduction of the UK Tax credit for high-end TV drama and animation has seen lots of American productions come to the UK to make shows for US audiences. Stateside production company Starz, for example, produces both *Da Vinci's Demons* and *Outlander*, filmed in Wales and Scotland respectively; both were intended for a seven-season run and cost well over £1m per episode, although *Da Vinci's Demons* was recently cancelled by Starz after three seasons. Disney and Lime Productions film the children's series *Evermore* in the north west, and *Sons of Anarchy* creator Kurt Sutter shot his new show *The Bastard Executioner* in South Wales' Dragon Studios. All of these productions will have a budget of over £1m per hour and, while some may not even be screened on UK terrestrial TV, they all need top UK crew.

In addition, these shows usually have far more episodes per season than their UK equivalents. Whereas a three-part BBC drama might be shot in 6 to 8 weeks with a single unit, US series are shooting for 20 to 30 weeks with multiple units running in parallel. They will be filmed in 'blocks'. So the first block might be episode 1 and 2, followed by a week break before the crew start filming episodes 3 and 4 in block 2. This has changed the job market so that more people have much longer contracts than previously known, and there is more second-unit or double banking work available thanks to these larger projects.

TV Comedy

Scripted comedy series like *The Inbetweeners, Peep Show* and *W1A* are produced for less than a prime-time drama series. A typical prime time BBC sitcom budget costs between £300,000 and £500,000 to produce six episodes, according to the BBC comedy commissioning website. Channel 4's producer support team confirmed that the broadcaster commissions narrative sitcoms between the £150,000 and £250,000 bracket. BBC One and BBC Two alone produce around 500 hours of comedy a year, although much of that includes low-cost panel shows.

The rates for working on a scripted comedy are similar to the weekly rates of working on a soap opera or daytime drama. (Again check the BECTU website for the most up-to-date information.)

Film

The film industry has seen a huge investment from inward production. The following graph shows the record-breaking production spend from 2014, which is double what it was in 2008 as a direct result of the Tax credit.

While the scale of UK feature films runs from the micro budget to the blockbuster, you can clearly see on the graph that 'inward investment' – mostly Hollywood money – accounts for the vast majority of production spend in the UK (89% in 2014).

The BFI Statistical Yearbook shows that of the 223 films made in the UK in 2014, just 17 account for the overwhelming majority of the production spend. Domestic UK features accounted for 154 of those films, with 80 being made on micro budgets of under £500,000, while 32 were co-productions with other countries and 37 inward investment films, mostly the big Hollywood blockbusters.

Over the course of reading thousands of CVs, I have picked up recurring career patterns. There are a number of crew members who tend to stay working at the same budget level, whether micro budget or blockbuster. Many of the micro budget crew aspire to work at the next level up, not just for the financial benefits that come with a bigger budget, but also for the difference it makes to their CV and the quality of colleagues and product.

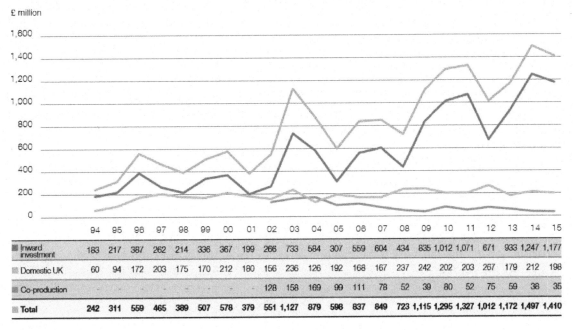

Figure 1 UK spend of feature films produced in the UK, 1994-2015, £ million

£ million

	94	95	96	97	98	99	00	01	02	03	04	05	06	07	08	09	10	11	12	13	14	15
Inward investment	183	217	387	262	214	336	367	199	266	733	584	307	559	604	434	835	1,012	1,071	671	933	1,247	1,177
Domestic UK	60	94	172	203	175	170	212	180	156	236	126	192	168	167	237	242	202	203	267	179	212	198
Co-production	-	-	-	-	-	-	-	-	128	158	169	99	111	78	52	39	80	52	75	59	38	35
Total	242	311	559	465	389	507	578	379	551	1,127	879	598	837	849	723	1,115	1,295	1,327	1,012	1,172	1,497	1,410

Source: BFI

Notes:

Data are rounded to the nearest £0.1m so may not sum exactly to the totals shown.

Films are allocated to the calendar year in which principal photography commenced.

Films with budgets under £500,000 are included in this analysis after 2008.

Numbers have been revised on the basis of new information received since publication of the 2015 Statistical Yearbook.

Inward investment feature films include inward co-productions and VFX-only films.

Measurement:

The above numbers include only the UK spend associated with productions shot or post-produced partly or wholly in the UK.

Spend is allocated to the year in which principal photography started or to the year in which the visual effects were undertaken in the case of VFX-only films.

Commercials

Commercials take just days to shoot but pay the best rates of any production, provided that the production company is registered with the Advertising Producers Association (APA) – 185 at the time of writing – who have very clear guidelines for crew payment. According to these guidelines, the average head of department will get paid around £400 to £500 per day and a director of photography (DoP) will take home a minimum £1,169 per day. As of June 2014, the daily rate for a runner is £182, but it's unlikely you will be working five days a week, every week.

Commercials are lucrative for the crew. Generally, they will shoot for one or two days and 'risk money' has been taken into consideration and included in the rate of pay, reflecting the fact that crew are available to work for short periods at late notice, and bring their expertise and skill to such a short term job. The other benefit of working with (good) APA production companies is that they typically reconcile freelance invoices within seven working days, or run a regular payroll for anyone on PAYE.

The big budgets on adverts do mean that a lot of expensive cameras and state-of-the-art post-production facilities are used. In turn this means that service companies such as camera rental and post-production houses make enough profit from adverts and long-running film and drama shows to support low budget productions and the occasional short film. Commercials help to indirectly subsidise low budget features and allow facilities companies to support the next generation of film-makers with in-kind services.

Some crew members do work across film, TV drama and commercials, but there are also a number of dedicated commercials crew who will only operate in that field. Below is a very rough approximation of how the work is balanced in terms of crew (this is not reflective of the size of the sectors, just the overlap):

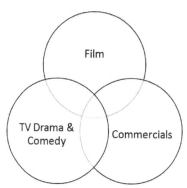

Over the years, I have noticed that an increasing number of crew members stick to their preferred field and there is decreasing overlap between these types of productions. While film and TV drama is buoyant, most of these crew members are unavailable to commercials production companies, but in leaner times savvy freelancers will court as many production companies and line producers as possible, across all fields. As a freelancer, it helps to build up a network of connections you can approach about the possibility of both short- and long-term work.

An important note: as we have now seen, there are many different types of UK production in which to build a career. For the purposes of this book, the definition 'film and TV drama' includes feature films with a budget of over £500,000, TV drama, TV comedy and commercials. News broadcast will be referred to as media, and everything else – including factual, light entertainment and documentary – will be referred to simply as TV.

The Job Market

If you want to get into the industry, it's important to understand the job market and where the openings lie. Getting an overall picture of the landscape will help you appreciate the size and scale of the business, and find the routes and the access points you have to getting work. It's very competitive, so a little knowledge will put you ahead of the pack.

I've examined figures published by the Department for Culture Media and Sport (DCMS), Creative Skillset, BFI, Office for National Statistics (ONS) and Higher Education Statistics Agency (HESA) to give a snapshot of the UK job market. There is an unhelpful European standard of collecting statistics for film, TV, photography, video and radio as one group, some statistics come from estimates taken from industry surveys, so we have to pick our way through a few stats for our focus on film and TV drama. Some of the figures are slightly hazy, so educated averages and estimates will be used where necessary as a guide.

The BFI publish an annual yearbook looking at the film industry in the UK. Their current estimate is that there are around 47,000 people working in film production in the UK, 51% of which are freelance.

In 2015 the Creative Skillset employment survey estimated that there were approximately 85,000 people working in TV (Terrestrial Broadcast, Cable/Satellite, Independent production, post production, animation and VFX). While that figure is only an estimate, for the purposes of this quick analysis we will add the figure of 85,000 from the TV sector and 47,000 from the film industry to give a very rough guide figure of 132,000 people working in film and TV production overall. There are far more jobs dependent on the industry, but these figures are meant only as a guide for those who work at the sharp end of production.

Let's break down those genres even further. TV is a wide-ranging, all-inclusive term encompassing everything from the high production values of *Downton Abbey* to the *Jeremy Kyle Show*. Broadly speaking 11 different genres of production in TV: drama, children's, comedy, entertainment, factual, learning, music, news, religion & ethics, sport and weather. If we divide our 85,000 TV jobs across those 11 divisions of production, this gives us an average of around 7,700 people per category (although obviously some genres will be far bigger than others). Given the huge output of content across all of the hundreds of channels available, that is actually quite a small number, and covers everything from development to post production across all the broadcasters and indie companies. A large proportion of these people are freelancers too; a subject we will explore later in the book.

We'll now delve even further into these statistics, and reveal more of the picture. There are four distinct areas that will affect any employment opportunities: location, gender, diversity and qualifications.

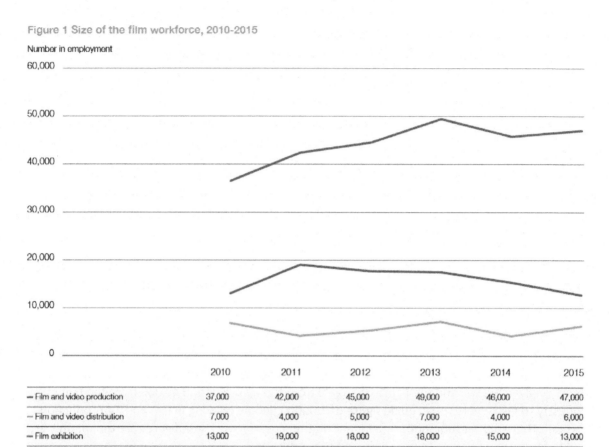

Figure 1 Size of the film workforce, 2010-2015

Number in employment

	2010	2011	2012	2013	2014	2015
— Film and video production	37,000	42,000	45,000	49,000	46,000	47,000
— Film and video distribution	7,000	4,000	5,000	7,000	4,000	6,000
— Film exhibition	13,000	19,000	18,000	18,000	15,000	13,000

Source: Office for National Statistics
Note: Figures have been updated since the publication of employment data in the 2014 Statistical Yearbook.

The Job Market In The UK

Unsurprisingly most of the creative jobs are in London and the South East. That's no surprise, as it's where the foundations of our industry were first forged and it still has some of the best facilities in the world.

Creative Skillset report that the number of jobs in London and South East makes up 53% of the national total. Which, using our estimated total of 132,000 people working in the industry, is just under 70,000 people. While London and the South East dominates the geographical spread of industry employment, the Midlands is currently at the bottom, as illustrated by the following Creative Skillset graphic.

2.4 Distribution of workforce reported in 2015 Survey, by nation and region

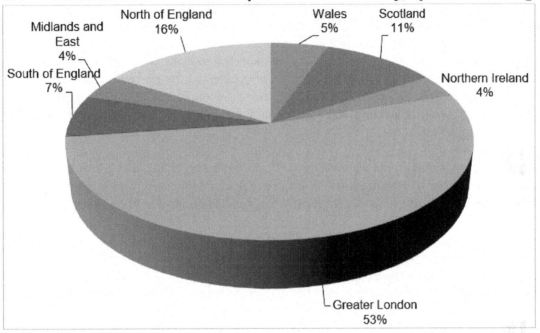

Base: estimated workforce reported by responding organisations

Thanks to Creative Skillset 2015 Employment Census for allowing us to reproduce this chart.

According to the DCMS, only 36.7% of the workforce is female in the creative industries: a far lower percentage than most other industries. The majority of departments are generally male-dominated, although make-up and costume have a far higher female-to-male ratio, and production offices are equally balanced. A 2012 BFI survey (*Succès de plume? Female Screenwriters and Directors of UK Films, 2010-2012*) also showed that women are massively under-represented in the key decision-making roles of writing and directing, particularly in low budget independent and major studio titles. A 2015 Directors UK report 'Cut Out of the Picture' highlights that women make up just 13.6% of working film directors. Additionally, the average salary of female freelancers is less than their male counterparts.

Equally damning is Creative Skillset's 2012 creative employment census, which revealed that just 5.4% of the entire workforce, around 7100 people, come from a Black, Asian or Minority Ethnic (BAME) background – far lower than the UK BAME population of 12.5% would seem to suggest. The top sector for BAME employment was in commercials and VFX, while SFX was at the bottom. In another depressing statistic, the average salary of BAME workers is lower than their white British male colleagues. Elsewhere, that same census found that just 5% of the overall workers considered they have a disability.

To take action against these disappointing statistics, the Creative Diversity Network was set up by broadcasters and the trade association Pact to monitor and encourage diversity in their organisations. In the summer of 2016, the CDN are expected to make two announcements. Firstly, the launch of Project Diamond, where production companies can use specialist software to monitor diversity on their own output, on and off screen. Secondly, The CDN will announce partnerships with commercial crew databases to make it easier for production companies to find diverse talent in the first place.

In August 2014, Sky announced it was setting itself a target quota of 20% BAME employment, and Channel 4 have also introduced measures to ensure that all independent production companies, which want the broadcaster's investment must make a real commitment to diversity.

It's also worth noting that around 78% of the industry workforce holds education qualifications from A-level to university degrees. So, as Conan O'Brien prudently noted in his 2011 speech at Dartmouth College, if you have a media degree, you now have a crushing advantage over 22% of the workforce.

We will come back to these figures later to unearth more details about the job market and industry as a whole. For now, let's take a look at the other end of the pipeline.

The Job Seekers

According to figures from the Higher Education Statistics Authority (HESA), in 2014/15 there were almost 17,000 graduates with some kind of media studies or film/photography degree about to hit the job market. And that figure does not include those who studied other relevant degrees, including production design, costume or English, or those who graduate from bespoke film schools like NFTS, The Met or LFS.

Whatuni.com lists 114 UK universities as having over 855 different types of film-related degree course, and 129 offering over 1000 different media studies degrees. While many people fall away from these fields following graduation, it's clear from the HESA figures above that there are a substantial number who do not. They are also joined by thousands of people with non-related degrees who are also drawn to careers within the industry, along with many more without any university education, those migrating from other industries and those who come from overseas.

Even a conservative estimate highlights that there are around 20,000 people attempting each year to squeeze into an industry of about 132,000 people, and they are trying to join the industry at a much faster rate than people are leaving or retiring. While there are still more people than can be accommodated at entry level, however, once you get beyond the bottom rung skills gaps begin to appear and opportunities become more visible.

It's also worth noting that the creative industries are not an immediately lucrative career path. In their 2013 study of wealth, the Office of National Statistics (ONS) canvassed graduates less than a year after leaving university. Those who studied dentistry were earning the most on average, a median amount of £45,600 per year, while those in the media industries were at the bottom of the list, earning just £21,000 per year on average.

Things do improve slightly with experience. According to the 2015 Creative Skillset Workforce survey, the average income for someone working in the film and TV industry is £33,900, with freelancers earning approximately £11,000 less than those in permanent employment, women earning £3000 less than men and disabled employees earning the least of all.

It's been this way for years. Back in the '80s, '90s and even the early 2000s, it was common practice for production companies to use free labour. There were so many fresh-faced graduates trying to break their way in that unscrupulous producers would offer them 'work experience', using an unpaid runner for as long as they possibly could. When one quit or moved on, they just hired another out of the stack of CVs sent to them every week.

Of course most people can't afford to work for free, so this meant the job market was awash with affluent graduates whose parents were able to pay for them to live while they worked for nothing. This practice is now, thankfully, being eroded, but the fact that it was those from a wealthy background landing most of the opportunities had a detrimental effect on diversity in the job market which lingers to this day.

Tax Credits: Their Impact On Your Career

In the last few years, UK production levels have exploded, creating more employment opportunities than ever before. This is largely due to our Film Tax Credit and its appeal to overseas production.

In 1995, the National Lottery Fund began supporting the UK film industry. The UK Film Council was established in 2000 to invest in domestic talent, including directors like Ken Loach (*The Wind That Shakes the Barley*), Shane Meadows (*This is England*), Andrea Arnold (*Red Road*) and Armando Ianucci (*In The Loop*). Overall the UKFC invested around £160m in 900 films.

In 2010 it was announced that the UKFC would be abolished, as the new Conservative and Liberal Democrats Coalition Government began their 'bonfire of the quangos'. There was much uproar, particularly as there was no indication of any future plans for growth, so there was fear that the film industry had been left blowing in the wind.

In 2005, five years prior to the closure of the UKFC, Gordon Brown, then Chancellor of the Exchequer, had announced his intention to introduce a tax credit for feature film production, after previously offering a temporary tax relief to film-makers when he first came to office in 1997. In essence, this new tax credit was a cash incentive for producers to make their films in the UK and its impact cannot be underestimated. Since its introduction, inward investment in UK productions has more than doubled, from £432m in 2008 to just over £1.47bn in 2014. The tax credit has elevated the industry towards capacity, with some productions forced to take their shows away from the UK as there is a lack of suitable space.

This graph (right) from the BFI Statistical Yearbook illustrates that huge growth.

Following the success of the film Tax Credit, Pact and several production companies lobbied the DCMS for a similar tax break for high-end TV and animation, and in April 2013 the scheme was expanded to include these sectors.

The TV Tax Credit is available to any high-end TV drama or animation that meets two sets of criteria: it must have a budget of at least £1m per hour and it must pass a cultural test to determine that it is a British production.

The cultural test, which is also applied to films applying for UK tax relief, is awarded on a points' basis. For example, a production is given four points if it is set in the UK, six points if it is in the English language, two if more than 50% is filmed in the UK, one for a British director, one for key crew and so on. There is a maximum of 35 points available, and a project will pass if it achieves at least 18 points. Those that do pass will then be eligible to claim back up to 25% of any UK core production spend.

Figure 21.1 Total turnover of UK film industry by sector, 1995-2012

£ million

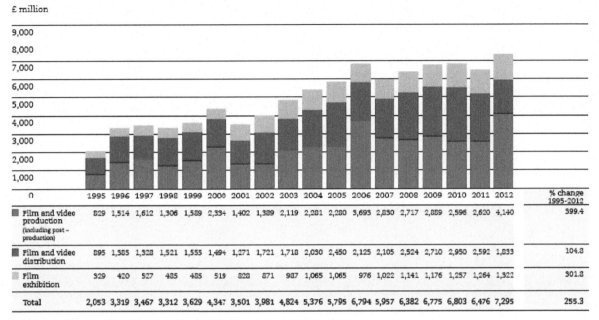

	1995	1996	1997	1998	1999	2000	2001	2002	2003	2004	2005	2006	2007	2008	2009	2010	2011	2012	% change 1995-2012
Film and video production (including post-production)	829	1,514	1,612	1,306	1,589	2,334	1,402	1,389	2,119	2,281	2,280	3,693	2,830	2,717	2,889	2,596	2,620	4,140	399.4
Film and video distribution	895	1,385	1,328	1,521	1,555	1,494	1,271	1,721	1,718	2,030	2,450	2,125	2,105	2,524	2,710	2,950	2,592	1,833	104.8
Film exhibition	329	420	527	485	485	519	828	871	987	1,065	1,065	976	1,022	1,141	1,176	1,257	1,264	1,322	301.8
Total	2,053	3,319	3,467	3,312	3,629	4,347	3,501	3,981	4,824	5,376	5,795	6,794	5,957	6,382	6,775	6,803	6,476	7,295	255.3

Source: Office for National Statistics Annual Business Inquiry and Annual Business Survey

Before the TV Tax Credit was introduced, accountants RSM Tenon estimated that an additional £350m per year would be spent on UK production, and that the UK economy would benefit from a return of around £1bn. per year including both UK and overseas producers. In reality the first full year of high-end TV drama production spend was £615m, with big TV productions like *24: Live Another Day, Game of Thrones, Da Vinci's Demons, Outlander, Galavant, Evermoor, The Royals* and *The Crown* taking advantage of the incentive. (To put that into perspective, the whole of the BBC One drama budget for 2011 was around £250m.) In June 2015, *Broadcast* magazine reported that for every £1 spent on TV drama, the tax relief has returned over £8.30 to the UK economy.

Huge numbers of overseas film productions have also been enticed to the UK. As a recent example, Disney's *John Carter* was originally set to film in the US but, when producers realised they could qualify for the Film Tax Credit, they relocated the shoot to the UK. The estimated budget of *John Carter* was $250m., and the majority of it was spent in Britain, using our locations, companies, crew and post-production facilities. That money then filters back into the economy, while the industry advances in talent development and skill, and the growth in infrastructure puts the UK increasingly ahead of rival territories. And of course, the more of these big productions that shoot in the UK, the more investment to the infrastructure, development of talent and opportunities arise for crew.

Two Women Who Changed the Film and TV Industry

Two of the most significant people to have contributed to the success of film and TV over the past 20 years have been women. You're sure to have heard of one of them, but possibly not the other. The first stood firm in contract negotiations, which subsequently breathed life into a flagging industry, and the other waged a long, hard campaign to change the TV landscape.

While success has many authors, I'm going to single out these two people as they made an enormous difference to the film and TV sector, which is in a far healthier state thanks to their efforts.

The Growth Of Film Production In The UK

When author JK Rowling insisted the film adaptations of her *Harry Potter* series were made in the UK, she transformed the British film industry by directly creating thousands of jobs, leading the Government to offer tax breaks to film-makers and motivating Warner Bros. to invest in the UK.

After Rowling insisted that the books be filmed here, Warner Bros. set up camp in Leavesden Studios near Watford in Hertfordshire, a fanfare move that effectively reminded the US that we have world-class crew and facilities.

After a few years of the Potter films driving the film industry, the Government finally saw its potential, and in 2007 launched Film Tax Credits as a further incentive to overseas producers to come to the UK. Production spend rose from just under £400m in 1998 to just over £1.47bn by 2014, with employment also doubling in this time period. At the end of the *Harry Potter* films, Warner Bros. bought Leavesden and invested £100m to turn it into a world-class film studio. The big-budget Tom Cruise movie *Live.Die.Repeat: Edge of Tomorrow* was the first film made at Warner Bros. Studios Leavesden (WBSL).

The Growth Of TV In The UK

You may not have heard of Eileen Gallagher, but her campaign to change the way broadcasters and independent production companies worked, transformed the TV landscape.

In 2002 and 2003 the Producers' Alliance for Cinema and Television (Pact) aggressively lobbied the Government to redress the imbalance between broadcasters and independent production companies. Eileen Gallagher, then chair of Pact, successfully persuaded then Culture Secretary Tessa Jowell into making delicate, yet significant, policy changes to the 2003 Communications Bill through a hard fought and quite brilliant campaign that has subsequently reaped huge rewards.

Before this policy change, broadcasters such as the BBC would either make shows themselves or commission an independent production company to do so. Like most commissions, the 'indie' company would work out the budget to make the show and add a mark-up; say, 10% of the budget. This 10% would keep the company afloat during the periods when they didn't have a commission, and the broadcaster would keep all the rights to the shows.

This led to many production companies running into cash-flow problems between commissions, with many going under. The 2003 bill changed the terms of the relationship, meaning independents can retain intellectual property after an agreed window of broadcast. This means that they can turn to the worldwide markets and sell proven content and programme ideas to eager overseas buyers.

This change of policy gave birth to the 'super-indies', as we know them now. It is no longer a time of feast or famine at the mercy of the broadcaster, but a steady and healthy growth of income based on intellectual property (IP), ideas and good content, and essentially rewarding creativity. Because indie producers can now sell to a much bigger market, they turn over hundreds of millions of pounds, have created thousands of jobs and have a much more secure business.

All this came about because Tessa Jowell heard Eileen Gallagher speak about the problem in 2002, and understood both the issues raised and the solution presented by Pact. The combined impact of the Film Tax Credit and the Communications Act of 2003 can be measured by both increased production spend and a rise in employment across the sectors.

Gallagher also directly benefited from her tireless campaign for legislative change. As well as being chair of Pact, she was CEO of Shed Productions from 1998–2008. Thanks to the new policy, Shed – like other super indies – was able to thrive and grow, and in 2010 Warner Bros.' parent company Time Warner bought a controlling share in Shed that valued the company at £100 million and then went on to purchase the whole company in 2014.

UK Production Boom

If you are looking to break into the industry, you need to know about the current levels of production in your local region, and what is likely to happen in the future. One important consideration here is the ratio between the size of the local workforce, examined in the previous chapter, and the volume of production in those areas, which is an indicator to the amount of opportunities that might available, particularly outside of London.

Northern Ireland

Northern Ireland has blazed the trail for film and TV production, leaving Wales and Scotland trailing in its wake. After landing the deal to host the production of *Game of Thrones* in 2009, Northern Ireland Screen has made the nation one of the most competitive filming destinations in the world. However, many of the crew members are brought in from England particularly at department head level.

Northern Ireland Screen set out a plan called 'Driving Global Growth', which ran from 2010 to 2014, and the resulting mixture of new, affordable facilities, labour, the tax credit and additional financial incentives meant that many producers now look to the region for film and TV drama. Several productions including *Game Of Thrones*, the BBC's *The Fall, Blandings, Line Of Duty 2, High Rise* and more, have recently filmed in Northern Ireland. In 2014, Universal filmed *Dracula Untold* in the Province, receiving £1.65m of investment from Northern Ireland Screen and returning approximately £15m to the local economy.

On April 1, 2014, Northern Ireland Screen unveiled a new strategy, 'Opening Doors', which will see £42.8m invested over four years, with a predicted return of £194m. Indigenous production has been an important part of 'Driving Global Growth' and will continue to be so; Sixteen South and Waddell Media are both big local employers and growing year on year.

In April 2016, construction began on a new studio complex in Belfast. North Foreshore Studios will contain 2 stages and office space.

Wales

The south coast of Wales has been home to several large-scale TV dramas in the last five years, most notably Starz production *Da Vinci's Demons*. A large-scale, multi-episode drama, was set to run for seven series, it was created by David S. Goyer (writer of *The Dark Knight*) and employed and trained a huge number of local people. After *Da Vinci's Demons* was cancelled, *The Collection*, a 1940's set drama about a fashion house in Paris, moved into the vacant Bay Studios in Swansea.

There is a wide range of locations in Wales, ranging from castles to coastlines and from modern to retro urban centres. Along with Bay Studios in Swansea, south Wales has benefitted from the emergence of 3 other studios along the M4 corridor in the last few years. Roath Lock is the BBC's multi-million-pound studio in Cardiff Bay is home to *Doctor Who, Wizards and Aliens, Casualty*, as well as flagship BBC drama *Sherlock*. Twentieth Century Fox revitalised Dragon Studios in Bridgend when they filmed *The Bastard Executioner*. The BBC production *Atlantis* was filmed in a converted supermarket distribution centre in Chepstow.

In February 2014, Pinewood studios announced a partnership with the Welsh Assembly to launch a brand new studio facility: Pinewood Wales is just five miles east of Roath Lock in Cardiff and consists of two 20,000 sq ft stages as well as office space and resident service companies. It has received a commitment of £30m from the Welsh Assembly and will be promoted to production companies worldwide. The Welsh Assembly Media investment fund, combined with the UK Tax credits, make south Wales a very attractive proposition for producers, who could save a considerable amount of money from their production budget. A new production company, Bad Wolf, led by Jane Tranter and Julie Gardner have a slate of over 25 high productions they intend to bring to Wales in the next few years.

According to the Welsh Government's creative sector team, there has been more than £150m of inward investment since 2010. During this time over 3,200 jobs had been created or safeguarded. With the influx of productions going to Wales over the next few years, there will be an increasing demand for experienced local crew.

The future looks bright for the industry in South Wales. Pinewood Wales will bring in bigger projects, and with training organisations like Cyfle, there will be increasingly more opportunities to grow and sustain the local workforce.

Scotland

Scotland is presently trailing behind other regions which can offer both facilities and cash. Creative Scotland has attracted a handful of incoming productions, including *Cloud Atlas, Sunset Song, The Railway Man* and, most notably, *World War Z*, which turned Glasgow into Philadelphia in 2012. (The grid layout of Glasgow's streets is similar to those of the US cities so can double as a location.) In 2010 the Scottish Screen Agency was absorbed into Creative Scotland and its staff downsized from 35 to 9. As a result, staff are 'over-stretched and under-resourced' according to producer Gillian Berrie, who is a member of Independent Producers Scotland (IPS).

There are only a few studio facilities in Scotland, most notably Film City in Glasgow and BBC Dumbarton studios. Pinewood explored opening a facility north of the border in 2013, but decided against it due to technical reasons. In the last few years, several feasibility studies have been undertaken by entrepreneurs eager to build a studio facility in Scotland; to date, none of those plans have come to fruition. In May 2015, shortly after the SNP landslide in Scotland, Culture

Minister Fiona Hyslop pledged that the Scottish Government will do more to strengthen the local film industry.

However, there are some large-scale productions currently shooting in Scotland. Starz are making big-budget period drama *Outlander* in North Lanarkshire, which has already been renewed for at least a third and fourth series – particularly good news when the economic impact of series one is estimated at around £20m. In March 2016, the Cumbernauld studio where Outlander is filmed, submitted planning permission to expand the Wardpark site to accommodate more Scottish production.

Just as indigenous production has been central to the emerging Belfast scene, Scottish producers, like Sigma Films (*Under The Skin, Starred Up*, which was filmed in a Belfast prison) can't currently rely on the limited infrastructure for growth and are engaging with Creative Scotland to stabilise and grow the industry. And much is expected from incoming director of Film & Media Scotland, former lawyer Natalie Usher, with Berrie describing the appointment as 'one of the best moves Creative Scotland has made.'

Scottish Enterprise, in partnership with Creative Scotland and the Scottish Government, commissioned a report by consultancy group EKOS, which recommended that Scotland 'should' have its own studio, and that a mixture of private and public investment is required to capitalise on the surge of interest. On April 9, 2014, Creative Scotland published a 10-year plan, which essentially set out the need to develop a strategy to be realised within the next decade. The first step was to create a £2m tax credit advance facility, then a £1m skills fund and finally, a £1.75m production growth fund was announced in October 2015.

I asked Gillian Berrie for her thoughts about this plan. 'There's no doubt we're lagging behind the other nations and regions but we hope to see some breakthroughs soon,' she said. 'We're working with Scottish Government and Creative Scotland to identify and access new funding streams, while Scottish Enterprise is investigating the creation of a super-infrastructure for the sector which will bolster the [forthcoming] studio. Together with a long term strategy for growth and focused leadership, we're expecting to see significant improvements in the industry's performance in the coming years. Scotland should be a major player.'

Notable English Regions:

North

Yorkshire was quick out of the traps when the UK Film Council was scrapped in 2010. Creative England had only just confirmed Caroline Norbury as CEO when Screen Yorkshire secured around £15m in funding (£7.5m from European Regional Development Fund, £7.5m of private investment) and started attracting lots of production to the region. Leeds has since been host to many TV dramas, such as *Peaky Blinders, Jamaica Inn, The Great Train Robbery, X&Y, Death Comes To Pemberley* and *Jonathan Strange & Mr Norrell*. Film-wise, David Heyman produced *Testament*

Of Youth in Sheffield; BBC Films/Punk Cinema made *Bill*, a feature comedy about Shakespeare in the region; and Yann Demage (*Top Boy*) shot his excellent debut feature *'71* in Yorkshire.

Screen Yorkshire recently announced a further £7.5m round of funding, effectively doubling their capacity. As well as welcoming outside investment, the organisation has also supported regional producers including Warp Films, which has become one of the UK's leading production companies in both independent film (*Four Lions, Tyrannosaur, Dead Man's Shoes*) and TV Drama (*Southcliffe, The Last Panthers, This Is England '86, '88 And '90*).

Leeds' Studio 81, and the nearby Prime Studios cater for most of the film and TV production in the area. A further studio facility opened in 2015 when a hangar at the former RAF Church Fenton airbase between Leeds and York was converted into a sound stage to film ITV's *Victoria*.

North East

The North East took a hammer blow at the start of 2014, with local production *The Paradise* being cancelled by the BBC after just two series. ITV then headed to the region with the epic *Beowulf*, which also got cancelled, this time after just one series. The region has a stable CBBC slate (*Wolfblood, The Dumping Ground*), ITV drama *Vera* continues to shoot there every summer and Company's *George Gently* is also filmed in Durham each year. There is a wide variety of locations and an accommodating screen agency in place for incoming productions, not to mention a small, regular workforce where all crew are known to each other.

North West

The North West is one of the biggest centres outside of London for TV drama production, with the late, great Victoria Wood's *Tubby And Enid, The Village, Foyles War* and a raft of CBBC commissions shooting in the region. The BBC, ITV, C4 and Sky regularly shoot high-end drama there, but studio space is still in demand. MediaCity does have studios, but they are mostly used by entertainment shows. They are also reportedly more expensive for the BBC to hire than the old studios at TV Centre, and some of the CBBC entertainment shows that were meant to move to Manchester are now 'on the road' given this cost. The team behind Manchester's Sharp Project have now opened the Space Project, a dedicated studio facility, in the city, which has attracted most drama productions. Ultimately there is a decent infrastructure in Manchester and good opportunities for entry-level crew with the BBC and ITV.

Liverpool has become a favoured destination for feature films in the last few years, mainly because of the period locations on offer. *Peaky Blinders, Florence Foster Jenkins, Film Stars Don't Die in Liverpool* and JK Rowling's *Fantastic Beasts and Where to Find Them* all made use of the city's buildings to replicate the early to mid-19th Century. Developers are currently working with Liverpool city council to convert the old Littlewoods building in Wavertree to a film studio.

Central

While Birmingham is home to *Doctors*, the area is overlooked by lots of production companies due to a shallow workforce and out-of-date facilities. Although ITV comedy *The Job Lot* was set in Birmingham, Big Talk moved production back to London because there was insufficient crew in the area. In a campaign backed by *The Birmingham Post*, local MPs raised a debate in Parliament in June 2015, questioning the BBC's local investment and claiming that the corporation wasn't spending enough in the region.

The lack of infrastructure in the region also means that few feature films shoot in the Midlands. The only recent films of note to come to the area include *The Girl With all The Gifts* and a stunt unit for *Kingsman 2: The Golden Circle*.

South West

Bristol is enjoying a busy time of late, with Mammoth Screen's *Poldark* coming to town for a third series. Mammoth Screen also shot *Agatha Raisin* around the Cotswolds for Sky, while Company Pictures' *The New World* made the most of the rural locations just outside Bristol. Disney brought to the area the large scale *Galavant*, a knights- of-the-round-table drama for a younger audience. *Wolf Hall*, the BBC adaptation of Hilary Mantel's novel, filmed in a number of National Trust properties around the west country including Lacock Abbey. The area boasts a variety of locations and studio facilities, such as the Bottleyard in Bristol.

South East

The south east is still the national leader in film and drama production. The highest concentration of crew and facilities are in London, and most major productions that come to the UK are based in Pinewood, WBSL or Shepperton Studios. 3Mills, Ealing, Elstree, Longcross, Twickenham and West London Film Studios host most smaller-scale Hollywood productions and British independent feature films, as well as catering for other international productions and TV drama. Large-scale film productions, including the likes of *Star Wars*, *The Avengers: Age of Ultron*, *Mission: Impossible – Rogue Nation* and *Pan*, are typically made in the capital. High-end TV drama is also based in London, such as Sky Atlantic's drama *Guerrilla*, based at Central St Martins, and crime drama *Fortitude*, which had a rumoured £25m budget and, although set in Iceland, both series were mostly shot in Hayes, Middlesex.

Film London and the modest powerhouse of the British Film Commission share offices in Finsbury Park, and are often conduits between the US studios and all of the UK nations and regions. The BFC are very often the first point of contact for many incoming productions, sometimes via their L.A. office. In particular, they help the US studios find what they need in the UK, making it an extremely important organisation for securing so many productions, which result in thousands of jobs.

Creative England is a government-backed organisation with a remit to facilitate film and TV drama (as well as animation and games) around most regions of the UK. (Film London operates only in the capital and Screen Yorkshire struck out on their own after the UKFC was dissolved.) For most people outside London and Yorkshire, Creative England is the pathway into film in the country, and their social-media feeds regularly advertise roles throughout the regions. They also run many training schemes and have many funding pots, and their current manager of Crew and Facilities, Nicky Ball, gives some great advice in the Pearls of Wisdom section of this book.

Are All the Jobs In London?

Looking back through our potted history of film and TV in the UK, you can see why so much production has been based in London. Nearly all of the financial and creative risks have been made in London, developing the infrastructure that now forms the backbone of the industry. In the same way that Silicon Valley is the centre of tech entrepreneurs, and Milan and Paris house the core of the fashion industries, London has always been the centre of UK production.

One practical problem facing most London crew is the rise in the capital's property prices. West London, with its triangulation of Pinewood, the BBC and Soho, was typically where most people would look for houses. Many are now priced out of the market, and we could be facing a very real issue in the next 20 years, where the talent can no longer afford to converge in the capital.

When I speak with people about London being the epicentre of film and TV production, they are generally unaware of the legislative changes that took place in 2003 to ensure that there was more work guaranteed for the nations and regions. (It's important to note, however, that this government policy against London's geographical production monopoly only affects TV, and not film.)

The 2003 Communications Act that we looked at previously not only contained new legislation on the way that programmes were bought and sold, but also stated that a substantive percentage of TV production had to occur outside the M25. (In order to qualify as an out-of-London production, the production spend in these regions must be at least 70% of the total budget, and over 50% of the crew must be based outside of the capital.) The Government gave the industry 13 years for these targets to be met, with each of the major broadcasters being given targets, with allowances for variables in the current broadcast environment, and facing financial punishments if they do not meet their quotas.

As an example of the impact of this legislation, the BBC's 2008 spend in London was around 65% of their overall budget. Now it's around 47%. While the capital is still the centre of UK production, much has been done (by legislation) to circulate the budget spend.

After the introduction of the 2003 Communications Act, many independent production companies also opened satellite offices outside of the M25 in order to meet their obligations. According to a 2013 Survey by Oliver & Ohlbaum for Pact, there are 202 substantial independent production companies operating outside London and 30 subsidiaries of production companies that are based in the capital. If you are based outside London, there has never been a better time to find work in film and TV production.

How The Industry Works

The Production Process; A Breakdown from Prep to Post

It is often said there are three general areas of film-making: pre-production, production and post production. In truth, there are many more pieces to the puzzle, such as development, financing, distribution and marketing. Many people entering the business find it hard to think beyond what's happening in front of the camera lens, and then only thinking of the final product being successful. For those who work in the business, even those who have worked in it for a long time, it is difficult to predict what will do well at the box office, receive critical adoration or top the ratings charts.

For many people success is measured less by the box-office takings for the finished film and more for the actual process of making it. If the wages are right, the people are talented and all of the components work in harmony from start to finish, then that makes for an enjoyable film-making process. On collecting his special BAFTA award in 2015, the screenwriter Jeff Pope said, 'In this industry, it's not what I've made, but who I have made it *with*, that really matters to me'.

As a new entrant to the industry, you may feel like you are almost insignificant to the process of film-making, but you would be wrong. All of the cogs must turn to make the machine move and your input, dedication and effort is needed just as much as anyone else's. This is a team endeavour.

Development/Pre-Production

Film is an expensive and risky business that takes a long time to piece together. In its infancy, a film is like a house of cards; delicately balanced and liable to collapse if one card is missing. A producer must initially acquire the rights to a story and develop a script, which must be good enough to attract key talent that will, in turn, attract investors. In the UK many independent productions are developed with the financial support of the EU Media Program/Creative Europe (the future of which is unknown at the time of writing), BFI, Film4, BBC Films and Creative England, their involvement often seen as a 'cornerstone' investment that will encourage further backing from other sources.

With talent attached, a project must be budgeted and scheduled properly by an experienced line producer and/or 1st Assistant Director. Budgeting at this early stage is all about feasibility. In any film, there are above-the-line and below-the-line costs. Above-the-line refers to the variable, market rate of key talent on a project; for example, Brad Pitt might cost £10m a movie, Bradley Walsh might cost £50,000. Below-the-line costs refer to crew members who would be interchangeable without it materially affecting the rate that you would pay them, and these rates are relatively fixed, with small margins for negotiation. The line producer would also determine budgets for each department and component such as studio space, art department, camera hire, costumes, post-production hire and everything else that might be required for that particular project.

Investors in independent film will appoint a completion guarantor: companies with very experienced production consultants that will 'bond' a production. For a retainer fee, which is proportional to the budget, they will review the script and schedule, stress test the proposed budget, oversee the key appointments and monitor the ongoing costs of the production. Once a bond company have reviewed all the documentation, they produce a 'letter of intent', declaring to investors that they will ensure that the project is delivered on time and within budget. If anything goes wrong on the film, they can be brought in to help the production team resolve issues. One of the completion guarantors' responsibilities is to oversee the appointment of 'capable personnel' in key roles, meaning that only experienced, proven personnel are appointed to the key, decision-making roles.

Once the green light is given to a project and the key artist availability lined up, the production office is created and the work begins. The hub of all pre-production activity, the production office is usually set up within a film studio, and within striking distance of key locations. Productions do sometimes set up in normal office space; the key is short-term rental.

Until this point, the production company is likely to have been shouldering the cost if it has been unable to obtain development funding, but at the point of commission a new ring-fenced company is created and registered at Companies House, this is often called an SPV (Special Purpose Vehicle). A bank account is then set up for the new company, and the production funds transferred from the investors; each production will have its own arrangements for how the funds are managed. There are several benefits to setting up the ring-fenced company, the main ones being to ensure there is no liability for the parent production company and that finances are easier to manage for the specific project.

The producers then set about assembling a team of freelancers for the project. The line producer will typically be the first of the freelance crew; sometimes called co-producers or unit production managers (UPMs), they oversee the budget and overall schedule. It's the line producer's job to work out how much prep time is needed for each department; they have to balance the budget with the needs of the production. Often, a 1st AD will be asked to provide a guide schedule well in advance, a location manager might also have set to work scouting for hero locations, and a production designer may be brought in early for more complex design jobs but, typically, the line producer is the first aboard. In the production department, they are usually followed by a production manager, production coordinator and production runner, with the coordinator seeking the roles of assistant production coordinator, production secretary, producers assistant, directors assistant and production assistants. The more people in the production office, the closer the project is getting to day one of filming.

In terms of practical logistics, film studios provide an infrastructure: stages to shoot on, local services companies on site and production offices. For example, there are over 200 small businesses with offices at Pinewood Studios, providing services ranging from camera hire to travel agents. There is also space for construction workshops, prop stores and fitting rooms. Studios also normally have flexible spaces available at short notice, allowing productions to keep everything and everyone within close contact.

In terms of hiring studio space, a UK-based producer will usually get in touch with a contact at their preferred studio to discuss options, while international producers will typically contact Film London or the BFC to help them find space. The space will incorporate office space, build space for sets and a prop store, all staggered according to the stages of production. In times past, producers would typically get their first choice studio and haggle down the rates. Now UK studio space is so in demand that many productions are not able to get their initial choice. (There are two new studios set to open in Scotland and Yorkshire to accommodate this spike in production.)

Productions are, however, requiring increasingly larger sets, so big that they might not fit into a typical studio, in which case empty buildings are often taken over and retro-converted to fit production needs. *Da Vinci's Demons* is made in an old car-part factory in Swansea, *Fortitude* is mostly shot in an old fruit-and-veg depot just a few miles from Heathrow and *Mr Selfridge* is filmed in an old carpet factory in North London. When BBC Drama *Waterloo Road* shifted production to Scotland from Manchester, they turned a former army barracks in Greenock into the fictional school, giving them space for offices and workshops and also buildings to accommodate the chaperones and tutors needed for the younger actors. Even if a production is set up in a studio, it doesn't always follow that they will film on the stages. Some shows are shot entirely on location despite having a base at a studio.

As a production nears the first day of filming, its crew keeps expanding. There are sets to be built, locations to be found, actors to be cast, cameras to be tested, lighting gear to be arranged, costumes to be fitted, make-up and hair to be designed and tested, and many large-scale productions will also be starting pre-viz. All of the prep needs to happen in stages, with people coming on board in time to prepare for the shoot, each individual having a negotiated start date. As crew are confirmed, they usually receive a standard deal memo, containing the basic information for terms of engagement; dates and rate are the most important factors. The contracts themselves may not appear until after filming has begun.

In the final run up to the shoot, the casting director will be confirming supporting cast, and the lead cast will be sent for insurance medicals; there is a list of approved physicians used by the industry. The walls of the production office will be covered in pictures of each cast member and their assigned number, with the lead actor always listed as number one. (We will look at actors' numbers in the next chapter.)

If the project requires it, the VFX supervisor will be now preparing for shooting. This may include using previs (short for Previsualization), which is a type of advanced animated storyboard of the film, as a guide for the shoot itself, and as much previs/VFX planning as possible is done prior to filming.

To give you an idea of the way the production swells, I've mocked up a pre-production diary (PPD) such as the one usually managed by the production coordinator and issued out to the key figures on a regular basis. For the sake of this example, I've created an entirely fictional project called 'SWITCH'. All of the documents are based on real templates and software but the names, numbers and details have been conjured from thin air.

It's quite a simplistic PPD, but covers from five weeks prior to the first day of filming. Most PPDs become very complex but this version is a good 'beginner' example. You can see that crew arrive in stages. Interviews and meetings are scheduled and that crew start in batches, as the production gets closer to the first day of principal photography.

	14 OCT MON	15 OCT TUES	16 OCT WED	17 OCT THU	18 OCT FRI	19 OCT SAT	20 OCT SUN
-5	0830, 1130 & 1400: Prod Secretary I/Vs: Hazel, Eleanor 0945: Ned & Alex C recce West London Studios pm: Alex C. meet Eleanor @ Prod Office Personnel start: Production Co-ordinator Art Director	1000: Isaac meet Alex C @ Prod Office 11:30: Rehearsal Space Viewing – Hazel, Eleanor @ Kobi Nazrul Centre	Location Recce TBC Louis, Zac, Eleanor 1500 & 1700: 1st AD I/Vs: Stefan, Eleanor Personnel start: Prod Accountant (p/t)	0930, 1100 & 1600: Editor I/Vs: Stefan, Eleanor am: Louise n/a	CASTING @ Central Stefan, Louise, Mary, Andre		
	21 OCT MON	22 OCT TUES	23 OCT WED	24 OCT THU	25 OCT FRI	26 OCT SAT	27 OCT SUN
-4	Personnel start: Costume Designer	CASTING @ Central Stefan, Louise, Mary, Andre		CASTING @ Central Stefan, Louise, Mary, Andre	PROSTHETIC FITTING @ Kristyan Mallet GEMMA Stefan to Rome		
	28 OCT MON	29 OCT TUES	30 OCT WED	31 OCT THU	1 NOV FRI	2 NOV SAT	3 NOV SUN
-3	INFORMAL READ (Ep 1) GEMMA, STEVE, ESTHER, DAN Stefan, Louise, Mary, Andre Personnel start: Production Secretary First Assistant Director Costume Supervisor		GEMMA n/a	VFX Meeting @ MPC Stefan, Louise, Emma, Amir			
	4 NOV MON	5 NOV TUES	6 NOV WED	7 NOV THU	8 NOV FRI	9 NOV SAT	10 NOV SUN

In the illustration above, the left hand column is counting down the weeks left until the first scheduled day of principal photography. The grey box starting on Monday 14th indicates the current day, and the PPD as it currently stands. It is regularly updated as each new event or appointment occurs.

It also contains a small example of the logistical challenges that a production coordinator might face, and their reliance on their production runner. The diary has a fairly innocuous entry on Friday 25th October: *'Stefan to Rome'.* Stefan is the director of our fictional production and has to get to Rome, and the production coordinator is asked to organise the travel. This seemingly simple request requires negotiation of the cheapest prices for booking cars to the airport, flights, car rental and the perfect luxury hotel, as well as writing up a travel itinerary and distributing it to all of the relevant parties who need to know where their director is.

The likelihood is that, after all this planning, Stefan will get to the airport only to find he has forgotten his passport, even after several reminders. At this point, the production coordinator has to send their runner to Stefan's house to collect the passport and frantically drive across London's Friday rush-hour traffic to get to the director in time for the flight. The result is that all of the production work that was meant to be completed by 7pm that day is delayed, and the production coordinator will be staying until 10pm to get it all done ready for next week.

The moral of this story is that the production office has to keep the show on the road no matter what diversions appear. A production runner could be asked to do anything that is required to get the job done, without complaint.

Our PPD is now counting down the last two weeks before the first day of principal photography:

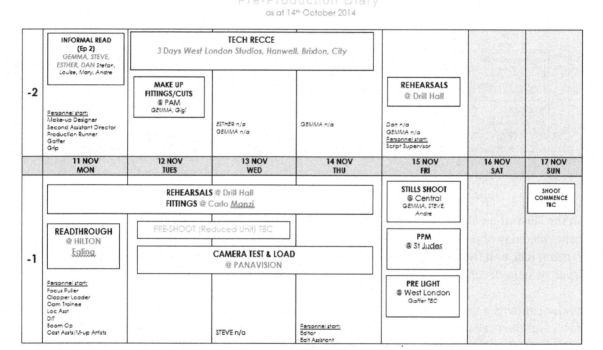

On 'SWITCH', as on all productions, each team will expand in scale as the production gathers momentum closer to the first shoot day, and so more job opportunities will arise.

In most cases, the person hiring for a production will be a freelancer, who will themselves be drafted in for a short-term contract. If you are sending CVs to the parent production company, the likelihood is that they will send them onto to the production coordinator, who may or may not distribute them onto the intended departments. Quite often, there are so many CVs being sent to the production office, that they easily get lost in the crowd, or ignored en-masse. A busy team may already have people in mind for many of the positions, or may prefer to use a diary service or crewing service to find someone for them, especially if they are looking for a specific skill set. If you do apply with your CV, you must do your research and determine the right person to approach within the department you are most interested in.

As an increasing number of crew come on board, the pre-production builds to a crescendo with three crucial components: read through, tech recce and pre-production meeting (PPM). It is unlikely that runners will be required to attend any of these elements, but production runners will certainly be involved in helping set some of them up.

The Read Through

The script read through is the first time that all (or most) of the cast are assembled together, and is sometimes called a table read. All of the actors read their parts, and any missing cast members will be replaced with a stand-in. The read through will be led by the first assistant director (first AD), who will read in the scene descriptions, and will be eagerly watched by the writer, director and producer. The script supervisor will be vigilant of timings for scenes, and the costume and make-up teams will be able to meet the remaining cast members for fittings and tests. For the second assistant director (second AD), it is an opportunity to meet the cast and discuss their needs. This is essential, as the second AD will be the primary point of contact with the cast members throughout the production.

The Tech Recce

The technical recce (short for reconnaissance and pronounced rek-e) usually happens at least a week before principal photography begins; earlier on bigger and more complicated productions. The heads of department (HoDs) travel together to each of the key locations: a touring party viewing all of the chosen venues at the same time, and some for the first time. It is an important part of the process as the director is available to all of the HoDs to answer questions, and physically display their vision for the film. The HoDs can now visualise the set or location, which will inform their decisions on things like lens choices, camera positions and objects that might need covering or removing, and are able to ask questions about the shoot and spot potential problems. There will be lots of notes taken and instructions relayed back to base for all departments

The PPM

The pre-production meeting (PPM) is again led by the first assistant director and includes the heads of department and often their seconds in command. This will happen after the tech recce and usually a few days before principal photography begins.

The first AD will proceed to walk through every single scene in the schedule order (not the script order), highlighting areas where clarification is required from certain departments or further discussion is needed. It can last for hours and the aim is to leave no stone unturned before the camera starts rolling. If there is an issue over how to shoot a particular scene, this is the opportunity to raise any questions. It may not get resolved immediately, but everybody leaves the room knowing what needs to happen, and who is taking responsibility for what. In theory, if the whole of the pre production has been smooth and communication between the departments has been fluid, then there will be few outstanding issues; if there are, then there is still time to raise concerns and address the problem. When the PPM is complete and the final issues have been resolved, the second AD will be able to finalise and distribute the call sheet for day one of principal photography.

The read through, tech recce and PPM are designed to pull together the strands of every department's prep for the film, and bring everybody together onto the same page. The volume of paperwork (which we will look at in the next chapter) reflects the fast evolving process. Barely anything, except an actor's improvisation, is left to chance, and every base is covered.

Production

'Filming is relentless by its very nature and you must meet that task with your own relentless energy'

Actor/Director Russell Crowe talking to the AFI in 2015

An average shooting day is called a 'straight' day, and is broken down into a schedule something like the below. Remember, this is just an example as very few filming days are the same.

06:00
➢ Facilities vehicles to be up and running (trailers, costume and make-up trucks, dining bus, etc.)
➢ Actors collected by 'unit drivers' (personal chauffeurs) from their home or hotel and driven to unit base

06:15
➢ Unit manager, second AD, costume and make up arrive and set up at unit base. Floor runners, location runners, costume and make-up trainees are expected to arrive at the same time or in some cases, before their HoD.

06:45
➢ First actors go into costume or make up.

07:30   Breakfast
➢ Breakfast for all cast and crew is served from the catering truck. Meals are then consumed in a specially converted double decker, known as the dining bus.
➢ All departments will be prepping their gear in time for call on camera, so some people will be grabbing breakfast on the run.
➢ Floor runners are expected to report to the second AD before call time.

08:00   Call time, location one
➢ Everyone is expected on set to start the first scene of the day. There may be a short distance to travel from the unit base, so transport and other essential vehicles will drive to the set. Stand-ins may be used to block through the lighting and rehearse the camera, while the director briefs the actors.
➢ Shooting starts, and continues until lunch time.

13:00   Lunch at unit base
➢ Even though an hour is scheduled, not everyone gets that much time; some of it is taken up by travel

- Many productions now prefer to shoot a 'continuous day', which means not stopping for an official lunch break and finishing one hour earlier. Lunch on a continuous day is consumed on the go.

14:00   Call time, location two
- Shooting takes place at the second location
- Moving locations is common, but when the facilities vehicles have to drive to the next place, that is called a unit move. It is not desirable, as the travel time cuts into the shooting day, but in some cases it is unavoidable.

16:30 Tea
- Sandwiches and snacks are provided for tea and mostly eaten 'on the run' while setting up. Food is reserved for those are unable to step away from set.
- A 'continuous day' will not stop for tea, instead craft services will be available all day.

19:00   Wrap
- Some crew members are lucky in that they are able to down tools and travel home almost immediately, but others will continue to work and reset for the next day. The camera will need to be broken down and put back on the camera truck, costumes washed, locations cleaned and call sheets emailed. The script supervisor will compile their notes for the day, ready to send to the editor. The cast members will be de-rigged: removing costume, make up, sound equipment.
- A rushes runner will then take the day's footage, called the rushes, and deliver it to the editor (or more likely the edit assistant), who will begin to import them to the secure AVID for the production. The DIT and production office will also receive back-ups. In years gone by, the rushes would be exposed film which was 'rushed' to a lab and processed in an overnight bath. Although some productions still shoot on film, the majority of film and TV drama productions now use a fully digital workflow.

As you can see, each day of filming is long and challenging. The European Working Time Directive indicates that crew must have a certain amount of time off, yet most official filming hours take that law right to its very limit, shooting as much as is reasonably possible in a given day. The fewer days a producer is employing crew, the cheaper it is to make a film.

Legally, crew should have 11 hours 'off the clock' meaning that they cannot start work until at least 11 hours after they have finished a previous shift. It is certainly not unheard of that this so-called 'turnaround' is broken, but it is unsafe for reasons we will discuss in the next chapter. A 'split' day is when filming takes place from noon to 11pm, or some other variation of time like 1pm to midnight. Unit managers, second ADs and costume and make-up artists will regularly work more hours than others as a basic requirement of their job. If you are keen to work in any of them, you need particular stamina.

When filming night scenes, the schedule has to work out how this can be done without compromising the 11-hour turnaround, and is typically done by bunching the night shoots together in the overall schedule. Going from shooting nights back to straight days is known as 'coming back around the clock', and gives you a feeling similar to jet lag.

Most productions shoot a five-day week, Monday to Friday, but there are variations on working patterns and each production has different requirements. The typical pattern of working across a two-week period is called an 11-day fortnight. It is a five-day week followed by a six-day week, or vice versa: for example, start shooting on Monday and work through to Saturday, take Sunday off and then back to work on Monday to Friday. As films usually shoot for at least six weeks, the shooting schedule might be something like five days one week, six days the next, and so on over the course of production. In this instance, it means 33 working days over a total of 42, and gives crew just nine days off in six weeks. Working 33 'straight days' can be an endurance on its own, and mixing in 'split' days and 'coming back around the clock' means it can be physically and mentally gruelling. Make no mistake, these hours are punishing.

Indeed, as an old boss of mine used to say: 'The only glamorous part of the film industry is when the people who didn't work on the movie walk up the red carpet'.

To cope with the demanding workload, almost every department has a budget for 'dailies': crew members brought on for a day at a time to cope with a particular scene or scenes. For example: scenes that require a lot of background artists, as additional runners are needed to shepherd the crowd, along with more costume and make-up artists, a 'B' camera team, etc. Whatever it may be, dailies jobs are common, and quite often late notice. The larger the scale of the film, the more dailies are needed.

Post Production

The Edit

At the end of every shooting day, the rushes are brought to the edit suite and are logged, transcoded and imported by the edit assistant. The editor will start reviewing the material from the moment they have it in the edit suite, and will work 'offline' to start assembling the edit. Because the size of the data that comes from set is so large, the editor will use lo-res footage to make an initial assembly.

This involves cutting a rough outline of individual scenes as they arrive, and constructing the overall film as the shoot continues elsewhere. (Many high-end editors try to be as close to the filming location as possible, but budgets do not always allow for that.) Picking out the best shots and piecing bits together, editors solve problems and give feedback to the director as they go. A very experienced feature-film editor told me that he aims to speak with his director at least twice a day. Many editors also try to get involved in a film as early as possible, even during script development and pre production; a voice from the edit suite can certainly help steer a project in the right direction before and throughout filming.

During the shoot, script supervisors will also send copies of their records to the editor. Their paperwork is used for continuity and story purposes, and gives an overview of what has been shot, how it was shot and details of each take. The editor can review the paperwork, and get additional pointers from the director via the script supervisor's notations.

Organisation is a key part of the editing process, especially when dealing with so much material, and the assistant editor is required to transcode the material, log shots and move the rushes into 'bins' to catalogue the material. They will also need to liaise with the production regarding logistics. Most projects have at least a first assistant editor, and depending on the budget level, you may find a second assistant editor and an edit trainee (A common route into editing is starting as a post-production runner and working upwards.)

Once the rushes from the final day of filming are imported, the editor has all of the assets to start work on a full assembly, and the director becomes available to get into the edit. What then occurs is a series of discussions and negotiations over every shot, scene and reel of the film. There will be lots of changes and it will be a laborious process; indeed, many editors prefer to be left alone. Tensions can easily build, particularly when creative decisions are at stake, so an editor must be a master diplomat.

At the end of this process, the editor and director will have assembled a fine cut and also a director's cut. That cut is then presented to the producer, who will give notes, and further cuts might be required. (In film, there may be several screenings of various cuts to test audiences, producers and other executives to hone the edit, but TV drama is on a much tighter schedule and may not have the benefit of test screenings.) Sometimes the director needs further outside input, and studios often retain the services of a supervising editor who can offer insight and wisdom to support the edit. Sometimes an edit lays bare the gaps in the film, and if there is budget for it, additional photography might take place.

When all of the parties are agreed on the final cut they sign off on the 'picture lock', which means that all of the edits will remain as they are on the same timecode until the final delivery of the film. The locked picture will produce the edit decision list (EDL), information about the timecodes of the locked picture. Once the post house has assembled the hi-res images according to the EDL, the colourist will then be able to start work alongside the DoP. This process is called 'the grade' and on feature films can take up to two weeks; a TV drama might only have the budget and schedule to grade for a couple of days. VFX companies will now also start to lock their work to the picture.

It is now the responsibility of the post-production supervisor to oversee the delivery of the final film, managing all of the various post-production departments to ensure that schedules are kept on course and that the budget is managed.

Sound

Audiences generally underestimate the power of sound in a movie. In the interview section of this book, double Oscar-winning sound mixer Chris Munro describes the importance of the audio experience to the finished picture. The big US studio movies have tended to give far more respect and credit to the sound teams than many UK productions have, recognising that good sound can absolutely transform a film. With the advance of home cinema and high quality flat-screen TVs the domestic experience of sound is also generally excellent on TV drama.

After picture lock, audio components are then required to match the visuals. First the composer is brought in to view the picture and start to work with the director. They will lay a temporary track down as a guide while they develop compositions for the score.

The sound designer will then begin to work on the audio elements and 'spot' the film with the director, working through the cut to identify exactly what is required. This will mean recording Foley, sound effects and additional dialogue recording (ADR), which will take place in specialist studio facilities. If the actors are unavailable for ADR in person, they are required to connect with the studio in what's called a two-way, via an ISDN line, to record the additional dialogue.

The musical score is usually recorded in more traditional facilities, such as Abbey Road or Air studios in London, and will vary in size and scope according to the requirements of the film and the budget available. Master film composers like Ennio Morricone and Hans Zimmer are vastly talented individuals who can enhance the film from the merely good to iconic.

The pre-mix is when all of the sound elements have been drawn together for an initial version, which might still include guide or temp tracks. When all of the parties are agreed on the audio elements–the original recording, the ADR, the Foley, the sound effects, and the score – the final mix can begin. Mixing the final cut together is still done against the locked picture, and the sound post-production team make different versions of the mix for the various versions they might be shown in. If, for example, the movie is available in all forms, there would be an ATMOS version for theatres capable of delivering that, then a 7.1 version for normal cinema, a 5.1 version and so on. There is also a mix for television, so the range sits within the permitted scale set by the broadcasters, and one for airline companies showing it in-flight. On certain airlines, and in particular territories, swearing and blasphemy might be dubbed out or replaced, which is all done in the ADR sessions.

The Finished Product

Once the component parts are completed, and the final audio-mix is laid-back to the picture, the online begins: this entails adding the captions, titles, end credits and legal and copyright notices to the conformed and coloured picture. The finished film is then delivered to the company in the format of their choice: if it is intended for cinema, for example, a digital cinema package (DCP) is required.

The post coordinator will inherit a large volume of paperwork from the production team, and will add their own before preparing all documentation for the production company. As individual involvement in a film project is mostly transient, it is essential that the documentation that accompanies a film is precise, clear and comprehensive. Should the production company be hit with a lawsuit of insurance claim months, or even years, after release, there needs to be a clear paper trail concerning all elements of a film.

If all has gone to plan with making the film, the distribution and marketing teams can now move into action and, hopefully, implement the ideas and plan that were born right back at the film's inception.

Obstacles
Of course, what you have just read is the idealised process of making a film or TV drama. No job is ever that straightforward, and there are myriad factors that can make the experience incredibly challenging and difficult.

At any single moment in the production process, you might encounter something that you never could have foreseen that will scupper your plans. People are human; mistakes happen; pressure of the work can spill into frustration and we are all prone to errors of judgement. Even the best-laid plans are easily upset when there are a lot of people and technology involved. For example, your leading actor might lose their false teeth the night before their close ups, a French air-traffic-control strike might leave your director stranded in Nice, an investor might pull the plug on the eve of filming or a local gangster might steal your generator truck for ransom: all true scenarios, unfortunately.

In his book *Creativity, inc.*, Ed Catmull, President of Pixar, confessed that a simple piece of mistyped code deleted over 90% of *Toy Story 2* just a few months before its completion. Two years of their work was wiped completely from their system *and* their faulty back-up system. If it wasn't for the technical director's personal back-up version saving the day, Pixar might well have vanished in 1998.

The overall moral of the story is to plan in as much detail as you possibly can, but learn to roll with the punches and keep your wits and humour sharp. Just don't expect a smooth ride: you will learn something the hard way on most jobs.

The Paperwork

This section concerns itself with a few of the key pieces of paperwork used in every film and TV drama production. If you are starting out as a runner, more than likely you will be handed some of this paperwork to photocopy without any explanation. It's expected that you know how to decipher it, decode it and act upon it if required. There are abbreviations and common shorthand used throughout. If you don't know what something means, don't be afraid to ask. Any production manager worth their salt would rather you do so rather than make a mistake. They would, however, also rather you look for answers yourself before asking.

I'm going to show you some examples of what this paperwork actually looks like, how it is used and the ramifications of any changes. You may have seen similar paperwork before on short or student films but I want to give detail and context to each of these key documents, looking at both what they do and how they are interpreted.

For the purpose of illustration, we return to our previous production 'SWITCH'. Again, all the paperwork in this chapter has been mocked up for this fictional movie.

Scripts

The script is the genesis of every project, and virtually all screenwriters and production offices in the industry use a program called *Final Draft*. Its software is compatible with industry standard scheduling software Movie Magic Scheduling, and we will look at scheduling in this chapter, too. In Final Draft, each page should, in rough theory, equal a minute of screen time. Feature length scripts are normally at least 90 pages long, and TV drama usually 40 to 60 pages per episode. When you get your script, your own name may be watermarked on every single page, to prevent leaking of plot detail to the press or online. Very large productions can be so secretive that many crew members are never issued their own script. One of the members of *thecallsheet*.co.uk once told me that on a particularly high-profile sci-fi film, his entire department was only allowed one copy of the script, which was locked in a safe, which itself was locked in a room within Pinewood Studios to which only one person had a key. In order for anyone in the department to read the script, they had to ask permission, hand over their phone and then be locked in the room with it. As you can see, protecting the plot is taken very, very seriously. You may be asked to sign a non-disclosure agreement (NDA), which is a legally binding document stating that you are not allowed to discuss the film.

The script, however, is never actually fully finished until the 'picture lock', when the edit is complete then the rest of the post production can start. The structure of the story and script can change in the edit, and dialogue might be slightly altered in ADR. A script can and will change during the production as the actors and directors flesh out the characters and plot, or the writer may want to make changes

Your first shooting script will be given to you on plain white paper and will be issued with a corresponding number, assigned against your name for the 'distribution list'. That is a huge spreadsheet of all crew, which the production office uses to track who has been sent which documentation, and when.

This 'locked' shooting script will be the base for all subsequent drafts and additions. Even if there are changes, the page numbers and scenes will remain the same; if a new scene is added, it will be called 'Sc. 5a' or 'Sc. 5b' and so on.

In order to make it clear what script elements have changed, and to save on huge wastes of paper, only the altered pages are re-issued. The right hand margin contains an asterix (*) next to the line that has been changed, to easily denote the alterations. Each script change is also printed on different coloured paper, easily identifiable within the original white shooting script. To complicate matters, the UK has a different order of colours to the US system.

The changes might be for dialogue, but they may also include new scene description that can alter the likes of location or props. It's important that you read all changes, as they may affect you and your department. When the script change is issued, there is normally a cover memo highlighting alterations to dialogue, location or action.

Let's use a crude example to realise the effect of a seemingly simple script change: in a scene in which one character shoots another, the director decides he wants a different weapon. The change is made from:

```
Delores shoots Juan with a revolver
```
to:
```
Delores slashes Juan with a knife
```

The knock-on effect touches almost everyone on set, and ripples through the departments. The stunt team need to change the fight choreography, under the watchful eye of the health and safety advisor or unit medic. The second AD now needs to arrange a rehearsal for the actors with the new prop, and the armourer needs to locate the type of knife the director wants to use. The make-up and SFX teams need to make new prosthetic wound moulds to place on the actor playing Juan, the costume designer needs to amend the costume, and they need to work out the continuity of blood splatter on Delores's shirt. The camera and lighting teams will need to work out the change of blocking in the scene, and may need to order different lenses and lights as well as thinking about the reflective surface of the knife blade. The art director will want more repeat props, as there will be more blood on set that will need to be cleaned before another take can take place.

It doesn't end there. This change will incur more time and monetary costs – including more SFX, more days for the stunt team, room hire for the rehearsal and more costumes –and all of these need to be factored in by the heads of department and, in some cases, negotiated with the production manager. The ripple effect might be felt even more keenly by all departments if they need to review their budget.

Pre-Production Diary (PPD)

Many people get their start as production runner and, while it's important to observe and absorb all the paperwork that passes through your hands, the pre-production diary (PPD) is one of the most important. It will give you a solid sense of what is on the horizon so you can anticipate and prepare accordingly. We looked at an example of the PPD in the last chapter, so flick back if you want to take another look at it.

The Schedule

Once you have a shooting script locked in place, the schedule is then worked out by the first assistant director using all the information contained within the script and details ascertained from the film's director and HoDs. They will go through every single scene and input it into their scheduling software, and the completed schedule is arguably a more important document for the crew than the script, as it is the skeletal framework for the entire shoot. HoDs have to be vigilant of both the story order and the schedule order.

The following is an example of what one scene might look like in a schedule. You can see that all of the elements are separated and accounted for, almost like an inventory for each scene. The final version of this is often called the 'full fat' schedule.

106 EXT Street	Day	3/8	1052hrs	Wardour St. W1
	Blue			Shots: :04

SGT. BOWSER chases DELORES & JUAN through Soho

Cast Members	**Props**
01.DELORES	10. Sgt.Bowser's walkie-talkie (F/P)
03.JUAN	**First AD Notes:**
10.Sgt. BOWSER	Location Street Closed to All Traffic
	Steadicam Seq. TBC (check with PM?)

Background Actors
     SWAT Team x 10
Stunts
     Stunts no longer Req. see Blue Pages
Vehicles & Vessels
     SWAT Truck x 1 (inc. Driver)
Armourer & Weapons
     Armourer Req.
     SWAT Team weapons
Camera
     'B' Camera req.
     Hand–held or easy rig – tbc
     Mini Jib & addtional Grip (pre–rig)
Wardrobe
     03. Juan's jacket (repeats)
Set Dressing
     Playback for Shop Windows Req.
Director's Notes:
     1. Hi Shot of chase (crane)
     2. Handheld or Steadicam of chase
     3. E/S of empty street (2nd Camera?)
     4.POV of chase through car windscreen

108   EXT Rooftop   Day   1   *0501   6th Floor MPC 127 Wardour

Sample breakdown of a 'Full Fat' schedule in Movie Magic Scheduling

Just as Final Draft is the industry standard screenwriting software, most schedules are created on a piece of software called Movie Magic Scheduling, which you can buy in the UK from Sargent Disc (who kindly assisted us in getting permission from Entertainment Partners to print the fictional schedule you see here.)

When the first AD creates the full fat schedule in Movie Magic Scheduling, they are also able to click a button to convert the information into a strip schedule. This is the boiled-down version of the full fat schedule, where you can get around 20 scenes on a single page. Below are the three scenes for our fictional movie 'SWITCH'. We will look at each block in more detail, but this is how it will appear on the page.

106	EXT	Street	Day 12	3/8	pgs	01, 03, 10	First AD Notes:
	SGT. BOWSER chases DELORES & JUAN through Soho			Blue		Wardour St. W1	Location Street Closed to All Traffic
108A	EXT	Rooftop	Day 12	1	pgs	01, 03	
	DELORES confronts JUAN on the Rooftop			Pink		6th Floor, MPC, 127 Wardour St. W1	
17	INT	Police Station	Night 02	4/8	pgs	01, 03	
	DELORES bails out JUAN			White		West London Studios,	

A strip schedule (or one-liner as it's often called), will start out in story order: scene one, two, three, four and so on. From that, the first AD will rearrange the strips into a shooting order and, contrary to what many people still believe, the majority of films are shot out of order.

When compiling a shooting order, every aspect needs to be considered, principally around artist, studio, location availability and, most importantly, budget. Cost implications mean that scenes are grouped together by location, so that the production only shoots in each place for the shortest amount of time.

As an illustrative example, all of the scenes in the Batcave would be shot in the same week, then the set would be taken down and the crew would move onto Bruce Wayne's mansion to shoot all of those scenes over a few days, and so on. A production would not want to rent expensive studio stages, build the Batcave set for the first scene and then keep renting it for another 15 weeks until you come back to shoot the next scene there. Likewise, renting the expensive house that doubles for Bruce Wayne's mansion only makes financial sense if you shoot all of those scenes in one go. This scheduling might mean shooting scene one of Batman entering the Batcave, then shooting the emotional final scene of the whole movie in the same set shortly after.

You also do not want to shoot the most difficult scene on the first day of filming or, if you can help it, the last. There are myriad factors to take into consideration to work out the right schedule and, just as the script will change on a regular basis, the schedule will also move around.

Schedule manipulation is also an important tool available to the director. Mike Leigh likes to shoot in story order, giving his actors a few pages of script at a time so they can 'become' the characters and live through the story. On *This is England*, Shane Meadows kept one of his actors isolated from the rest of the cast for weeks, then surprised them all by throwing them together into a scene while the cameras were rolling, it had a devastating effect, provoking genuine reactions.

There is another obscure piece of paperwork to come out of the schedule called the doods, which stands for 'day out of days'. Although it sounds like a terrible B-movie, it is in fact a document that shows which actors are working on what days, and is required only by certain departments. (The doods is further explained in the glossary at the back of the book, which lists man the important terms used within the industry.)

Practically speaking, there are different ways of setting up your schedule, depending on the production and the first AD's preference. Let's have a look at an individual line from our schedule, below:

106	EXT	Street		Day 12
		SGT. BOWSER chases DELORES & JUAN through Soho		
108A	EXT	Rooftop		Day 12
		DELORES confronts JUAN on the Rooftop		
17	INT	Police Station		Night 02
		DELORES bails out JUAN		

We can see that each 'strip' relates to a specific scene, the number of which is given on the left hand side. If there is a 'pt' next to the number, this indicates that the shoot is for part of a scene: if a scene is two people talking in a house and they open the door to a large crowd, it would be broken into its two respective parts.

If the scene number has 'A' or 'B' next to it, that indicates that it is an amended scene not in the original script, as we looked at previously.

Moving across the line, 'INT' means interior filming and 'EXT' means exterior filming. If you see 'INT/EXT' it means that you will be doing both within the one scene: a character walking from their office and exiting the building onto the street.

The text on the right of the line, in this case 'Night 2', indicates the point that we are at in the story. The script is broken down sequentially, and each scene given as part of the chronological order of the story, so 'Day 1' would be the first scene and so on. This is included for the sake of continuity, and to follow where we are in the order of the film at any given point. Although not visible on the printed page, the daylight scenes are coloured yellow and the night time scene strip is blue.

The next box along the line features the page length of the scene, and also includes the script version that it appears in:

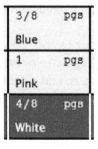

You will recall how in the previous script section we noted that a page could be broken down into eighths? We can now see from this the proposed length of this particular scene in the final film. As an example, a scene in a police interrogation room might contain lots of dialogue between investigators and the interviewee, so it might be 3 and 6/8pgs in length, while a scene with a character walking down the street might only be 1/8pgs. The first assistant director will be able to judge how much they can film in any given day, and so each of these strips will be moved about in order to fill each day.

The final panel gives us information about the cast members who are involved in the scene and its location:

01, 03, 10	First AD Notes:
Wardour St. W1	Location Street Closed to All Traffic
01, 03	
6th Floor, MPC, 127 Wardour St. W1	
01, 03	
West London Studios,	

The numbers on the left (01, 03, 10) refer to the named cast members who are involved in this scene. Each character in the script is assigned a number that will stay with them throughout the production. If a character that appears in the first draft of the shooting script is suddenly written out before production, the number goes with them to avoid confusion. Sometimes, the volume of background artists required might also be included in this box.

Colours are used to identify the changes as new schedules are issued. Unlike script amendments, where just the new pages are printed, the entire new strip schedule from the date of issue to the end of production will be distributed to the crew.

Ultimately, the strip schedule gives all the essential information required for a scene at a glance. It's condensed into a format that will be repeated for every single scene, and because of its concise nature will be used in the daily call sheet rather than the full fat version.

The Call Sheet

This is a concise document, usually just a couple of pages, distributed to all members of crew for every single day of shooting and covering every essential detail. If you ask any production coordinator or second AD a question about filming times, locations or schedules, they are likely to say 'it's on the call sheet' without looking up at you. A paper version will be handed out individually, and an email version is sent to every member of the crew at the end of each working day.

There are so many variables when filming, such as actor's availability, weather and locations, that all schedules have the potential to be changed at the very last minute. Most of the time, these tweaks are minor but all information must be correct at the time of publication. The details for the next day of filming, therefore, might not be locked down until very late in the day. There is little point in publishing something at lunchtime that might well change completely by 4pm. So the production manager or coordinator and second AD will work to lock down the next day's call sheet an hour or two before wrapping. The production runner will then print off or photocopy the document, and rush them around the set putting them into the hands of all the crew. There is also an email copy in case you don't receive it by hand, and further amended call sheets can be sent digitally if there are any urgent last minute changes. Thankfully, amendments are rare.
The call sheet is vital to the smooth running of the production, and all information must be clear and unequivocal therefore a form of shorthand is used to convey all details.

Let's take a look at a sample call sheet made up for our fictional film 'SWITCH'. (Every production will have their unique call sheet, but this particular template is available for free download on *thecallsheet.co.uk*.) Most of the document is self-explanatory but, if you haven't seen one before, it can look intimidating and confusing.

In essence, every call sheet gives you who, where, when, what and how of the day's filming. We will look at the individual segments:

Fictional Films

'SWITCH'

Production Office: Room 101, West London Studios, London W7 9PP
TEL: 020 7946 0000 FAX: 020 7946 0001

Director : Producer (s) :	Stefan Sucre Dan Mallett	**Call Sheet 01**		Sunday 17th November 2014	
Line producer: 2nd Assistant director: Prod coordinator: Location manager Unit manager: 3rd Assistant director:	Eleanor Howard Luke Roxburgh Alex Todorova Martha Smith Jojo David Hattie Jenkins	07700 900 123 07700 900 456 07700 900 789 07700 900 101 07700 900 121 07700 900 314		**UNIT CALL** Breakfast from Lunch: Estimated wrap	**0800** 0700 1300 1900
Weather: Overcast early, bright sun by afternoon		Min Temp: Max Temp:	11 13	Sunrise : Sunset :	**0722** **1609**
UNIT BASE:	Howard Street NCP - London W1V 9PL				
LOCATION 1:	Wardour Street, London, W1. *Closed to traffic*				
LOCATION 2:	6th Floor, MPC, 127 Wardour Street, W1				
LOCATION 3:	West London Studios, London, W7 9PP				
UNIT NOTES: 1) Scott Mogul from Universal set visit **2) EPK Crew filming interviews with cast from 11am today** **3) There is no Congestion Charge on Sundays**					

SHOOTING SCHEDULE

SCENE	SET	SD/TIME	PG CT	CHARACTER
106	EXT. STREET Sgt Bowser chases Delores and Juan through Soho	D10	3/8	1, 3 ,10
108a	EXT. ROOFTOP Delores confronts Juan on the Rooftop.	N12	1	1, 3
	UNIT MOVE to LOCATION 2			
17	INT. POLICE STATION Delores bails out Juan	Day/Night Scene Day	4/8	1, 3
		Total	1 7/8 pgs	

No	ARTISTE	CHARACTER	P/UP	M/UP/HAIR	COSTUME	TRAVEL	ON SET
1	GEMMA TOWNES	Delores	0600	0630	0730	0750	0800
3	GIL HERON	Juan	0600	0730	0700	0750	0800
10	FEMI KUTI	Sgt Bowser	0630	0645	0730	0750	0800

SUPPORTING ARTISTES:

CHARACTER	AGENCY	SCENES	CALL @ U/B	COST	M/UP	READY
10 x SWAT Team	Mad Dog	65	0800	0800	0900	0900
2 x Male Police officers	Mad Dog	17	1400	1400	1430	1500

TOTAL = 12

ART DEPT	As per Production designer (07700 900 920)	To include playback in shop windows and dressing of rooftop garden Armourer: Tim Wesson (07700 900 920)
PROPS	As per Prop department (07700 900 920)	Various props on rooftop garden and police station
ACTION VEHICLES	As per Action car company contact (07700 900 920)	Police car and SWAT truck to unit base for 0800
CAMERA DEPT	As per Director of photography (07700 900 920)	B Camera crew: Operator: Bruce Fernandes (07700 900 920) Focus Puller: Oli Neighbour (07700 900 920) Crane from Crane-o-Vision to be deliver to set for 0800
COSTUME	As per Costume designer (07700 900 920)	Additional Dressers - Chris Chapman (07700 900 920) called to unit base for 0800

The block at the top of the page is 'who, where and when'. Some of this information will remain on every call sheet of the production, such as the film title, director, producer, production office and the key contacts and telephone numbers:

Fictional Films

'SWITCH'

Production Office: Room 101, West London Studios, London W7 9PP
TEL: 020 7946 0000 FAX: 020 7946 0001

Director : Producer (s) :	Stefan Sucre Dan Mallett	**Call Sheet 01**		**Sunday 17th November 2014**	
Line producer: 2nd Assistant director: Prod coordinator: Location manager Unit manager: 3rd Assistant director:	Eleanor Howard Luke Roxburgh Alex Todorova Martha Smith Jojo David Hattie Jenkins	07700 900 123 07700 900 456 07700 900 789 07700 900 101 07700 900 121 07700 900 314		**UNIT CALL** Breakfast from Lunch: Estimated wrap	**0800** 0700 1300 1900
Weather: Overcast early, bright sun by afternoon		**Min Temp:** **Max Temp:**	11 13	Sunrise : Sunset :	**0722** **1609**
UNIT BASE:	Howard Street NCP - London W1V 9PL				
LOCATION 1:	Wardour Street, London, W1. *Closed to traffic*				
LOCATION 2:	6th Floor, MPC, 127 Wardour Street, W1				
LOCATION 3:	West London Studios, London, W7 9PP				
UNIT NOTES: 1) Scott Mogul from Universal set visit **2) EPK Crew filming interviews with cast from 11am today** **3) There is no Congestion Charge on Sundays**					

Top Block

The rest of the information in the top block is changed daily according to the requirements. Each filming day is given a number (this is call sheet number 1), plus the day and date of filming. The unit call refers to the time when everyone must be ready to start work, and we can see that the breakfast catering truck is available from 7am. The sunrise and sunset times are obviously crucial when filming exteriors, and the weather report will indicate if you need to bring wet weather gear or sunglasses.

The middle part of the top block indicates the day's locations. The unit vehicles such as the make-up and costume trucks, dining bus, cast trailers, production offices, Winnebago's and honey wagon will be set up at the unit base, and we can see the locations are nearby. Often – and especially in city centres – it can be difficult to park a unit base right next to your location, so there will usually be minibuses shuttling back and forth.

The lower part of the top block contains a few key notes for the crew, which will change daily. Here, note one indicates that the studio boss is on set today, so everyone needs to be on their best behaviour. Note two states that the electronic press kit (EPK) crew will be on set; they are a separate company hired to film behind the scenes footage, and will usually attend sets on multiple days during production. The final note about the congestion charge is a useful piece of information, and prevents crew asking the question of the busy production coordinator.

The middle section of this page contains the 'what' of a call sheet:

SHOOTING SCHEDULE

SCENE	SET	SD/TIME	PG CT	CHARACTER
106	EXT. STREET Sgt Bowser chases Delores and Juan through Soho	D10	3/8	1, 3 ,10
108a	EXT. ROOFTOP Delores confronts Juan on the Rooftop.	N12	1	1, 3
	UNIT MOVE to LOCATION 2			
17	INT. POLICE STATION Delores bails out Juan	Day/Night Scene Day	4/8	1, 3
		Total	1 7/8 pgs	

It details the scenes that are scheduled to be shot today, the details having been extracted from the strip schedule, and a notification of the unit move for the final location. (Hopefully you can make sense of the content in this section now, but look back a few pages if you are still unsure.) Our second scene of the day on the 'EXT ROOFTOP 'is a new scene not in the original script, and we know this because the number of the scene is 108a. We know it features two of our lead actors, indicated by the numbers 1 and 3, and it's on Day 12 of the story, so we can check it against continuity.

Just below the strip schedule is the final part of the call sheet and it will run over to the next page. This details the 'how' of the days shoot:

No	ARTISTE	CHARACTER	P/UP	M/UP/HAIR	COSTUME	TRAVEL	ON SET
1	GEMMA TOWNES	Delores	0600	0630	0730	0750	0800
3	GIL HERON	Juan	0600	0730	0700	0750	0800
10	FEMI KUTI	Sgt Bowser	0630	0645	0730	0750	0800

SUPPORTING ARTISTES:

CHARACTER	AGENCY	SCENES	CALL @ U/B	COST	M/UP	READY
10 x SWAT Team	Mad Dog	65	0800	0800	0900	0900
2 x Male Police officers	Mad Dog	17	1400	1400	1430	1500

TOTAL = 12

We can see a new table with the name of our (fictional) actor along with their character name. Each piece of information along that row refers to that actor's specific timings for the morning: when they are picked up by their driver ('P/UP') and when they need to be taken into costume and makeup. Before the AD publishes these numbers, they will have devised timings in consultation with the costume and make-up designers respectively.

The next block contains specific details for our supporting artistes: how many are required, the agency they come from and the time they are expected to go through costume, make-up and be ready on set. The number of background artists will have been stipulated in the schedule at the outset, as we saw previously.

The next section (*below*) is a line-by-line account of departmental responsibilities. The name and number of the head of department is listed, plus the details of what is specifically required on that particular day. All of the departments will already have prepped what they need but, again for the sake of absolute clarity of communication, everything is laid out here:

ART DEPT	As per Production designer (07700 900 920)	To include playback in shop windows and dressing of rooftop garden Armourer: Tim Wesson (07700 900 920)
PROPS	As per Prop department (07700 900 920)	Various props on rooftop garden and police station
ACTION VEHICLES	As per Action car company contact (07700 900 920)	Police car and SWAT truck to unit base for 0800
CAMERA DEPT	As per Director of photography (07700 900 920)	B Camera crew: Operator: Bruce Fernandes (07700 900 920) Focus Puller: Oli Neighbour (07700 900 920) Crane from Crane-o-Vision to be deliver to set for 0800
COSTUME	As per Costume designer (07700 900 920)	Additional Dressers - Chris Chapman (07700 900 920) called to unit base for 0800

We can see that today, the art department need some dressing in the shop windows seen in scene 106 and that they have an armourer on set to provide the knife for scene 108a. The prop department have instruction, as does the action vehicle company for cars that appear on camera. We can see that the camera department have brought in some 'dailies' crew to man the B-camera.

Each line of the call sheet contains specific instructions and responsibilities for every department involved in the day's shoot, and these continue right to the end of the second page. Here, we can see that the rushes runner has specific instructions to collect the data or exposed film from the set and deliver it to the post production facility: an extremely important job.

We can also see that the next section clarifies how many meals the caterers need to provide for the day. The catering numbers on this particular job are quite straightforward, but on days with lots of background artists, a second or third catering truck may be needed. If you have a lot of background artists on a given day that also means that costume, make up and assistant director 'dailies' will also be on set and will need feeding too.

After the catering numbers is another strip schedule, the 'advance schedule' for the following day, Monday 18th November. This is another reminder to all crew as to what is next on the horizon, and if any additional requirements are needed.

The final section on this call sheet belongs to the unit drivers: each one is named and has clear instructions of who to collect and when to get them to set. The second AD will be in near constant contact with them to ensure they are where they should be

MAKE UP	As per Make up & hair designer (mobile number)	Prosthetic leg required, squibs and additional blood.
ELECTRICAL DEPT	As per Gaffer (mobile number)	Dimmer board Op (TBC) called to set for 0800
GRIP	As per Grip (mobile number)	Crane Supervision.
SOUND DEPT	As per Sound recordist (mobile number)	To include;
STANDBY'S	Grade: Name (mobile number)	
LOCATIONS	As per Location manager (mobile number)	*Access to walkway for lighting, kitchen extractors turned off please Artiste / VIP Green Room @ MPC 3rd Floor Background holding adjacent Holio restaurant*
SECURITY	As per Location security contact (mobile number)	To include information on security personnel
MEDICAL	Unit Nurse / Vet - (mobile number)	called to Unit Base @ Unit Call
FACILITIES	As per location facilities company Transport captain: Name (mobile number)	1 x artist trailer/ production office/ make up/ costume/ 3 way/Honeywagon/
RADIOS	c/o Walkie company (telephone number) Contact	Channels: 1 + 2: A.D's 3: Lighting 4: Locations/ Security 5: Art/ Props/ S'bys 10 x Pairs to be distributed and collected by a department
RUSHES	Camera & Sound Rushes to be collected from the camera truck on wrap by Ambrose Bash(07700 900 920) & delivered to Production office / Editors.	

CATERING: C/o Catering Company - Head Chef: Name (mobile number)

Breakfast available from:	0700 for approx	100 x cast & crew
Lunch available from:	1300 for approx	100x cast & crew
Tea & Sandwiches available from:	1700 for approx	100 x cast & crew
Tea, Coffee, & Water to be available all day on set & @ Unit Base		

ADVANCE SCHEDULE: Monday 18th November UNIT CALL : 0800

SCENE	SET	SD/TIME	PG CT	CHARACTER
2	EXT. FOREST Delores and Juan escape the masked man	D1	1/8	1, 3 , 15
3	EXT. FOREST Juan kills the masked man	D1	3/8	1, 3, 15
4	EXT. FOREST Juan and Delores find an old abandoned car	N1	4/8	1, 3
		Total	**5/8 pgs**	

BERT WOOSTER – 1ST ASSISTANT DIRECTOR

TRANSPORT :

TIME	UNIT DRIVER	CONTACT	PASSENGERS	FROM	TO
0600	BILL RICKMAN	07700 900 151	Gemma Townes	Home Address	Unit Base
0600	IAN KINGLSEY	07700 900 617	Gil Heron	Home Address	Unit Base
0600	BEN HURT	07700 900 181	Femi Kuti	Home Address	Unit Base

C/o Additional Transport 1 x 12 Seater Minibus. Driver : Barry Bethel (07700 900 920) To standby at Unit Base from 0700
1 x 12 Seater Minibus. Driver : Wanda Trump (07700 900 212) To standby at Unit Base from 0700

The studio and any financial backers will also receive copies of the call sheet via email, as well as a daily production report, which is usually compiled by the production manager and signed off by the line producer, but not shared with any other crew. This report logs and records all of the actions from the day's filming (what's been shot, what hasn't, what dailies crew came aboard, which actor turned up late, etc.) and outlines any adjustments or amendments for future planning.

The people responsible for financing the whole picture can use these two documents – the call sheet (what we intend to shoot) and the daily production report (what happened and any significant changes) – to monitor the production without needing to be present on set at all.

Sides

'Sides' are script pages that are issued along with the daily call sheet. It's not the entire script, just the scenes that are being shot that day as listed on the call sheet. 'Sides' are usually issued to those departments who will need to monitor continuity, and also for the actors to have a simple reminder of their lines.

Movement Order (MO)

The movement order, which is always attached to the call sheet, is the instruction on how to get to the unit base and key filming locations. The term is another one from the days of military personnel organising the crew, but is essentially the paper form of sat nav.

The MO will contain a map with the unit bases and locations specifically marked out, and a point-by-point series of driving instructions. The instructions do not start with an address tailored to specific individuals but will pick up from the most common route of entry for the crew. For example, if a production is filming on the Clifton Suspension Bridge, the directions might begin from central Bristol.

Most of the time, the unit base is a car park or a field, somewhere where you can park up lots of big trailers and trucks, so it might not have a postcode you can set in your sat nav. There will also be specific instructions on the MO about exactly where to park your vehicle, and any special considerations for travel or for the location. And if you live in an area that is popular for filming, you may also have seen the fluorescent arrow signs fastened to lamp posts that direct the crew to the base and locations.

As with the PPM, no stone is left unturned and there is no opportunity for anyone to say that they did not have the information to get to work on time.

Risk Assessment

This is a health and safety imperative that all companies must observe to ensure their employees are working in a safe environment. The film and TV industry have to issue one for each day of filming, because every day is different. You might be working with stunts, weapons, underwater, at height, with cranes, with animals – every day contains a new adventure and a new potential risk. It's important that you look at the paperwork to see where the dangers might lurk on set.

Departments and Roles, From HoD To Junior and Everything in Between

'A film is a paradox; it needs many people to make it, but it has to have a single voice'
- *Ken Loach, speaking with Cillian Murphy as part of the BFI 'In Conversation' talks, May 2015*

Making a film or TV drama requires a very wide range of expertise. Each production relies on a team of specialist technicians and highly skilled crew, assembled for a precise amount of time and then disbanded to look for other projects. Almost everyone is freelance.

If you're reading this book, you will likely have a good idea of what you want to do in the industry. Lots of people want to become directors, cinematographers or producers, but many of the people I speak with get their first taste of the industry properly and have their heads turned by another role that they hadn't previously thought of. Quite often seeing certain individuals at work inspires people to follow a different path.

Even if you do continue in your desire to be a director or DoP, you will certainly need to know and understand all of the other departments, their structures and hierarchies. All departments should aim to work in harmony, as they all want – and need – the end result to be as good as possible. As most of the workforce is freelance, there is also a financial imperative to perform well within a team, and any personal issues must be put aside for the benefit of the overall.

This section will give a basic guide to the different departments, the job roles that are in each and how they are structured in the hierarchy. Some are clearer than others, but the chain of command usually follows like this: everyone on set is there to service the vision of the director, but the producer is everyone's boss which is why we will look at this job role ahead of all others.

Below the director and producer, there are heads of department. These are the people at the top of their respective tree, utilising their experience and expertise to enable the director to achieve their vision within the constraints of the budget. All heads of department must have the requisite experience for the job, in order for the producer to satisfy their obligation to the financiers of the production, whether that is the broadcaster, studio or private investors. That experience is built up over years working through the ranks. They must effectively manage their own department, and that means choosing the right team.

Later in this book, there is an interview with the one of the world's leading chief electricians (or Gaffer), John Higgins. Speaking about his role as a head of department, he says: 'Avail yourself of the best crew around. The choice of crew is very important as a reflection of you'. I want you to keep that advice in mind; always try to think of the employer's perspective in terms of approach and conduct. You are representing your head of department as well as yourself.

We are now going to look at each role on a film set from top to bottom, grouped by department in alphabetical order. Not all of the job titles examined on the next few pages will be needed on all productions, and there are a few highly specialist roles that are not included either.

With an increasing number of individuals in the business, it is very rare for people to get their first role (on a proper production) at anything other than entry level. No matter where your role is in the chain of command, however, it is important to show deference to your superiors and treat everyone with respect, no matter what their role or department.

Through *thecallsheet.co.uk*, I see a lot of reasonably well-established people from the world of television try to jump across into film or high-end TV drama. I have never known of any production personnel who have made such a transition and remained at the same grade. The production manager of *Gogglebox*, for example, would never be considered by the producers of film or high-end small screen drama for the same role: the paperwork, systems, methods, demands and protocol are just too different. If an individual is serious about that move from television to film, then they would need to drop down at least two grades, and face a drop in pay, to even be considered for employment. That's not to say the production manager of *Gogglebox* isn't perfectly adept at their job, it's just a different role with different procedures and protocols, which can't be learned overnight.

The one key role that doesn't require a full description in this breakdown is the role of the screenwriter. You know what they do, and if it were not for them and their talent there would be nothing to produce.

Producer

The role of the producer is difficult to distil into a few words. Essentially, they are the driving force behind every project, from picking up the rights to a script and developing it, to raising finance, picking cast and key crew with the director, steering production and post, making distribution and marketing decisions and selling the film to the market. They do all of this while trying to oversee every penny and keep every stakeholder on their side. The producer is a shipbuilder who hires a director to steer the vessel, and their influence permeates through every part of the process.

Each production is a business in its own right. Some are backed by movie studios, others are supported by broadcasters and some have to find ways of making their film through independent means. Whatever the case, producers shepherd each project from conception to the market and it requires a very driven character to make that happen. Producers must be entrepreneurial, diplomatic, ruthless, charming and passionate about making films. It is their responsibility to keep their head above the cloud of production and focus on the story they want to tell, making sure that they don't mess it up. This involves taking many difficult decisions and managing multiple relationships, not only over a course of one film, but with a view to being able to make more.

Initially, producers will scour for material, commonly through reading speculative (spec) scripts and books that could make a transition to the screen, or by finding screenwriters who have completed manuscripts. In the case of studio projects, which usually concern a concept, individual, product or character that has an existing market, the producer will be given those assets to work with. Producers have several projects they are developing at any one time, and acquiring an 'option' for material is a race no one wants to lose.

From there, they will develop a script with screenwriters, or a mood/look book explaining the story, and prepare it to take to potential cast and directors. By attaching key talent to a project, the producer is in a better position to approach financiers; in the UK, this means the likes of BFI, Film4 and BBC Films. TV drama producers can approach the domestic broadcasters and also pitch to international broadcasters at markets such as MIPCOM, which is held in France each year.

If finance is raised or a green light given by a broadcaster, the producer will then usher the project into production. Once they appoint a line producer they will be able to delegate much of the work to them to take care of, but they will still have a series of high-level creative decisions to make. Throughout the entire production process, they will be aiming to retain their vision for the story, and ensure the whole thing stays on course and on budget. In post-production, the producer will be working with the editor and director to deliver the best possible product. There are usually many opinions upon what exactly this is, and this is a tough test of a producer's diplomacy and belief in the project.

Once the final cut has been approved, and the elements such as VFX and audio are added, the film is ready. In the case of a TV drama, it is now ready to transmit. In the case of the studio film, it is ready for release. If it is an independent production, then the producer will either sell it directly or through a distribution company.

At the point where the film is released, any income will be distributed back to the original stakeholders in the order specified in their contract. There are usually complex financial models in place to divide the box office, DVD and VOD (video on demand) sales, and the last financier in is often the first to be paid back. The producer cannot afford to burn bridges with financiers if they want to go to them for their next project, but they also need to do effective business with them and that means learning the complex art of negotiation.

The producer lives with each project for years, even when there is no money in it. They are the boss of the whole production and their ability to get a project off the ground is what opens up the possibility of employment for others. They are the central cog in the big machine of production.

Accounts Department

ABOUT

The accounts department is far more involved in the navigation of a film than you might think. The production accountant answers to the investors of the production while managing the day-to-day spending. As well as the traditional 'bean-counting' for the various stakeholders, they produce cost reports and analysis that enables the line producer to manage the production smoothly and spot any problems on the horizon.

Every single production is set up as a new company, so if the movie gets into financial difficulty or flops at the box office the debt and liability is contained within this 'ring-fenced' company and the parent company is legally and financially distanced from the problem.

Because a company is ring fenced, the production accountant manages a massive turnover in cash in a short space of time. The 'company' goes from nought to sixty in the space of a few weeks, and the accounts department must be reactive to that. They are often the early warning system for productions that are getting out of hand.

If you are starting out as a runner, you may well be given a cash 'float' to buy things for the production. You will need to reconcile that float with all of the receipts to the accounts department.

ROLES

Production accountant (Head of department)
Oversees all financial aspects of production including budget analysis, forecasting, cash flow, payroll, cost reports and providing updates to key principle

Assistant production accountant (Second in command)
Supports the production accountant throughout all aspects of financial management

Accountants assistant
Assists with the payroll, petty cash reconciliation and other day-to-day duties on a production

Cashier
Deals mainly with reconciling floats and managing on-site cash

Trainee accountant/cashier

KEY SKILLS: good head for figures; excellent organisational skills; methodical; ability to react quickly for the good of the production

SOFTWARE KNOWLEDGE: Sagepay, Excel, Movie Magic Scheduling, budgeting, bespoke payroll software

QUALIFICATIONS:
AAT (Association of Accounts Technicians) NVQ, APATS Course (The Production Guild of Great Britain), CIMA (Charted Institute of Management Accountants).

Action Vehicle Department

ABOUT

Working in collaboration with the production designer and/or the stunt team, the action vehicle coordinator will source, maintain and manage vehicles that will appear on screen. From single saloon cars to fleets of period vehicles, this department will have contacts throughout the automotive world to find the right vehicles for the character and the story.

Once the car is sourced, it may be used for stunt purposes (in which case multiple vehicles may be required for continuity), it may be rigged with heavy cameras attached to the bonnet or doorframe or it may simply be driven along the street.

Commonly, an action vehicle is placed on a low-loader, in order to film a character driving. The 'action vehicle' is placed on a flatbed trailer or attached by an 'A-frame', which is towed along by a larger truck with safety harnesses at the rear enabling key crew to ride along. The camera and lights will be rigged on the back of the towing vehicle, looking back at the action vehicle and the clear view behind it. The flatbed trailer is only a few inches from the ground, giving the appearance of being on the road. Depending on conditions outside the vehicle, the lighting department often place discrete fluorescent tubes inside the car to illuminate the actor.

'Hero' vehicles, such as James Bond's Aston Martin, will be well maintained during the shoot in order to ensure continuity. A good understanding of health and safety is also required.

ROLES

Picture car supervisor (Head of department)
Sources and manages vehicles and crew, oversees budget

Picture car driver
Highly trained driver with mechanical skills

Low loader driver
Expert driver

KEY SKILLS: mechanical skills, logistics, contacts, understanding of story, clear communicator, good with actors, knowledge of health and safety practices

SOFTWARE KNOWLEDGE: Microsoft Office

Art Department

ABOUT

Headed by the production designer, the art department is responsible for the overall look and appearance of the film including set design, props, set dressing and special effects. The production designer will oversee all facets of this, by sub-contracting further heads of department to complete specific duties, for example, a construction manager/company to build the sets.

ROLES

Production designer (Head of department)
Oversees all visual elements of sets and locations

Supervising art director
Oversees the art department and supports the art directors. Usually only required on large scale features

Art director
Manages and orchestrates the department, chooses crew and suppliers and supports the production designer

Standby art director
Ever present on set to adjust, arrange and organise the visual elements and monitor continuity

Assistant art director
Supporting the art director, duties vary depending on budget level of the production

Draughtsperson
Creates detailed and technical drawings of the set design

Graphics
Design, create and print signage and artwork for the production

Art department coordinator
Usually only required on larger scale productions to manage the workflow and communication

Art department runner/trainee
To support the team, often taking on small creative jobs as well as menial duties

KEY SKILLS: creative, resourceful, eye for detail

SOFTWARE KNOWLEDGE: AUTOCAD, Photoshop, Illustrator, InDesign, Sketch Up

NOTE: the art director will bring in additional departments depending on what is needed for the individual production; although they are their own departments, they report to the production designer. We will expand the set decorator's role and the props department later in the list.

Assistant Directors

ABOUT

The AD oversees schedules, operations and logistics, and organises on-set activities. Split into first, second and third assistant directors, they each have a different and specific role to keep the schedule on course.

The AD department are responsible for scheduling the entire shoot on paper, as detailed in the previous chapter. On set, the first AD will never be far from the action. They organise and orchestrate the rest of the crew to meet the director's vision, and have a plan B if they can't. They also help facilitate relationships between the director, DoP and actors.

The second AD will not be on set. They operate at unit base, welcoming the actors and overseeing them through costume and make up, as well as organising all of the transport and writing the next day's call sheet. They will be in regular contact with their first AD and liaise with all departments throughout the day to make any necessary adjustments or changes to the schedule and call times for cast members.

The third AD is the on-set contact between the actors and the AD team. They will organise the distribution of walkie-talkies, and on-set duties include managing background action.

The AD team will need floor runners for a variety of tasks, and expect them to display determination, charisma and a cool head.

ROLES

First assistant director (Head of department)
Schedules the shoot and is the director's right-hand person throughout filming

Second assistant director (Second in command)
Manages actors' transport, scheduling and writes the call sheet

Third assistant director
Right-hand person for the 1st AD on set; escorts cast members and manages background artists

Floor runner
Background management, lock offs and general running duties – including making tea

Set PA
Working under the instruction of the 3rd AD to work with background artists and locking off

Base runner
Supporting the second AD at unit base

Note: larger US studio feature films are increasingly employing additional 2nd ADs to work on set and additional 3rd ADs to at unit base. These are known as Floor 2^{nds} and Base 3^{rds}.

KEY SKILLS: attention to detail, strong leadership qualities, calm under pressure, quick witted, quick thinking, forward planning, diplomatic and a problem solver

SOFTWARE KNOWLEDGE: Movie Magic Scheduling, Final Draft

Camera Department

ABOUT

The director of photography is considered one of the most important roles on a film or TV drama. When the producer and director are sketching out their wish list of crew, the DoP is at the top of the list. Think of the influence of Roger Deakins on the Coen Brothers, Emanuel Luzbeki's visionary approach for Alfonso Cuaron and Alejandro González Iñárritu, or the visual style that Barry Ackroyd brings to a Paul Greengrass film.

The DoP will work closely with his own team and the Gaffer, who is the chief electrician, to create the lighting for the whole production. It's not just about understanding shot composition and lighting, however, it's being able to work closely with the director and actors and remaining sympathetic to their needs. These are soft skills that take time to hone.

The typical route in to this department is as a camera trainee, and the majority of film and drama is shot on the ARRI Alexa. If you are interested in this department, take time to understand the equipment and the suppliers.

There may also be 'B' and 'C' camera crew, if extra coverage of a scene is required.

ROLES

Director of photography (Head of department)
Works with the director and gaffer to compose the lighting, and the grip to determine camera movement

Camera operator
Frames the shots and manipulates the camera during a take

Steadicam operator
Usually brought in for dailies, as and when required, to move the camera smoothly through a shot

Focus puller / first assistant camera
Keeps the image sharp or soft as required, by measuring distances from lens to actor, and moving the focus of the camera during takes

Second assistant camera
Claps the board and logs takes. Also manages the lenses and upkeep of the camera equipment and works with the video assist to feed video village

Digital imaging technician (DIT)
Oversees the safe transferral and management of the data between camera and post production

Camera trainee
Assists the second assistant camera to manage the equipment and board

Camera car driver
Drives and manages camera truck; collections and drop offs

KEY SKILLS: keen eye for images; ability to work to a high standard under time pressure

EQUIPMENT: sound knowledge of all cameras, lenses and equipment

Catering

Providing catering for film and TV crews can be an incredibly challenging job for any chef. Unlike restaurant chefs, who work in the same building each night, film caterers day will usually start their day around 4am. They have to travel to remote locations in a mobile kitchen, come rain or shine and deliver top quality food.

It is their job to provide a range of options for breakfast, lunch and afternoon tea as well as provide hot drinks, water and snacks that can be consumed on the run, throughout the day. Crew members will line up outside the catering truck at meal times to collect their meals. If cast members are still in costume, make up or even in their trailer, a runner will be asked to fetch them tin-foil wrapped meal for them from the truck.

Hot breakfast is usually served at least 30 minutes prior to the unit call time, so that can mean that anything up to 100 crew and cast will need to be served in a relatively short time frame. Any delay might mean that crew don't get fed and that can have a knock on effect to individuals and in the worst case scenario, the entire unit.

The caterers must prepare their menu in advance and carefully select an inventory that can provide enough covers and be stored in the truck. Film caterers require logistical ability to match their culinary skills. Catering trucks usually need a minimum of 3 cooks to function smoothly.

An army marches on it stomach and crew members will spend longer on set than they will at home, so they expect to receive decent meals provided by the production. Good caterers can transform the morale of the crew.

Casting Department

Casting begins very early in the film's life cycle, and continues until well into production. Casting directors are sometimes consulted by producers before the script is issued to any agents, for their suggestions and advice. Successful casting is a vital part of getting a project off the ground in the first instance, as investors are unlikely to be interested until a lead actor is attached.

Casting for the principal roles on a film or drama happens during pre production, and the casting department work tirelessly to get credible actors in front of the director. The castings often take place in city centres, away from the production office, and tapes (or secure links) of likely candidates are distributed to key stakeholders for viewing.

We examined the geographical-industry dominance of London in the last chapter, and it's very pronounced in casting. The majority of actors, directors and producers live in London, so most casting jobs are based in the capital

Although there is a special alchemy that many good casting directors have, most of their skill is hewn from an appetite for the industry and years of experience.

Casting for background artists is always performed by specialist agencies, on the instruction of the 2nd AD. Supporting artists (SA's) not the responsibility of the casting director.

ROLES

Casting director (Head of department)
Works with the director and producer to find, suggest and test actors for the roles

Casting associate (Second in command)
The right hand of the casting director, responsible for day-to-day functions such as arranging sessions, organising deal memos and liaising with the production team

Casting assistant
Supports and aides the casting team

KEY SKILLS: great communicator, unflappable, able to multitask, passion for actors and acting

SOFTWARE KNOWLEDGE: rudimental editing software such as iMovie; secure online video portals

Clearances

ABOUT

Clearance is a little known but vital part of the film-making process. Every character name, brand, logo, piece of archive footage or company name that is visible on screen needs to be cleared. This means that production needs either permission from the existing copyright owner, or creates their own version which is then cleared through a series of research checks so it doesn't conflict with any existing copyright. It takes a lot of experience to know what type of clearance is needed, and how to obtain it. This is why you often see obscure brands or companies in films.

Construction Department

ABOUT

Working directly under the production designer and art director, this department is responsible for building safe and believable sets and scenery. The process starts with the designs handed over by the art director or draughtsman; these are then turned into blueprints by the construction manager, before being built by the team.

The majority of this work is done in a separate construction workshop, pre-fabricating many elements of the set before assembling them on the stage or location.

ROLES

Construction manager (Head of department)
Oversees the build, translates the art department's design into a safe and functioning set

Assistant construction manager (Second in command)

Standby carpenter
The on-set carpenter, who must be ready to react quickly to any changes and maintain current sets

Supervising carpenter
Oversees any wooden construction

Chargehand carpenter
Foreman of the carpenters

Carpenter
Creates sets and structures for use on screen

Trainee carpenter
Supports the team and undertakes basic carpentry duties

KEY SKILLS: carpentry, knowledge of blueprints, creative, calm under pressure, safe working practices
QUALIFICATIONS: CITB awarded NVQ

Costume Department

ABOUT

The costume designer must choose and create clothing that best represents the characters on screen. Precision is vitally important, as the look of a costume can reveal a character's profession, location, age, or personality before they have even opened their mouth.

Depending on the requirements of each specific production, the costume will be either selected 'off-the-rail' from shops or hire companies, or may be designed from scratch. Either way, there needs to be more than one of each item, each properly fitted to the individual actor.

A costume designer will typically start prep after the production designer, and will work with them to ensure that the costumes compliment the sets in terms of colour and theme. When these elements work in harmony, it is far easier for the DoP to capture the colour palette on screen.

Alongside the creative elements, the costume department oversee multiple practical considerations, one of the most important of which is preparing the costumes on a daily basis and monitoring continuity as the shoot continues. They must also ensure that all hired costumes are correctly stored, managed and returned in good condition; a huge undertaking if you consider the sheer volume of clothing that's used on a film or TV production.

ROLES

Costume Designer (Head of department)
Designs and creates the look for each character

Costume supervisor
Responsible for managing the team, overseeing continuity and undertaking administrative tasks like organising actor fittings

Wardrobe supervisor
Oversees the inventory, mends and accessorises the costume and dresses actors

Costume Standby
Stays on set with actors to maintain continuity and make running repairs

Costume daily
Brought in to dress on large-crowd days

Costume Maker
Creates unique garments and apparel to the costume designers' specifications

Costume assistant
Provides general support such as researching costumes as well as adapting, mending and dressing

Breakdown artist
Will give costume 'character' by distressing, dyeing or ageing specific garments

Costume trainee
Entry-level role to help support the team

KEY SKILLS: interested in clothing history and design; creative, organised, good communicator; confident and comfortable dealing with actors.

Editing Department

ABOUT

The editing department gradually assembles the footage shot by the director and crew into scenes, sequences, acts, and into the final film or episode.

Typically, the edit happens away from the set, where the rushes can be viewed and assembled in calm isolation. Feedback is given to the director by the editor, and there is a constant dialogue between the two. After filming is completed, the relationship between the director and the editor becomes the central part of making the film.

The editing department is usually very small, revolving around a single individual and editing software, but the editor relies on their team to process all of the technical elements efficiently and flawlessly. Each day, the rushes are brought from the set to the awaiting edit assistant, who will carefully transcode and log the footage into the Avid, and rough assembly will commence immediately.

The process of editing goes from assembly to rough cut, to fine cut and eventually picture lock, with lots of tweaking, tuning and maybe some test screenings along the way. Large studios also tend to employ a supervising editor to help oversee the post-production process, offering additional help and support if required. The length of the editing period is impossible to define, as every project has unique individual requirements as well as budgetary and schedule restraints. On larger productions, the editor will often speak with the director before a single scene has been shot, offering suggestions about how scenes might work once in the edit room. Indeed, several high profile editors have told me that they aim to get as involved as early as possible, so they know they will have footage they can work with later down the line.

Usually, the route into the department is through trainee status, working up to edit assistant. Edit assistants take a long time to make the transition to editors, as the nuanced skills of the job take a long time to learn.

ROLES

Editor (Head of department)
Cuts the film from assembly to picture lock

Assistant Editor
In charge of the ingest, logging, paperwork and technical, as well as liaison with suppliers and production

Second edit assistant
Supports the edit assistant

Edit trainee
Supports and assists the team

KEY SKILLS: storytelling, composition, technical proficiency, creativity, diplomacy

SOFTWARE KNOWLEDGE: AVID, Adobe Premiere, Final Cut Pro (FCP)

Colourist

ABOUT

After picture lock, post production moves to sound and any required VFX. One of the other core processes in post is to 'grade' the picture, which is the responsibility of a colourist.

The colourist will first balance the look of the footage taken from different days under different lighting conditions to ensure continuity from scene to scene. Using specialist software, they will be able to manipulate the colour palette of shots, lighting and shading, so controlling the grain and texture of what has been filmed and enhancing the visuals that have been captured on camera. A grade can be used to create an even tone, or to make a high impact.

A good example of the impact of the colour grade is Danny Boyle's 2007 sci-fi film *Sunshine*. The interior of the spaceship was intentionally designed in muted greys and blues, so when the audience first see the blazing yellow and orange of the sun on screen it is a very powerful visual moment. The work of the director of photography and the production designer was successfully underscored by the colourist, maximising the audience's experience of the film.

KEY SKILLS: creativity, attention to detail, ability to follow a brief

SOFTWARE KNOWLEDGE: Baselight, NuCoda, DaVinci Resolve

Electrical Department

ABOUT

After a DoP has decided how a shot should be lit, they will tell the chief electrician – known as a Gaffer – exactly what they are looking for. It is then the responsibility of the Gaffer to ensure this look is achieved by setting up the correct lamps, reflectors, filters and other necessary devices for the filming of the shot in a safe and considered manner.

The equipment used by the department varies in size from small, battery-operated torches to enormous 135kw wendy lights which are powered by a 450k generator truck. (To give you an idea of scale, OFGEM states that the average UK house uses 9kWh of electricity per day.) As almost every set up requires multiple lights, a huge amount of electricity is running through the set. The Gaffer must calculate how to safely distribute this electrical output to the different lamps.

Lights come in a variety of different types, such as 'daylight', 'tungsten' or 'fluorescent', and give off either a warm or cool glow. The use of coloured gels, diffusers, shutters and shades can further manipulate the output of the lamp and the 'colour temperature' it emits.

The Gaffer is responsible for anticipating the requirements of the shoot and ordering the correct equipment. The skills and knowledge needed to do so successfully are developed over many years.

ROLES

Chief Lighting Technician (Gaffer) (Head of department)
Liaises with the DoP to set up the lighting and power for every shot

Best boy (Second in command)
The right hand of the Gaffer, with duties including the ordering of equipment and management of labour

Electrician ('spark')
Takes orders from the Gaffer and best boy to set up lighting arrangements as required

Lighting rigger
Builds scaffold and secures lamps at height

Genny op
When a large generator is required, a genny op is in charge of setting up and maintaining the power source

KEY SKILLS: knowledge of safe working practices; physical strength and stamina; able to follow direction

CERTIFICATES INCLUDE: City & Guilds certificate, CITB, NVQ, SITAC/JIGS approved (rigger), HGV certificate (genny op/lighting truck driver), CISRS (rigger)

Grip Department

ABOUT

The grip is responsible for the secure mounting and movement of the camera. Whether that is setting up a tripod – tall or short 'legs', as they are known – track and dolly or crane, the grip must ensure that the shot can be made safely.

If the director and DoP want a smooth shot, where the camera moves alongside a character, they may opt to lay down a track. Track generally comes in standard 2ft, 4ft, 6ft or 8ft pieces, straight or curved at either 20 or 30 inches width. The track is levelled out using rectangular wooden blocks called pags and angled wedges, and a 'dolly' is placed on the track. A dolly is a small, heavy cart with dedicated support and fittings for the camera to be attached, and the grip will push or pull this alongside the action as required.

Not only is the safe assembly of track and mounting of the camera part of the grip's job, but they must also match the movement of the action perfectly for each take.

A fully loaded camera, the most important device on set, is expensive and heavy. The most commonly used ARRI Alexa camera costs over £50,000; lenses can be valued up to £25,000 and follow focus kits, viewfinders and on-board monitors costing thousands more. The accumulated weight is over 10kg; if the fitting is not secure, the crew, cast and camera are in danger.

ROLES

Grip (Head of department)
Sometimes referred to as the 'key grip'

Dolly grip
Responsible for the tracking and pushing the 'dolly', which runs along the track

Crane grip
Works with the crane

Grip assistant
Supports the grip in assembling equipment and laying track

Grip trainee
Entry-level position, supports the team

KEY SKILLS: engineering, safe working practices, physical strength

CERTIFICATES INCLUDE: NVQ – levels 2 & 3

Home Economist

ABOUT

Home economists are expert chefs, skilled in the art of presenting food. Predominately working in commercials and for magazine editorials, the 'home ec', will have several portable kitchen appliances to style any food in shot to make it look at its most appetising and desirable.

Locations Department

Location management is one of the most challenging jobs in the industry, and is the link between the 'outside' world and a production.

A script may call for the use of a particular location, and the location manager is responsible for finding options to present to the director. Once a location is chosen, the department will then have to liaise with a variety of people including the property owner, local council, community and police.

Whereas filming in a studio allows for complete control over the environment, the same cannot be said for shooting on location. Not only will the location department have to source and secure an external site, they will have to find a suitable unit base to park the facility vehicles, leaflet-drop the neighbourhood to inform people of possible disruption, deal with property owners, write up the movement order for every filming day, and make it simple for crew and cast to access.

As an example, think of the famous scene in *Notting Hill* where Hugh Grant walks through the local market as seasons change. The film's location manager Sue Quinn had to convince 100 market traders and countless residents to allow filming to go ahead; that's a lot of individuals to appease. Payment helps, of course, but not all films have mega budgets and many location owners can be aggressive negotiators too.

ROLES

Location manager (Head of department)
Finds the key locations and liaises with the director, production team, property owners, council and police

Unit manager
Manages the unit base and supports the location manager

Location scout
Tasked with finding locations and researching the viability to shoot

Assistant location manager
Helps scout for locations, writes movement orders and supports the location manager

Location runner
Assists the location manager and unit manager in the smooth running of the department

Location marshall
Usually brought in for large-crowd days to help with locking off, parking and traffic support

SOFTWARE KNOWLEDGE: Microsoft Excel; Microsoft Word; online location libraries

KEY SKILLS: diplomatic, charismatic, local area knowledge, budget management, excellent communicator

Make-Up and Hair Department

ABOUT

The make-up and hair designer is responsible for creating the look for each character on screen. The department must be skilled, not just in make up, styling, haircutting and wig application, but also have experience in prosthetics and special effects.

The make-up designer will usually take around two to four weeks to prep a normal drama production, and longer for period and sci-fi pieces. Research is key to ensuring accuracy and authenticity, and they will discuss each character with the director, creating mood boards or look books even before they meet the actors.

As many actors shoot projects back to back, sometimes compromises may need to be made over their look. For example, an actor might be growing their hair long for a leading role on a major movie, so will have to wear a bald cap to achieve the cropped cut for the small indie production they are shooting first.

One of the unseen but vital roles of the department is to deliver the actor to the ADs ready for the shoot, meaning that actors do a lot of their final preparations in the make-up room (or Costume truck). The ability to create the right environment for the actors is a subtle skill that comes with experience.

The make-up department is usually among the first crew members to get to unit base, and work longer hours than many on set. Make-up trainees are expected to keep up with the pace, and get involved in making up background artists and minor cast members.

ROLES

Make-up and hair designer (Head of department)
Creates the look for each character, makes up key cast, monitors continuity and manages the team

Make-up supervisor
Organises crew, liaises with the second AD and manages continuity

Make-up artist
Makes up key cast members and monitors continuity

Prosthetics/life casting

Depending on the requirements of the production, either an individual or a company is brought in to create, apply and maintain prosthetics

Wig maker

Usually brought in for complex period pieces, to adjust, modify, bake and apply wigs

Make-up trainee

Supports the department and makes-up background artists

KEY SKILLS: steady hand, cool head, good with actors, attention to detail, knowledge of make-up application and hairdressing, knowledge of prosthetics

KIT: all make-up artists are expected to have their own basic kit of brushes and essential tools

Medical Department

ABOUT

All productions employ medical personnel to be present on set at all times, usually in the form of a unit nurse who is the first line of medical care for cast and crew. Thankfully, they are not in constant action, but supply running support to keep the company ticking over. For action sequences, paramedics and even fire-safety officers will be on standby on set.

Unit nurses are fully trained, and are often former NHS workers who have branched out into film and TV. Some people make their own way in to the business, others use industry agents like Millstream to get into the industry.

KEY SKILLS: good bedside manner, confidential, committed, familiar with filming set ups

CERTIFICATES INCLUDE: Registered Nurse with the Nursing and Midwifery Council (MWC); HCPC registered

Playback Department

ABOUT

Sub-contracted by the art department or set decorator, the playback department is needed when a screen displaying any form of content is visible within a shot. A basic example is when a character is watching TV, but it can be more complex than that: a character using an air-traffic-control radar or FBI computer, for instance.

Whatever content is seen on screen, it must be approved for usage by the content owner, which is the responsibility of the production department, and then played in such a way that it will not scan or distort when filmed. This is usually undertaken by an individual, although additional technicians may be required on more complex shoots.

Later on in the book, there is an interview with *Prometheus* set decorator Sonja Klaus, who worked closely with Mark Jordan's company Compuhire, to fit out the entire spaceship set with practical screens. Mark Jordan's work can also be seen in the Milano spaceship in *Guardians of the Galaxy.*

KEY SKILLS: good working knowledge of most kinds of software and hardware; very technically minded

Previis

ABOUT

Previsualization, or previs, has existed since the start of filmmaking, with storyboards and replica models being used to plan a shoot. Modern previs uses digital technology, and enables a director to explore, devise, develop and express their vision for sequences of their film. Previs companies work closely with the director, production designer and VFX supervisor to create the template for complicated sequences. Indeed, in a 2011 interview with American Cinematographer magazine, Avengers director Joss Whedon described previs as an "invaluable tool to get everybody on the same page."

Previs is aimed at speeding up the filmmaking process. Previs artists and editors generate advance animated storyboards so that a director can see and test concepts quickly, determine how best to tell the story and make the most of their time on set. They can also work out potential camera angles and edits, and discover what coverage they might need.

At the time of writing, there are four principal methods of previs. The first is the advanced animated storyboards; the second utilises motion capture; the third is a method of studio filming called Simulcam, where computer-generated footage can interact with live characters; and the fourth is virtual reality (VR). With VR, a director can view a 3D-modelled environment to explore what their set might look like, and make changes before a physical set is ever built.

The previs team will select the most appropriate method, and can deploy the technology is during one of four stages of the filmmaking process.

Previs is sometimes used to create a proof-of-concept sequence, so that studio executives can see a director's vision before deciding to greenlight an expensive project. This process is known as pitchvis.

Traditional previs is used during development and pre-production, as described above, while the third stage is termed tech-vis and is used to determine how to shoot scenes within the bounds of the available technology.

The final stage, post-vis, is used at the end of the shoot, when temporary animation is inserted into the offline edit as a guide, primarily for the editor and VFX department to help them render computer generated images perfectly, but also to enable the director, studio and test audiences to understand the finished product.

Previs Supervisor (Head of Department)

The previs supervisor is responsible for the creative direction of previsualization projects. They collaborate with the director and VFX Supervisor, and liaise with other HODs to help visually conceptualise the film. Supervisors have overall responsibility for the management of the previs team.

KEY SKILLS: Strong storytelling skills; strong knowledge of cinematography and shot creation

Previs Production Management

The production manager and production coordinators keep track of the budgets, schedule and talent resources. They also track the progress of each previs shot throughout production.

KEY SKILLS: Strong project management skills.

Shot Creator

Previs shot creators produce previs shots by piecing together elements, setting them in motion and 'filming' them with virtual cameras.

KEY SKILLS: Animation; an understanding of digital cinematography - camera movement, lenses, lighting and composition - and storytelling.

Asset Builder

A special breed of 3D modellers, previs asset builders create environments, props, characters for the shot creators to use.

KEY SKILLS: A strong sense of design; an understanding of topology, rigging, lighting, texturing and surfacing.

Previs Editor

The previs editor cuts together the sequence, adding dialogue, music and sound effects. They participate in story discussions with the previs supervisor, VFX supervisor and director, and can suggest additional shots.

KEY SKILLS: Strong storytelling skills; strong sound design skills; some knowledge of cinematography and VFX.

Junior Shot Creator or Junior Asset Builder. (Entry-level roles)

Production Department

ABOUT

The central hub of any production; this department is the engine of the film-making process. It has responsibility for controlling the budget, working out the overall schedule, communicating to the crew and managing each step in the production process.

As discussed earlier, the producer is the driving force behind the director and always looking at the bigger picture, and it is the team a producer assembles that actually brings a project together over the course of months or even years.

The line producer – also called a co-producer or unit production manager (UPM) – keeps a firm hand on the tiller, budgeting the entire film and managing the key relationships between heads of departments, investors, actors and agents. They are usually very experienced in film making, finances and diplomacy, and will assemble the team that manage and co-ordinate the entire cast and crew.

ROLES

Line producer/co-producer/UPM (Head of department)
Budgets, supervises and manages the crew

Production manager (PM) (Second in command)
Monitors budgets and negotiates with suppliers, departments and individual crew

Production coordinator
Oversees the tidal flow of information throughout the production, coordinates the cast and crew, travel and accommodation as well as equipment, transport and logistics

Assistant production coordinator (APC)
Organises travel and accommodation for cast and crew, and supports the coordinator.

Travel coordinator
On larger productions with multiple locations, a specialist travel and accommodation coordinator is utilised

Production secretary
Provides administrative support to the PC and APC, and manages the diaries of the key crew

Production assistant
Provides administrative support to the PC and APC

Production runner
Helps with administration, research, catering, fixing, driving and anything else that is needed

KEY SKILLS: organised, diplomatic, strong attention to detail, stamina

SOFTWARE KNOWLEDGE: Movie Magic Scheduling, budgeting, Final Draft, Microsoft Office

Post-Production Department

ABOUT

The post-production process for film and TV drama is usually longer than the filming period. There are many elements that need to be pulled together for picture, sound and VFX, and it's the post-production supervisor's job to oversee the delivery of the final film.

The post-production team are responsible for budgeting, planning and scheduling the completion of the film, liaising with all departments, edit suites, studios and post houses to ensure that each one has the correct assets and direction to complete their work in line with the schedule.

All of the film's assets will be delivered to the production company, including all of the rushes and relevant paperwork needed to meet the production's legal obligations, contracts, errors and omissions (E&O), agreements, licenses, insurances and financial records. Instructions for future recoupments and royalties must also be arranged.

All major studios will have rigid policies and procedures in place for delivering the film and its assets; independent producers will have more flexibility.

ROLES

Post-production supervisor (Head of Department)
Oversees the team and manages the relationships with the key film-making talent to ensure that the film is delivered according to budget and schedule

Post-production coordinator
Supports the supervisor and manages the flow of information and paperwork

Post-production secretary/runner
Supports the supervisor and coordinator

KEY SKILLS: planning, broad technical knowledge, project management

SOFTWARE KNOWLEDGE: Microsoft Office, diary management tools

Publicity Department

ABOUT

The unit publicist usually begins working on the film in pre production, and external publicity companies will be engaged early on to start capturing assets that can be used for marketing nearer release. This may include acquiring interviews with the key cast and crew on set and often in costume. These interviews and general behind-the-scenes footage are taken by an Electronic Press Kit (EPK) crew on either an exciting filming day, or one that is quiet enough that the production can release actors for short periods to be interviewed while in full costume and make-up.

While the film is being made, the unit publicist will start working on strategies for their release campaign. A photographer will be embedded in the crew, taking shots throughout filming that can be used in publicity material.

On bigger projects, the publicity process might include creating teasers that are distributed through social media, arranging interviews between lead actors and journalists, and organising talk-show appearances. Within the industry, PR companies might also organise screenings for BAFTA and Oscar voters, as well as managing various red carpet events.

ROLES

Unit publicist
Strategist and creative mind behind the project's publicity, and manages the budget

Unit stills
Photographer working on set, shooting behind the scenes and press images

EPK crew
Digital crew who film and edit behind-the-scenes footage and interviews

KEY SKILLS: understanding the film and how best to target its audience, campaign strategy, contacts, creative marketing

Script Supervisor

ABOUT

There is usually only one script supervisor on set at any one time, working alongside the director, and their role is crucial and often unheralded. The script supervisor diligently ensures continuity, not only between camera set ups or for a particular scene but in the context of the entire story. They provide an extra pair of eyes and ears for the director, recording details and providing notes for the editor as well.

During prep, the script supervisor will work out the running time and effectively 'lock' the script for continuity, which costume, makeup and other departments will use as the master continuity framework.

For every scene being shot, the script supervisor takes detailed notes on specially created templates to log and record what happens in each take. They also 'mark up' the script, recording additional details on the script pages, copies of which are sent to the editor who can see which takes the director particularly liked, for example, or in which take an actor might have missed their mark or fluffed a line.

The role of script supervisor requires immense concentration, memory and focus. When the crew heads for lunch or leave upon wrap, the script supervisor will still be writing notes. It is a highly specialist role and requires an almost obsessive attention to detail because not only do they act as an essential bridge between director and editor, but they will also be able to assist other departments with questions of continuity.

ROLES

Script supervisor

Script supervisor's assistant
Shadows the script supervisor for training purposes

SOFTWARE KNOWLEDGE: Final Draft. There are various continuity apps available online, although many prefer paper notes

KEY SKILLS: keen observation, diligence, attention to detail

Set Decoration And Props

ABOUT

This department works directly with the production designer, but has a specific brief to use props to help convey character and make locations look entirely authentic.

The set decorator has to think very carefully about the characters and the locations in order to choose the right props, which may result in hundreds – or even thousands – of different props being rented from large prop houses.

ROLES

Set decorator
Uses props, artwork and anything at their disposal to create a believable, authentic set

Prop buyer
Works with the set decorator to hire or purchase the items for the set, then manages and organises them with the props team

Prop master
Manages the inventory of props and oversees their safe transportation to and from sets

Standby props
Present on set to react to any changes or requirements, and to provide any necessary repeats. For example, if a character smashes a glass, standby props will clear up the mess and give the actor the replacement fake glass.

Set dresser
Deploys the props and artwork around the set to make it look real, usually not present during filming, but prepares the set for the next day

Prop hand
Responsible for the safe transportation and security of the props

KEY SKILLS: sharp eye for character, budget management, expansive knowledge of props and set dressing, good knowledge of prop hire company stock

SOFTWARE KNOWLEDGE: inventory software, spreadsheets

Special Effects Department

The SFX department are responsible for the live-action effects that happen on set and, unlike computer-generated VFX, all of their work happens in-camera. This can include effects like the spinning corridor of *Inception* to the fake snow of *Snow White and the Huntsman* to the explosions of *Skyfall*.

Special-effects technicians work closely with the director, production designer, construction department and often the stunt team to realise each of the effects. It takes a lot of creative thinking and imagination to realise a director's vision within budget.

Special-effects workshops are used as testing ground for complex shoots. The team behind *Gravity*, for example tested several rigs on the stages at Elstree studios long before they settled on the light-box solution used for eventual filming at Shepperton. As digital technology has evolved, the industry has moved away from older techniques such as miniatures and matte painting, but skills such as model making, life casting and animatronics are far more developed than ever before.

ROLES

Special effects supervisor (Head of department)
Heads up the creative solutions, and manages both budget and crew

Senior technician
Leads the operations and organises the team

Technician
Operates the relevant machinery, rigs and pyrotechnics as required

Trainee
Supports the technicians

KEY SKILLS: creativity, basic engineering, problem solving

CERTIFICATES INCLUDE: JIGS – The Joint Industry Grading System (graded at one of the four levels listed above)

Production Sound Department

ABOUT

On set, the job of the sound department is to capture the highest quality recording of the action and dialogue, free from interference and background noise.

The production sound mixer must decide on how best to capture the on-set sound, within budget. Equipment used will normally include radio microphones, a boom and directional microphones, all feeding into a mixing desk and recording device, which will be synced with the camera's time code. They will also provide actor earpieces, if required, as well as capture atmosphere sounds from locations. The phrase 'wild tracks' is called over the radio to let everyone know to remain entirely silent for a few moments so they can record the natural background environment.
In this book, the sound department is split into two categories: the on-set team (production team) and the studio team (post-production team).

ROLES

Production sound mixer (Head of department)
Responsible for the clean recording of dialogue, action and wild tracks

Re-recording mixer
Completes the final mix of the film

Sound assistant
Fits microphones, logs tracks, monitors levels and supports the sound mixer

Boom op
Holds and points the boom microphone, ensuring it remains out of shot

Sound trainee
Assists and supports the sound mixer

KEY SKILLS: a good ear, technical know-how, diplomatic, sensitive around actors during performance

HARDWARE KNOWLEDGE: microphones, mixer, sound cart, cables and leads

Post-Production Sound Department

ABOUT

At the end of principal photography, the supervising sound editor (or sometimes sound designer) takes over the responsibility for the audio of the project.

During filming, the production sound mixer will have aimed to capture the cleanest sound possible, but this isn't always possible: background noise such as traffic and planes may have been inadvertently picked up along with the actors' dialogue, and this will have to be removed. Additional sound and music will then be added to the film, and the supervising sound editor will first conduct a 'spotting' session with the director to identify what is required. They then hire a series of lieutenants to edit different elements of the soundtrack. These different types of editor are listed below. (If the budget allows, these editors will also utilise additional engineers and assistants).

Once all these elements are completed, the film is handed over to the re-recording mixer (listed on the previous page), who will balance everything into one final mix and lay it back to picture.

ROLES

Supervising Sound Editor (Head of department)
Leads the sound editors both creatively and logistically

Dialogue editor
Replaces audio, edits lines and uses alternate takes so that every line of dialogue is delivered to maximum effect.

ADR editor
Responsible for additional dialogue recording, also known as 'looping' (in the US, this is termed automated dialogue replacement)

ADR recordist
Works with the ADR Editor to capture replacement, additional and alternative dialogue

Sound effects editor
Identifies where additional sounds are required, which were not captured during filming, then creates, edits and implements these sounds working with library audio and the Foley editor

Foley editor
Recreates sounds that were not caught in recording such as footsteps and punches

Foley recordist
Captures the recording of bespoke sound effects for the production

Music editor
Alongside the director, spots and identifies where music is required, and sources viable, affordable options

KEY SKILLS: highly developed 'ear' for audio; creative, technically minded.

SOFTWARE KNOWLEDGE: ProTools, compressors, basic video playback and numerous technical elements

Storyboard Artist

Not used on every production. Some directors never use Storyboard artists, some rely on them heavily and some directors bring in someone to help with specific sequences, such as an action scene.

The Storyboard artist comes on board the production at a very early stage and works closely with the director to listen to their description and visualize the given sequence. As well as being highly skilled artists, they must also have excellent knowledge of the filmmaking process; be creative, personable and an incredibly fast worker.

The novelist Ernest Hemingway once said that "writing is rewriting" and the same is true for storyboard artists. They will undertake constant revisions of the action, helping the director nail-down their vision.

The director can then share that vision with the heads of department as a basis for them to realize the action on set. Frames can indicate action, camera moves, design elements and stunt ideas.

David Allcock is one of the world's most renowned Storyboard artists and is interviewed later in this book.

KEY SKILLS: Artistic, sound knowledge of filming techniques
SOFTWARE: Photoshop, Corel Painter

Stunt Department

ABOUT

The role of the stunt performer requires strength, stamina, conditioning, attention to detail and acting skills.

All UK stunt performers must be registered with, and hold qualifications from, the Joint Industry Stunt Committee (part of the Joint Industry Grading Scheme), which is also overseen by the Equity Stunt Committee. Stunt performers must be trained and qualified in at least six of the following: fighting, falling, riding and driving, agility and strength, water or one other miscellaneous field such a parkour. There are three levels to the JISC qualifications: probationary, intermediate and full membership, and only those with the latter can act as stunt coordinators.

Stunt coordinators have the responsibility of devising and planning the stunt, including considerable risk assessment and safety management, working first with the director, then production, ADs, art department, costume, make-up and camera teams to execute the stunts. Stunt coordinators are also often brought in as the second unit director, responsible for a separate unit dedicated to shooting the stunts of the film.

The stunt performers will often double for the main cast so will need to understand the character and take direction. The ability to mimic the leading actor's physique and mannerisms while fighting, falling off a building or riding a motorbike through a fire is not to be underestimated and, unlike any other department, stunt performers are registered with actors union Equity.

ROLES

Stunt coordinator (Head of department)
Plans the stunt, oversees safety management and hires the team

Stunt performer

Rigger
Specialises in rigging for stunts; JIGS registration required

KEY SKILLS AND CERTIFICATIONS: as described above

Transport Department

ABOUT

The unit transport department usually consists of two different teams: the unit drivers who ferry the cast and crew between locations, and the facilities-vehicle drivers. The art department and camera team will have their own drivers whose duties extend further into their departments.

The unit drivers are managed by the second AD and production coordinator, and tasked with transporting the key cast and director from home to unit base. Once they are delivered safely, the driver can often wait on standby for their actor, or be asked by the second AD to make further collections of other cast members. They need to be discreet and sensitive to the needs of the talent and ready to go at a moment's notice.

Minibus drivers are also overseen by the assistant directors, and shuttle between set and unit base, carrying crew members, cast, background artists and occasionally delivering costumes, make-up, paperwork, spare radio batteries or food.

The facilities drivers are responsible for the large trailers that make up the unit base. They will work together to ensure that the vehicles are maintained and moved as required by the production. Most of the time, all of the vehicles will be hired through the same facilities company, and will come with their own staff. The unit manager directs the movement between locations, and the configuration of the vehicles when parked. Forward planning is required, so that the vehicles are lined up in such a way so that any needed elsewhere, or to be an advance party to the next unit base, can be easily moved. Generally speaking, however, they will move in convoy.

Depending on the needs and budget of the production, the vehicles may include the following: artist trailer (for lead actors), three-way trailer (split into three sections for supporting cast), costume truck, make-up truck, production truck, dining bus (coach converted with tables) and a 'honeywagon' (mobile toilet).

KEY SKILLS: clean driving licence, excellent road knowledge, discretion, forward planning

VFX

ABOUT

VFX has been crucial to the growth of the UK film industry. Many international producers bring their shows to the UK just for post production, without having shot a single frame on these shores. The skills and talent available, together with the financial incentives, have seen the UK become a world leader in VFX.

There are many massive VFX houses such as Dneg, Framestore, MPC and Cinesite that are headquartered in London but have an international pipeline of talented artists in places such as Singapore, Montreal, Vancouver, Bangalore, Mumbai and Beijing. There are also many smaller, boutique VFX houses based in London creating Oscar- and BAFTA-winning effects, such as nvizible, the Senate, Blue Bolt and Lola. It is not uncommon for one VFX house to sub-contract work to other vendors.

Due to shrinking budgets and competitive tax incentives from overseas, however, many VFX houses walk a financial tightrope. Rhythm and Hues, the company behind the jaw-dropping effects that were the backbone of *Life of Pi*, went bust just a few months after the film was released in 2012, laying off hundreds of staff after 25 years of business. Just a month later that film went on to win several Oscars but neither DoP Claudio Miranda nor Director Ang Lee remembered to thank the company during their acceptance speeches. VFX is a tough business.

Working in VFX can be very intense: it's a challenging working environment and there is a lot of pressure to meet deadlines. As we've seen, it's not always valued so highly by some film-makers and studios are likely to move VFX to wherever the tax incentive is more attractive.

The volume of different roles in VFX is considerable. On most projects, VFX is separated by sequence, and each sequence will have an assembly line in which each department does their work then passes on to the next. Quite often, a previs company (separate from a VFX company), will have begun laying out the look and feel of the film. Within the VFX company itself, it starts with research and development, takes modelling, rigging, lighting, shading and animating and will ultimately all be put together by the compositor. A sequence or shot may not take the exact same route along the assembly line but they will all end up with the compositor at the end, who will also have to make up the time if deadlines have been missed along the way.

The entire department is led by the VFX supervisor, who is the point of contact with the director, producer and production designer. This means that the VFX supervisor will be involved early in the film's pre-production, testing, budgeting and even working with the previs team.

ROLES

VFX Supervisor (Head of department)
Creates the look and oversees the team making the shots

VFX Production Department
Consisting of line producer, production manager, production coordinator and production assistant, this department keep track of the budgets, schedule and talent resources

Concept artist
Works with the supervisor and director to create look and feel during development and pre-production

VFX Artists
There will be 'lead' artists for each group, responsible for the department's output

Rotoscope: hand-tracing individual elements in-shot frame by frame
Model makers: creates shape of VFX characters
Riggers: creates framework for models
Effects TD: implements lighting and shading into shot, and maintains continuity
Matchmovers: used by 3D productions to track camera movement
Painter: paints out unwanted shot elements frame by frame
Matte painters: creates backgrounds
Animators: animates the characters
Compositors: Gather, arrange and assemble all of the different VFX elements into the final shot
Runners: Supports the artists, assists with technical support and basic VFX duties

SOFTWARE KNOWLEDGE INCLUDES: Mari, Maya, Nuke, Houdini, Studio Max, ZBrush, XSI, Motionbuilder, Softimage, Smoke, Flame, Inferno, Adobe Creative Suite

Video Department

ABOUT

'Video village' is the viewing area where a director, producer and script supervisor can watch the action as it appears in the DoP's viewfinder. The video assist operator will take a live feed from both the camera and sound mixer, either through cables or transmitters, and will set up monitors as required. The video department works closely with the camera department and the monitors will be calibrated to reflect what the DoP is viewing.

Many drama productions are shot on a single camera, so video assist is relatively straightforward. On large productions, however, video assist operators will need to pull feeds from multiple cameras, mix shots and overlay feeds. The video assist will work with the director not only to provide a live stream, but also to review material for continuity and playback at any speed, and some video assists will be able to offer a quick and rough assembly edit on set, and even print screen grabs.

Heads of department will also look in on the monitors in order to check how their work appears on camera, so it is not an area where a runner should be loitering – however tempting it might be.

ROLES

Video Coordinator (head of department)
Responsible for providing a suitable viewing area, editing, mixing, overlay and playback

Video Assist
On larger productions, an assistant will be need to set up monitors and cabling

KEY SKILLS: technically minded, editing knowledge, good understanding of cameras, cranes and motion control; discrete, diplomatic

HARDWARE/SOFTWARE KNOWLEDGE INCLUDES: Qtake, Cinelog, Final Cut Pro, Realtime Editing

CHAPTER 2

Getting Work

Now we've covered the history and present-day status of the industry, the production process, the departments and their roles, and the paperwork, you should now have a more comprehensive understanding of UK film and TV drama production, including the entry level access points for each department.

It's important to remember, however, that there isn't a one-size-fits-all process for breaking into the industry. You should never assume that you will land a job as soon as you start looking, particularly as there are so many people trying to do the same, but there are certainly things you can do to increase your chances of getting work and staying employed.

The next three chapters are dedicated to helping you land your first job in the industry, combining practical advice, such as writing CVs, finding openings and managing bookings, with first-hand knowledge from a wide variety of experienced industry professionals. I have conducted interviews with a variety of successful individuals from across the entire industry, and collected over 50 exclusive pearls of professional wisdom from across the sector.

Almost all production crew are freelance, making themselves available for the productions they really want to work on and only taking a holiday when they are sure they will not miss out on work. The average independent feature film or TV drama takes 4 to 12 weeks to shoot, and freelance crew will always be looking to line up the next job. There is little security as a freelancer, and even experienced crew must jockey for position to get on to the good jobs and fill employment gaps. Succeeding in this competitive environment relies heavily on word of mouth and personal connections. It is, therefore, important to know how to successfully network, and continue to build your network of contacts: skills we will also examine further in this chapter.

It's a fact, no matter who you know, that most film- and TV-drama crew hire people who already have experience elsewhere, as they don't always have the time to train people on the job, and they prefer to use people who they know will not let them down. As a freelancer, you must seek out relevant training yourself, either from learning on-the-job or attending training events, which will inevitably incur cost implications.

Creative Skillset is the industry training organisation and there is a quote from its CEO in the Pearls of Wisdom section of this book. They support the industry through skills training and education, offering a comprehensive guide to courses across most fields of film-making. Creative Skillset evaluates training courses and ensure that they are meeting the industry standards. If those courses pass the evaluation, they are given a seal of approval in the form of the Creative Skillset 'Tick'. The organisation is backed by the Government so you should also be able to find information about available funding for training on these approved courses. It can be difficult for freelancers to commit to training courses when paid work takes precedence, but it's worth exploring what options are available.

If you have absolutely no experience, make sure you carefully consider the positive skills you can offer any potential employer. To help you do this, take some advice from Laszlo Bock, head of recruitment for Google, who outlined the four factors he considers before hiring anyone in his 2015 book *Work Rules!* He receives around 2 million job applications per year. For each one, he firstly assesses the candidate's ability to absorb information, secondly identifies their leadership qualities, then determines whether their personality and outlook are a good fit for the company before finally examining their particular expertise. In making their 5000 hires per year, Google prioritises a candidate's intelligence, character and people skills before their specific abilities to do the job they are applying for. Similarly, the film and TV drama industry also places a high value on so-called 'soft skills' like social interaction, sensitivity and good communication. Teams in film are often small, dynamic and under intense pressure so it's as important to get on well with your colleagues as it is to do your job properly.

The hard work doesn't end when you get that first job, however, and we will also examine the physical and emotional impact of working in such a demanding industry. Many seasoned professionals have told me that many of their trainees are simply not prepared for the energy and stamina that is required on a film set.

The working hours on a film production have a special exemption from the European Working Time Directive, the law that governs the working conditions of most industries. Film and TV freelancers are considered to be in the same category as hospital or care workers needed to give 'round the clock' services. So, most of your non-industry friends may clock off at 5pm and head out for dinner and drinks, you will need to be prepared to start much earlier and finish much later than them, and initially, for less pay too.

Which Route to Take?

When people are starting out, they can be unsure of what job title to give themselves or what jobs they should apply for. Most people want to end up at the same place but take different views on how to get there. Some are willing to start at the bottom and climb their way up, and others prefer to seek opportunities at a higher level immediately.

As a newcomer to the industry, you may have your heart set on a particular role such as directing feature films. After you gain some experience in the industry, however, a sense of pragmatism is likely to kick in and you may find regular work in another role. Just as an actor might become typecast, crew members can become pigeonholed in one category and, if you are making a good living, your career targets may well shift and there is nothing wrong with reassessing your goals. You may discover, for example, that you make a superb production manager or location manager: roles that you may not have been fully exposed to in student or short-film production.

Whatever your end goal, the best initial route into feature-film or TV-drama production is as a runner or trainee. Although the temptation may be to look for roles at a higher level, particularly if you have worked on a lot of student or short-film productions, there is simply no substitute for professional real-world, on-set experience.

In his 2009 book, *Outliers*, author Malcolm Gladwell suggests that to be a genuine master of something you need to have accumulated 10,000 hours experience of actually doing it. He cites the eight-hour sets the Beatles played in their Hamburg club days, and schoolboys Bill Gates and Bill Joy working with early computers, as examples of the fact that the more exposure you have to something, the more challenges you overcome and the more skills you learn.

The film and TV drama industry undoubtedly, if unconsciously, subscribes to this doctrine. There is no doubt that to be an effective head of department, one that inspires trust and belief in their team, you need a huge amount of experience across a wide variety of productions.

For his MA dissertation *Living on the Edge: A Study of Freelance Workers in UK Film and TV*, former BBC producer James Mackie took an industry survey about the life of a freelancer. It includes the following observation: 'To get into television, it is virtually essential to establish some credentials by working as a runner before moving up. There are very few cases where transferable skills from previous experience are valued. It is also very hard to leave film and TV at a later stage – the skills are not seen as transferable, and the working habits are difficult to break out of.'

It's essential to view the initial steps of your career through a pragmatic and practical lens, putting employment first. What you will learn on a proper set will translate and inform your personal projects down the road, and you will also make contacts that can help you make those projects a reality. As an example, take a look at Matt Kirkby, the UK Director of the 2015 Oscar-winning short film *The Phone Call*. Kirkby was a commercials director at Ridley Scott Associates (RSA), and made his zero-budget short by pulling in favours from his regular crew, and securing A-listers Sally Hawkins and Jim Broadbent through his contacts in commercials.

As you embark on your career in film and TV production, it's important to stop and assess your current situation at regular junctures. There are no annual work reviews or appraisals, and sometimes the only feedback you will get is not being asked back to work on the next job. It's also essential to listen to senior professionals in the business at every opportunity, acting on their advice and always showing respect. Humility, gratitude and manners go a very long way.

The Importance of Being a Runner

As mentioned, when you leave school, college, university or film school, no matter what your grades are, it's likely that you will be starting out as a runner. Lots of people hate the thought of being a runner, and try to either bypass the stage or get promotion as quickly as possible, but if you can embrace it, you will find that being a runner is a positive and vital part of your professional education.

Don't Rush

Whatever you learned about film and TV before you got into the industry, you will find that the practical experience of being on set is very different. You need time to find your feet and learn the ropes: running is the perfect job for that. Give yourself at least six months to absorb life in the professional environment, learn the un-written rules, the hierarchies and structures across film, TV, commercials and promos. The learning curve is steep and you don't want to have any big knowledge gaps that could be exposed later on, so make sure to soak it all up.

If you aspire to be a director, and simply can't wait to get involved, then I would recommend you make short films and absorb all of the information on film making that you possibly can. For aspiring directors, I also recommend working with local theatre groups while earning a living as a runner. Managing and manipulating a performance from an actor takes skill, and it's one you can learn by spending time on by rehearsing plays. Directors like Sam Mendes, Danny Boyle and Stephen Daldry all come from a theatre background, and their intimate relationship with their actors is evident in every scene. (There is a paid, training bursary available for young theatre directors through the Regional Theatre Young Director Scheme, find the link in the back of the book.)

Find A Job You Love

The industry needs all kinds of specialist skills, and there are hundreds of roles, each suited to a wide range of personality types – you may find you are brilliant at something you had never previously considered. Take your time and be curious about everything that's out there. It's important to find something you love, because you will be spending every waking hour doing it.

Develop A Sense of Perspective

There are many people – your competition – who resolutely do not want to be a runner. Every production manager has met their fair share of recent university graduates asserting 'actually, I'm a director of photography'… they will usually be told to stick the kettle on.

If you are employed as a runner, concentrate on being reliable, friendly, trustworthy and unflappable before you start shoving your show-reel or script into the hands of everyone you meet. Prove you are indispensable, and you will be the first one getting the call for work on the next production. That gives you a really solid grounding on which to build.

The step up from runner, be it to production assistant, production secretary, third AD or an assistant will always be a bigger leap that you imagined. These roles carry extra responsibility, and the skills you will have learned as a runner or trainee will help you make the transition.

Building A Network

As a runner, you are likely to be placed on lots of jobs for short periods and will get the chance to mix with other entry-level colleagues. Don't see other runners as rivals but as allies. Keep in touch with the good people you encounter, help each other find work and share advice, and that growing network will become incredibly useful as you all start moving up through the ranks. If they get a call about a job they are unavailable to do, they may recommend you for the role instead, and vice versa. You may even start employing one another on future projects.

Genre Jumping

There are not many senior positions where you can jump between genres. People often end up working on a cycle of one particular type of production and stay there. It's much harder to jump from say, factual TV to features without taking a step (or three) down the ladder.
Runners are in the unique and fortunate position of being needed on all genres, regardless of previous experience, and are likely to be working on a TV series one day and a commercial the next. You can flit between the genres and gain experience from each before settling into the one that feels like home.

Film Schools

There are different types of education establishments in the UK offering a range of training, and each has a slightly different relationship to the industry. There are various three-year degrees, including technical courses, such as sound technology, and those that focus on the cultural impact of film and media on society. (Courses that have the Creative Skillset 'tick' indicate the training body's coveted kitemark of quality.) These courses produce a volume of new entrants to the industry each year, although many also come from the UK's dedicated film schools, to which this passage is dedicated.

The UK's film schools, which are mainly in London, offer MA courses lasting from one to three years. Courses generally focus on directing, screenwriting or more all-encompassing aspects of filmmaking. Producer and film blogger Stephen Follows assessed over 600 international film schools in 2014 and in that study (published on his website, stephenfollows.com), he found that the cheapest UK film-school courses cost an average of £10,165 per year and the most expensive cost £19,076.

The Director Paul Thomas Anderson (*Boogie Nights, Magnolia, There Will Be Blood*) famously dropped out of film school after just two days, and publically derided them in a 1999 interview with film critic Elvis Mitchell, while promoting his film *Magnolia*. In fact, there is so much information available online about film and TV it seems that accessibility to in-depth details about any aspect of film-making is available for free. That's not to say, however, that film schools do not have a place in the modern industry: Beaconsfield's National Film and Television School (NFTS), for example, have exceptional tutors and an established pipeline into the industry, while Ravensbourne, Falmouth, Brighton, Bournemouth, Westminster, Wimbledon and Nottingham universities also have excellent courses with direct links to the industry.

Many graduates of the UK's other film schools find themselves emerging into employment no-man's land. This is because film school graduates are more likely to label themselves with a job title, be it 'director', 'producer' or 'cinematographer' when first entering the job market, rather than presenting themselves as a runner, assistant or trainee. Having paid many thousands of pounds for a film-making education, and having learned many skills along the way, they are reluctant to start at the bottom. The problem is that commercial film and TV drama productions must use experienced professionals as department heads, as determined by the financial backers or broadcasters and to them film-school experience simply does not count.

It's simply not the case that you can pay for a short cut into the industry by attending film school. Approaching the job market with an inflated job title and little real experience is extremely unlikely to pay off. What a film school can offer, however, is a collaborative, encouraging environment in which to foster creativity, experimentation and theoretical knowledge.

When deciding whether to attend film school, it's important to do your research. Look at the teaching staff in your chosen institution: do they have personal experience of the industry, are they able to impart their knowledge to their students in a meaningful and useful way and are they offering realistic advice about starting out in the industry? Find out how many recent graduates have actually gone on to find work within their chosen field, and speak to some of them about their experiences if you can.

If you do decide to choose film school as your route into the industry, remember that the skills you are learning are likely to come in handy later on in your career, rather than at the beginning. For example, you might be able to operate AVID or Pro Tools by the time you graduate, but the equipment knowledge you'll need for your first job will likely extend to a kettle and a photocopier. If you are realistic about what it takes to get your foot in the door, are happy to stick it out and show you are keen, you will surely get the opportunity to use all that you learned at film school (or university).

Alongside film schools are dedicated make-up schools, and they have a far higher success rate of getting their students into the industry. The training is very focused and the tutors are all professional make-up designers on constant look out for good trainees. Students, therefore, have the opportunity to impress potential employers while still in the classroom. These institutions also have a direct line to the industry, and will be contacted by designers looking for trainees to work on projects, usually for dailies' work with lots of background artists. (In contrast, production companies rarely have the need to source runners from film schools, as they have so many entry-level individuals vying for their attention.) Graduating make-up school students expect to find work as trainees, and have realistic ambitions for their first job.

Of course, not all film schools – or indeed students – are created equally, and the skill set that is needed to get your very first professional job will not necessarily be the skill set that you graduated with. If you do decide to attend a film school, it's important that your expectations are realistic and that you pay equal attention to developing those all-important 'soft' skills we discussed earlier.

Making Contacts and Networking

'It's who you know, not what you know', so goes the old adage about success and, generally speaking, it holds true for the film and TV drama industry. Most work is found through word of mouth.

I have read a great deal of advice about networking along the lines of 'keep hold of unit lists and call, email and connect with people via Twitter, Facebook and LinkedIn after a job'. I have also met a number of individuals with a pathological zeal to make you their contact, who then expect to be hired instantly. Some people approach networking as a competition to collect as many business cards as possible but, while self-promotion is definitely a big part of getting work, this is not the whole picture.

Quite often, the most effective way of networking and accumulating contacts is overlooked; to be as good as you can possibly be at the job you have been employed to do. It really is that simple. Once you get into the industry, work as hard as you can. No one expects you to know it all on the first day, you just need to show common sense, initiative and drive.

The greatest calling card you have is your work, and the effort and intelligence you put into a task or the initiative you demonstrate in getting out there and doing something. A great work ethic gets noticed, and makes you more likely to be recommended by your colleagues and superiors. A verbal endorsement from one production manager to another is a far more effective way of advancing your career than grabbing a thousand business cards.

A solid network of contacts built through hard work will also be obvious from your CV, which we will look at later. Most industry employers will view any name listed on your CV as a potential referee, and will likely know them personally, or know someone else who worked on the production. If they are considering hiring you they may talk to those people, so it is essential that you have made a good, strong and lasting impression. Working hard and getting on well with people is, therefore, the most effective method of networking there is.

If you are a graduate of a film and TV course, then your network begins with your fellow graduates. Several of you are likely to be looking for similar industry roles at the same time, they will be going through the same peaks and troughs of establishing a career as you are. You can help each other by sharing advice and experiences. If one of your friends in your network lands a job, there may be an opportunity for them to put your name forward for additional roles. Equally, if they get a call about work and they are unavailable, they could give your name and number to the employer as a recommendation, and vice versa.

A few years ago, I interviewed James Graham, former Vice President of Amblin, whose talent was originally spotted by Frank Marshall and Kathleen Kennedy in the 1980s. They moved him to LA to work with Steven Spielberg on productions including *Who Framed Roger Rabbit* and *Back to the Future II* and *III*. Here's what he says about starting out at Amblin, as an associate producer on Spielberg's 1998 film *Empire of the Sun*:

'I knew that I was a hard working individual and happy to work 20 hours a day using whatever intelligence or learning I had. I was first and foremost a good listener, I must have had ears like Dumbo the elephant, in not only listening to what they asked me to do, but also trying to listen through the task and anticipate what they really wanted a day or a week from now. That was probably the thing that helped me a lot, thinking around the problem.'

The full interview with James is in the next chapter, and I urge you to read it. As he says, and it's worth repeating, you are more likely to get noticed and be remembered for being good at what you do, rather than your ability to 'network' long after a job is finished. Focus on doing the job right before working out your email campaign strategy.

Networking Events

Networking events often fill people with dread: you may have to go on your own, and you will have to spark up conversation with total strangers. It can feel awkward and contrived but, if you can hurdle your shyness, it can reap huge rewards, particularly as so much of this business happens face to face. While networking events might not yield any immediate benefits, relationships can be sparked that build and mature over time.

That being said, you do need to pick the right events to attend. The various guilds all organise their own, so keep an eye out for specific events where non-members may attend. There are lots of pop-up events too, so keep a watch on social media for interesting opportunities. If you can, attend British Video Expo (BVE) in either London or Manchester and head for the production show section: there's always interesting talks and technology on display, and lots of organisations also take stands. BVE is huge but it usually runs for three days so you can get around lots of talks. There is also a handy list of the guilds and notable networking events and courses in the back of the book.

Another very useful event to attend is an industry talk: a question and answer session with a film-maker about their latest release, for example. The majority of these talks happen in London, with BAFTA and Directors UK hosting some very insightful discussions, but increasingly events are springing up all around the UK. The BBC often has talks on drama in the regions. Creative England hold regular networking nights at different locations around the country and BAFTA also hold many talks outside of the capital. As well as getting an insight into production, there is usually an opportunity to grab a drink and mingle.

Whichever event you attend, it's important to approach it with enthusiasm. If you are on your own, and feeling a little shy, arrive early as this gives you a better chance of speaking to other individuals who are also arriving on their own. Remember that the majority of people at these events are open to conversation, so don't be afraid to say hello.

There are a few things to think about when communicating in these environments, however. Firstly, make sure you are presenting yourself in the best possible light, giving the other person all the practical information they need to forge a mutually beneficial relationship while also allowing your personality to shine. Communicate clearly, and be sure to ask questions and listen to the answers; engage with the person you are speaking with, and don't look around the room to see if there are any better prospects. Don't pretend to be an expert in something you're not (and that includes being honest about your job title on your name badge, particularly as you could easily come unstuck), and if you don't know something that's being discussed, ask: people love sharing their opinions. Attending a networking event is planting a seed for the future, and people have to trust you to want to continue contact afterwards.

A final, important piece of advice from my personal experience: be sure to seek out and thank the organisers putting on the event. Not only is that good manners, but chances are they know a number of people in the room and will happily make introductions.

Short Films

Short films are a great way to get some practice, experience and, hopefully, make a few contacts. To some, however, working on shorts is a slightly contentious issue, as it often means unpaid labour. Most professionals will have worked on short films at some point in their career, in the spirit of collaboration, but are able to do so because they have plenty of paid work.

There are, unfortunately, some unscrupulous and inept producers and directors out there churning out endless short films, which are no more than vanity projects. When considering if you are going to give your time, effort and skill for free, you need to be sure that the project is worth it, and offers you a long-term investment in your career. Below are some of the things to look for.

Short-film producers often 'crew up' using resources like Shooting People and mandy.com. Often they offer no pay, and the only incentive for crew is 'experience', perhaps a credit on IMDb and a copy of the film on DVD. The following sample advert is similar to what you might find on one of the above-mentioned websites, which is reasonably typical of its kind.

Camera Assistant

Rate	Expenses only We have no budget for this great little short thriller, but we have a fantastic script and will be entering it to all major short film festivals
Budget	£0
Details	All cast and crew on this short film will be offered: *Expense agreements for all personal costs* *A copy of the finished film for show-reel purposes* *Credits listed on IMDb*
Shooting in	London

In this sample advert, the return for your time would be an appropriate credit in online listings and a copy of the film for your show-reel. Firstly, runners don't have show-reels and secondly, no one in the profession gives a hoot if your short films are listed on IMDb. Both offerings are arbitrary and shouldn't factor into you accepting an unpaid role. The expenses will cover your travel costs, and the production should also provide food and drink so that the crew is not out of pocket.

For a project such as this, your involvement would be down to your individual judgement. If you know the producer or director, you may wish to help them achieve their vision as well as gaining experience and banking a favour for later in your career.

If you have no personal connection to the project, you face some different criteria. If you accept there is no payment, you could politely enquire what other benefits you are likely to get. For example, find out if there are professional crew working on the short, as you want to work with people who you may be able to learn from, impress and connect with for future (paid) work.

Indeed, good short films will use seasoned professionals who are collaborating on the project for similar reasons as yourself: returning or banking favours or because of a personal connection. American editor Tom Cross offered his services to Director Damien Chazelle on the short film of *Whiplash*, for example, on the understanding that if it be taken on to a feature film he would edit that too. This agreement paid off when Cross won the Oscar for Best Film Editing in 2015.

In the UK, DoP Laurie Rose was working in TV when he teamed up with Director Ben Wheatley on the micro-budget feature *Down Terrace*. Looking for more creative projects, Rose posted a call out on Facebook for Feature scripts. Wheatley responded immediately and they worked together to make the entire film on a shoestring budget. *Down Terrace* launched Wheatley's career and Rose has gone on to shoot all of his films including *Kill List*, *Sightseers*, *High Rise* and *Free Fire*. Their collaborations have also brought Rose's talent to the attention of others, and he has worked on projects as diverse as *Him & Her, Made of Stone*, *Bill* and *London Spy*, for which he won a TV Craft BAFTA in April 2016.

If you believe in someone's talent, then it's far easier to take a calculated gamble on whether to get involved or not. If you're looking for more concrete clues, however, then take a look at the equipment being used. Key members of staff at the larger camera-hire companies and post-production facilities are encouraged to spot talent, and if they are backing a short film by loaning equipment or services it means they are making a long-shot, long-term investment in the people behind the project. They want to help nurture the next generation of film-makers, who will likely pay for their services if their careers take off. If companies such as these are supporting a project, it's a good indication that you may wish to get involved.

The upshot is that good short films can be a great opportunity to gain experience, support talented colleagues and make useful and helpful new contacts. But, as positive and productive as they can be, it should never be confused with paid work.

No production manager working on a commercial project should ever ask you to work for free; if they do, make sure you contact BECTU. Work experience is, of course, a great scheme for those in full-time education, and a valuable tool for your CV, but you must be sure that these placements are genuine. Work placements usually last around one-to-two weeks, and Skillset guidelines state that they should last no longer than 160 hours in total.

Unfortunately, there are companies offering work experience to those long out of the education system, taking advantage of the eagerness of the candidates and scarcity of opportunities. Make sure you do not succumb to the temptation to work for a company for free outside of your education, just for the experience, as this not only sets back your own career, but skews the job market for everyone else. There has been far too much exploitation in the film and TV industry, and there is no place for it now or in the future. Commercially-made productions are a business and individuals should be paid fairly for their time, expertise and effort.

How to Write a Great CV

Writing a good CV is vital to all job seekers, but particularly to those starting out. When you are a newcomer to the industry, you will be sending your CV to complete strangers in the hope that yours stands out enough to encourage the (usually extremely busy) recipient to pick up the phone.

Most crucially, a CV should be kept simple and easy to read, allowing the reader to glean key information about you quickly. It's no secret that an employer will most likely spend 30 seconds to a minute examining your CV, so it needs to provide the basics front and centre. You've only got a small window of time to impress them, and give them an incentive to read further. As your career develops, the style and format of your CV will evolve; something we will look at further on.

One quick note for aspiring VFX artists; you will need an impressive showreel to accompany your CV. Make it short (between one to two minutes) and as good as it possibly can be. VFX companies are likely to look at a reel before considering your CV. You will still be starting out as a runner, but a great showreel will help you get your foot in the door.

Here, we will look at the basic CV elements that I have heard most employers talk about and, crucially, explain why they want to see the information presented in a certain way. If you can start to think about your job search from the perspective of the person doing the hiring, you can engineer your approach and CV to best suit their needs. Seeing it from the recipient's perspective is a refrain you will see time and again in this chapter: it's crucial.

For example, the reams of paperwork that professional production people are familiar with is incredibly concise. A typical call sheet, for example, will be densely packed into the shortest space possible, with most being two pages long, and contain the information needed to instruct hundreds of people through a complex series of events across an entire shooting day. If you are a production team member, you are used to dealing only with the pertinent information; it's not surprising, then, to find that they expect such precision in your CV. If your CV looks shabby, poorly designed or padded-out, it will be binned.

Having read thousands upon thousands of CVs over the years, and having spoken with many head of department across a multitude of productions, I am about to provide practical, useable advice about creating a CV that will get you noticed. It's worth noting, however, that the tips presented here only paint half of the picture; the actual content of the CV is obviously down to you and your experience.

Writing Your CV

Before we even get to the contents of your CV, we need to establish its ideal length and format. As a new entrant, a CV should only be one page of A4 paper; we have just discussed the necessity of being concise. As your career grows, your CV will expand as the credits pile up; you will also find that your name and reputation begin to precede you.

I once received a 12-page CV that had its own cover page and index. That's far too much information for anyone to digest, let alone someone working on a fast-paced production who has hundreds of CVs to get through. You must learn to be economical with your information, and focused in the way you present it.

Your CV should be saved and sent in .PDF format, as this is far more clear than a word document, with the document title being your name, role, month and year (e.g. Jane Doe Graphics CV Jan 2016.pdf) so that your CV is easily discernible to the recruiter in the sea of others it will be joining. Make sure when saving your document that it hasn't added an additional blank page at the end – a common mistake, this looks sloppy and can point to a lack of attention to detail.

This is a visual industry, and a bad font – such as Comic Sans and Heavy Heap – can count against you. Be sure to opt for a font that is clean and easy to read: Arial, Calibri and Verdana are always good choices. Another good reason to use .PDF format for your CV is so that you can see exactly how it appears to the end user.

If you are including a website or profile link in your CV, make sure you test it beforehand and get others to do so as well.

The Headline

The header of your CV should include the most pertinent information to a recruiter: your name, age, location, contact details, the role you perform (e.g. runner), driving ability and if you have your own car. The reader will then know immediately who you are, what you do and how to get in touch.

Your name should be the first line of your CV, in a slightly larger font; after all, as a freelancer your name is both your business and your brand.

However rightly proud you are of your degree achievements, it's not necessary to include your honours alongside your name – e.g. Jane Smith BA (Hons) – rather they should be detailed in the education section of your CV. When your career has really developed, and you no longer need this book, and you have joined a guild, you may wish to write those letters after your name. For example, 'BSC', which stands for British Society of Cinematographers, is a prestigious membership, and well regarded throughout the industry.

After your name, you should state very clearly what role you do, making sure it best applies to the skills, experience and credits you will be listing in the CV below. Absolutely do not call yourself a film-maker: the term implies that you are an auteur who can pick and choose projects at will.

Job Title

There is a huge difference between life in the film and TV drama industry and other forms of filming. If you've shot a few shorts, or your graduation film, on a Canon 5D, that does not make you a cinematographer. If you have cut together a few clips from a wedding on Final Cut Pro, that does not make you an editor. It sounds obvious, but I receive so many CVs from people who have no basic grasp of this fact, listing themselves as a producer, director or editor – and even, in one memorable case, a non-existent director of cinematography – although they had no professional experience. It immediately strikes a reader into thinking that the person has no understanding of the industry, and is arrogant enough to think that they don't need to learn the ropes.

I hope you are in no doubt about the situation by now, but let me clarify things for you once again. You will not walk straight out of university or film school into a head of department role on a serious, large-scale commercial project. Graduates may be full of enthusiasm because they have talent, fresh ideas and a great student project but that has no bearing on the broadcasters and financiers of film and TV drama, who will only back projects with experienced crew. As we saw, one of the key elements of a production securing finance is to demonstrate that their HoDs have a proven, successful track record.

(Of course, if you want to shoot or edit shorts or wedding videos in your spare time, then create a second CV with cinematographer as your job title. It will likely impress a bride, or secure work on a short, but don't send it out to commercial productions. For these, you will need a CV with 'camera trainee' or 'runner' across the top, to indicate your lack of real-world experience.)

Naturally, it can be tempting to put a slightly more advanced role on your CV, but resist jumping ahead of yourself when you are at entry level. Production assistant in UK film and drama is NOT an entry level role, neither is second assistant camera or third AD. A runner is an entry-level position, and don't try to bypass it. If an employer has a third AD role to fill, they may ask an experienced and capable floor runner to step up, but that experience is still required.

There is absolutely no shame in being a runner and taking your time to work up the ladder. The production manager, HoD or supervisor to whom you are sending your CV was probably a runner themselves at one point, and will do all they can to help hard-working and dedicated newcomers to the industry. They can spot trouble and bad attitudes a mile off, particularly as the decisions they make about who to recruit directly reflects back on them.

Contact Details

It's not enough to simply include your contact details in the body of the email when you send your CV; you need to make sure your mobile number and email are clearly visible in the document. When you save it as a .PDF, you can include a hyperlink for your email address to make it even more convenient to contact you.

Make sure you choose your email address carefully, and keep it professional as it may need to last you a long time. Think twice about putting your job title in your email, such as johnsmithrunner@gmail.com, as it will become obsolete as you move up the ladder, and certainly do not up-sell yourself in email address, for example using johnsmithdop@gmail.com if you are a camera trainee.

It's advisable to use a free email provider like Gmail, as they are more successful at getting messages through the strict spam filters of production companies. If you are still a student, switch from the .ac.uk address as soon as possible.

The standard format for any mobile phone number on a call sheet or unit list is as a five-three-three formation (e.g. 07700 900 123). This is a (maddeningly) small detail that will appeal to fastidious production team members.

You don't need to list your entire postal address on your CV, just your area, town or city is fine. Nor do you need to list your NI number on your CV.

Personal Details

Age

Most productions are looking for runners over the age of 21 for insurance purposes, and are also interested in the maturity of their candidate in terms of their professional outlook. If you are coming into the industry at a later stage, this can be a positive as extra-life experience is a plus, and there is a real-life example of this later on.

Driving Ability

Many runner jobs involve driving. In a survey conducted with employers by industry analyst Stephen Follows, he found that most employers said that being able to drive was more important to them than a university degree. That's not to say your university degree is useless, far from it, but you need additional practical skills, which you need to perform certain roles. As a recent graduate, you will not be entrusted to hold the camera and a shoot a scene, instead you will be asked to take care of the things that need doing, which often includes ferrying around people and things. And if you are working at a studio like Pinewood and Leavesden, you will probably need a car just to get to work on time.

Some productions will want you to have your own car, and some will hire one for you. Most car-hire companies will not allow someone under the age of 21 to drive one of their vehicles, due to increased insurance costs.

Location

Where you live can be a key factor in finding employment. Productions usually want runners based in the area and possessing local knowledge and, as the working hours are so long, don't want someone who has a lengthy commute each day. Filming is a marathon endeavour so they want someone who will be fresh on set or in the office each morning. Driving into work from a distance also increases the chances of late arrivals, which is an absolute taboo when filming.

I regularly see applications for entry-level jobs from people who live nowhere near the area the job is based. That person may have emailed hundreds of applications without success, and I would urge you to see why from the employer's perspective. If an employer sees that you are not based nearby they are not likely to read further as they will already have many applications from locals, and are unlikely to shoulder the responsibility of you potentially moving hundreds of miles for one short-term job, or any travel costs. In this case, a rejection is nothing personal; it's down to geography. You are much more likely to find work if you focus on your local area.

Credits

The main content of your CV will be your credits, i.e. your professional work. This does not mean short films or university projects; employers can tell the difference, and don't like it when an amateur credit is 'passed off' as a pro-credit. One day's experience on a professional production is worth more to your CV than 10 short films.

Even if you don't have any professional experience at all, I still would not recommend listing your university work as individual credits. Instead, include them within your education section later on in your CV.

If you have no professional experience then highlight other personal achievements, and the motivations behind them. Do you have any language skills? If so, detail them and mark them clearly as basic, intermediate, fluent or mother tongue. Have you ever volunteered anywhere? Do you have a CRB check? Do you have any software skills beyond the usual Microsoft Office? Again, put yourself in the position of the employer and highlight what is relevant to them.

If you do have credits or employment history to list, then everything should be in chronological order with the most recent first. If your most recent project hasn't been released yet, say so and put the estimated release or TX date on it. You can list any projects on which you have worked, even if you did not get an actual on-screen credit for it, but be clear about the level and length of work you did. Never lie about a credit on your CV; you will always get found out.

The listed credits must have some context, and all the relevant information for the department: the title and nature of the production, production company, dates worked and role performed, and the names of the director, producer and head of department. Below is an example; you do not have to lay it out exactly like this in your CV.

Title:	Downton Abbey 5
Production Company:	Carnival, ITV
Format:	6x60m ITV Drama
Dates:	Jan 14 - Jul 14
Role:	Floor Runner (2nd Unit)
Producer:	A N Other
Director:	A N Other
Head of Department:	A N Other

Giving the names of the director, producer and head of department is important because it's a small industry, and people know each other. If you have worked under someone the employer either knows or recognises, that is a positive association. It also gives them somewhere to turn for an easy reference.

How you arrange your credit information on the page is down to your personal preference. Ensure that the information is clear and the format is repeated and standardised for each credit. Ask people you trust to scan your CV for 30 seconds and tell you what stands out.

There is a tendency for listing achievements within a credit, but this is usually unnecessary. A production manager might be tempted to say things like 'booked crew, organised insurance, managed budget', but this is what every single PM does on every project. If you only have a few credits, however, you may wish to include a very brief line of context, for example, 'crowd runner for over 200 background artists'.

Indeed, if you've worked dailies or crowd on a project, you must make that distinction clear. Never claim to be part of the main team if you were not; these falsehoods have a tendency to catch up with you. To avoid making this mistake, use the job title that is given to you on the call sheet and include the additional detail in brackets: 'additional floor runner (dailies)' or 'costume trainee (second unit, dailies)'. Only ever use the title given to you by the production: if you were a runner then say so, even if on-set you found yourself doing the work of a third AD.

Use your judgement when deciding which credits to include. I've received CVs with porn channel productions included; unless you're applying for a job on an adult movie or late-night TV, leave these off your CV.

Personal Profile/Biography

If you are going to include an 'interests and hobbies' section, don't be boring. If you were a former barrister or built shelters for refugees in Indonesia – and I've seen both – you could certainly consider putting that in. However, the reality is that I hardly ever read anything in these sections that actually stands out.

Personally, I rarely read all of the mini biographies but some people do. Whether or not to include one is a question of personal taste; you must decide what works for you, and act on feedback.

If you do include one, never refer to yourself in the third person, and do not include that standard line: 'I am passionate about a career in the media'. Media is not film and TV proper, and all runners are notionally passionate. Other hot words to avoid include: 'confident', 'dynamic', 'skilled' and so on. Try to actually display these traits in your CV by showing that you've gone the extra mile and volunteered, led, organised, contributed and taken part. Back up your assertions: show, don't tell.

Be careful too about your phrasing. A sentence such as: 'I want to develop my career as a producer' can be read as an indication of the direction you want to take, but some could infer that you are using their production simply as a means to spring-board your own success. A production manager needs to be clear on what you can do for them, and not the other way around. They are paying a person to do a job; if you do well, then they will be only too happy to help you find more work.

If you have something genuinely interesting that you would like to include in your CV, which doesn't fit easily into the other sections, then it may be worth considering a personal profile. If you are merely following a standard format, then think carefully about whether it actually adds anything to the reader's understanding of you and your achievements.

Important Information

Not only can flat blocks of text can be off-putting to a reader when they have a stack of CVs to get through, but important information can get lost in a sentence and may be served far better as a bullet point. For example, if you've done the latest BBC Health and Safety course, or you're a member of The Association of Motion Picture Sound (AMPS) or have been DBS checked, that information can get lost in the paragraph. Make sure it stands out:

• BBC Health and Safety trained (2016)
• Associate Member of AMPS
• DBS checked (2016)

References
List your references by name, company and occupation at the bottom of your CV. Many people prefer to keep their email address private, so it's perfectly acceptable and advisable, to state 'contact details on request'. The names and grades of those referees should be a reasonable indicator for the reader.

When you are starting out in the industry, references can be useful but they can also work against you if handled incorrectly. Let's say you have a few jobs under your belt by this stage, including a couple of months working at the BBC. That will really stand out on your CV, and I would expect one of your references to be from this production, but if I find the references are from your sixth form tutor and holiday job employer, it would raise questions. Make sure you get professional, industry references on your CV as soon as possible, as it gives a very positive impression.

It's worth noting that employers will consider any name mentioned on your CV as a potential reference, and could get in touch with any one of them for 'unofficial' feedback.

I have on occasion seen quoted testimonials from recognised industry individuals included in a CV. For example, a brief line from a producer to say that: 'Jane Smith was a hard-working, cheery and level-headed runner on our shoot. I look forward to working with Jane again, and I recommend her for any production running work in the future.' I think this can be a very positive addition to a CV, an industry endorsement which encourages me to consider the individual in greater detail. Obviously, you need to have done a really good job and have a great relationship with the HoD or producer before you ask for such a quote.

Education

This is a section that will probably only feature on your CV for the first couple of years of your career. No one will be concerned about your degree if you can demonstrate plenty of professional experience, and you'll know when the time has come to remove the section.

When you start out, your education is one of the most important parts of your life and, whether you are coming from university, college or school, will be the cornerstone of your CV experience. The vast majority of new industry entrants, however, have some kind of degree in film or media studies.

You only need to mention the name of the institution, the years you attended, the course title and the grade/award achieved. Some employers think highly of certain courses and institutions; others may be more interested in your result.

Often the CV that stands out from the pile is from someone who has studied an entirely different subject, purely because it bucks the trend. A different skill set might also be useful for the role. If you studied Law, for example, you might be considered for a research job, and if you studied English you might be considered for the role of an assistant script editor.

If you have no other experience outside of education to include in your CV, then you could describe the work undertaken as part of your course. Just be sure to be concise. As an employer, I will be more interested in the things you did outside of the curriculum, such as setting up any organisations or clubs, volunteering or learning a language. An employer will also be impressed if you have managed to find some work in professional TV or film production in your university holidays, or if you undertook some relevant work experience as part of the course.

Once you are happy with your CV, you can begin to start sending it out. Get into the habit of continually updating it; you may find that you will need to amend it for specific job advertisements to highlight your suitability for a job.

Five Different Types of CV

I see a lot of CVs that are sent to *thecallsheet.co.uk* – over 10,000 in the last couple of years alone – and, while it's good to have variety, some are definitely better than others.

Now that we have taken an in-depth look at creating a strong entry-level CV, it will be useful to see what other CVs might actually look like on the page. What follows is examples of the five different types of CVs I most commonly see, and we will examine their key differences depending on what each candidate does, their level of experience and the type of productions they work on.

Not one of these five is better than the other: each has a unique impact and suits a particular stage in a career. They are not intended to be copied, rather used as inspiration for your own personal document.

CV # 1: The Entry-Level CV (Sample)

Kelly MacDonald

Make-up Assistant
London based, willing to travel
M: 07900 100 450 e: kellym@mac.com w: kellymacmakeup.com

Delamar Academy Graduate
(Year course 2015/16)

Skills include:

- Hairdressing
- Prosthetics
- Casualty FX
- Beauty/Fashion

Age: 25
Full & Clean Driving Licence, Own Car
Illamasqua 2 Day Training Course
Full beauty kit & small prosthetic kit

DATE	TITLE	ROLE	DESIGNER	PRODUCTION COMPANY
June 2016	"Insert Title"	Make-up artist (Dailies)	Loz Schaivo	BBC/Tiger Aspect
Feb to June 2016	"Insert Title"	Make-up assistant	Catherine Scoble	Warp Films
Nov 2015	"Insert Title"	Make-up trainee	Deb Taylor	Silver Films
August 2015	"Insert Title"	Make-up trainee	Lois Burwell	Disney
July 2015	"Insert Title"	Make-Up artist	Lydia Pett	A small film co
May 2015	"Insert Title"	Prosthetics	Kelly MacDonald	Tiny pictures
May 2015	"Insert Title"	Make up designer	Kelly MacDonald	Speck pics

OTHER EMPLOYMENT

MAY 2011 – JUL 2013	The Red Lion Pub, Ealing	Bar staff
OCT 2010 – APR 2011	WH Smith, Bradford	Retail staff (part time)

EDUCATION

2009 – 2011	**CITY OF BRADFORD COLLEGE** (A-LEVEL)
	Media Production (Merit)
	English (Distinction)

PERSONAL INFORMATION

I have volunteered for charity, assisting victims with severe burns with the application of camouflage make up. I regularly face-paint at children's parties and provide bridal make up at weddings.

Important things to note:
• Name, role, location and contact details prominent
• Details of most recent relevant training clear
• Driving details prominent
• Clear credits, laid out in reverse chronology with the most recent at the top
• Description of role, with named head of department for each
• Brief indication of other employment and education

CV #2: The Experienced CV (Sample)

Natalie St John
PRODUCTION COORDINATOR

Mobile: 07700 982 336   email: natsj@hotmail.com

Personal Statement: Over 5 years' experience as a production coordinator. Worked for BBC, ITV, Sky One, Channel 5 and Channel 5. Specialise in large scale entertainment format shows. I have experience with Booking crew, International Travel and Accommodation, hiring equipment, Clearances, Post Production Paperwork and music licensing.

TV

AS PRODUCTION COORDINATOR

Britain's Got Talent 5 Feb- May 2014	Syco TV ITV Studios	Producer: Syd Sydenham Director: Dani Dagenham PM: Ben Brockley
	*Key coordinator on all rounds and live finals *Managed team of over 40 junior crew *Wormed 'Pudsey'	
Strictly Come Dancing 6 Jun – Dec 2013	BBC	Series Producer: Cecilia Oxbridge Series Director: Bruce Oldboy-Network PM: Brian Whiteman
	*Key coordinator for all live TX *Coordinated all VT teams and spin-off teams *Slept in office on 19 occasions without crying	
Friday Download	Saltbeef TV CBBC	Producer: Sam Spencer Director: Jeff Yooftoday PM: Diana Murphy

This type of CV is quite common in factual, light entertainment and comedic TV production. CVs for drama and films tend not to include the bullet-point details.
Important things to note:
• Contact details prominent
• Productions listed in reverse chronology with the most recent at the top
• Details of the director, producer and HoD
• Brief description of the major obstacles and task undertaken
By this point of Natalie's career, she no longer needs a specific section for references. Most of the names contained in the CV should effectively be sufficient as referees

CV #3: The Commercials CV (Sample)

Prestige Diary 01900 9-2-5 9-2-5

Frazer Marcus
Digital Imaging Technician D.I.T

frazerDIT@gmail.com

COMMERCIALS

Brand	Title	Production Co	Director	Producer	DoP	
Guinness	Time	Rattling Stick	Daniel Kleinman	Johnnie Frankel	Ben Davis	*Alexa*
Pepsi	Messi & Co	Partizan	James Joy	Audrey Hepburn	Chaz Kirwan	*Arriflex, Aaton*
BBC	Wimbledon: 'Play'	Red Bee	Billy Norris	Pearl Barley	Paul Lucan	*Alexa, Phantom*
The Guardian	360 news	Academy	Steven King	Tim Temper	Alice Duggan	*Sony PD150/170*
Guinness	Time	Rattling Stick	Daniel Kleinman	Johnnie Frankel	Ben Davis	*3D rig (Paradise)*
Pepsi	Messi & Co	Partizan	James Joy	Audrey Hepburn	Chaz Kirwan	*Arriflex, Aaton*
BBC	Wimbledon: 'Play'	Red Bee	Billy Norris	Pearl Barley	Paul Lucan	*Alexa, Phantom*
The Guardian	360 news	Academy	Steven King	Tim Temper	Alice Duggan	*Sony PD150/170*
Guinness	Time	Rattling Stick	Daniel Kleinman	Johnnie Frankel	Ben Davis	*Alexa*
Pepsi	Messi & Co	Partizan	James Joy	Audrey Hepburn	Chaz Kirwan	*Arriflex, Aaton*
BBC	Wimbledon: 'Play'	Red Bee	Billy Norris	Pearl Barley	Paul Lucan	*Alexa, Phantom*
The Guardian	360 news	Academy	Steven King	Tim Temper	Alice Duggan	*Sony PD150/170*

MUSIC VIDEOS

Artist	Track	Production Co	Director	Producer	DoP	
Coldplay	Blandy Bland	Gutterfish	Wizard + Foy	Carly Knox-Fopley	Marco De Gale	*Canon XL1*
Kasabian	Spinal Pap	Fluiditiy	Bolo Yueng	Juan Riquelme	Simone Lowden	*Arriflex SR3*
Little Mix	Hollow Vessels	fineSLICE	Paul Pewter	Ian Cannisters	Lewin Buckaroo	*Alexa*

Camera familiarity:
Sony PD150/170, Sony DSR 390,400,450 Sony HVR Z1E, Cannon XL1/XL2,, Arriflex D21, Arriflex 16SR3, AATON XTR, RED ONE +(MX), Paradise 3D rig, Element Tech 3D Rig, Pace 3D Rig, Arri 2C 35mm, Cannon 5DMk2, 7D, Arri Alexa

Editing software:
Avid, Final Cut, Adobe Premier Pro, Photo Shop and Adobe, After Effects

Mobile: 07700 942 840

Important things to note:

• This type of CV is often laid out in landscape, and is never longer than three pages
• Commercials happen so frequently that dates are excised and credits are densely packed
• Brands and script names (and sometimes even ad agencies) are listed
• Diary service is listed as the primary point of contact
•Specialist skills and equipment are listed

The production companies listed on a commercials CV are the first thing the producer, director and PM will look at, and many focus on picking the more fashionable individual, rather than the most skilled.

CV #4: Very Experienced CV (Sample)

Lesley Buckham DoP

BSC, GBCT

CV Summer 2015

www.lesleybuckham.com

Feature Films

'Tails You Lose' *Fox/StudioCanal*
Dir. Simon Harden Prod. Laurie Bagshaw UPM. Allen Harris

'Pride and Prejudice' *Working Title/Universal*
Dir. Tony Huu Prod. Roger Garvey UPM. Barnard Willow

'Mission Impossible 10' *Paramount/Skydance Productions*
Dir. Eleanor Brown Prod. Tom Cruise, Pauline Wagner UPM. Freddie Pearce

'Clash of the Galaxies' *Marvel/Disney*
Dir. Simon Harden Prod. Laurie Bagshaw UPM. Allen Harris

'Balero' *MGM Productions*
Dir. Irena Todarova Prod. Martha Joseph UPM. Matt Roxburgh

TV Drama

'Westminster Village People' *BBC*
Dir. Simon Harden Prod. Laurie Bagshaw UPM. Allen Harris

'Murder Scene' *ITV*
Dir. Tony Huu Prod. Roger Garvey UPM. Barnard Willow

'Baked' *HBO*
Dir. Maggie Cullaine. Prod. Tom Cruise, Pauline Wagner UPM. Luke Edwards

Important things to note:

- This CV is very simply laid out and doesn't require lots of explanation
- The names mentioned speak for themselves
- Experienced CVs usually contain an association with guilds (in this case BSC and GBCT)
- The footer of this CV contains the contact details for Lesley's agent

CV #5: The Art Department CV (Sample)

Important things to note:
• Informative, interesting and clearly demonstrates ability
• Compels the reader to engage with the information
This style of CV should *only* be used by the art department, and is not suitable for most other departments.

How to Write a Great Cover Email

Most job applications these days are sent by email, with a cover note in the body of the email and a CV attached. If you are emailing a job application there are likely to be hundreds of others heading to the same inbox, so you need to make sure that your email grabs the attention of the recipient and gets you on their shortlist.

Your email should be informative, concise and interesting enough to entice the reader to open your CV, which in turn, should convince them to pick up the phone.

Below is an example of a simple, effective cover email:

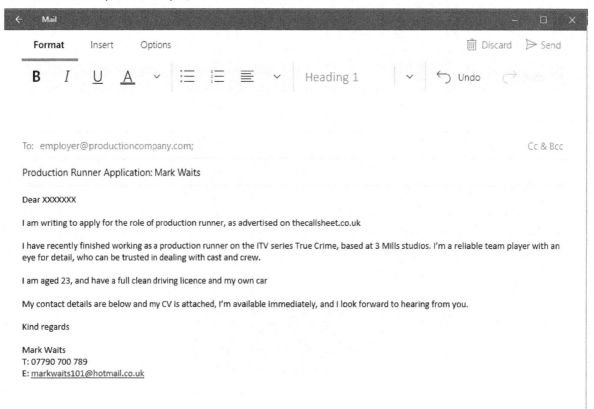

To: employer@productioncompany.com;   Cc & Bcc

Production Runner Application: Mark Waits

Dear XXXXXXX

I am writing to apply for the role of production runner, as advertised on thecallsheet.co.uk

I have recently finished working as a production runner on the ITV series True Crime, based at 3 Mills studios. I'm a reliable team player with an eye for detail, who can be trusted in dealing with cast and crew.

I am aged 23, and have a full clean driving licence and my own car

My contact details are below and my CV is attached, I'm available immediately, and I look forward to hearing from you.

Kind regards

Mark Waits
T: 07790 700 789
E: markwaits101@hotmail.co.uk

10 Top Tips

I see plenty of bad cover emails, which don't address the criteria that the job poster is looking for, so here are my top 10 tips to making sure your email catches the attention of any potential employer:

1. The only document attached to your email should be a CV in .PDF format. Put your cover letter in the body of the email.

2. Understand and address the job description, and tailor every cover email to each individual role. It's painfully obvious when an applicant has used copy and paste.

3. Be concise. Too much waffle shows poor communication skills, so always stick to the point.

4. Tell them where you saw the job, and why you are applying. If you have enjoyed the company's previous productions, you could include a sentence about how much you admire their output.

5. Briefly describe your recent work experience and how it highlights your suitability for the advertised role. Remember, if you don't have the experience they require, your application is likely to be ignored, so make sure your skills stand out.

6. If you can drive and are over 21, make sure you mention these facts in the cover letter. It's one of the first things that a production will look for, and immediately ticks an important box.

7. Spell check! Triple check your own spelling, and don't rely on your computer's spell checker. Always read and re-read your cover letter before sending it. A free web app called Grammarly is very useful.

8. Mention your availability, especially if there are specific dates in the job post. If you are definitely not available for the advertised dates, it's simply not worth applying.

9. Make sure that the job title you have given yourself within your CV and email match the title of the job post. If your CV says you are a production manager, and you are applying for a runner position, an employer is not likely to continue with your application.

10. Be sure to put your full name, email address and mobile number at the bottom of your email, and a link to your website or online profile if you have one.

Always remember that the aim of a good cover email is to direct the recipient to your strong CV, which will encourage them to call you in for interview. You don't have to tell them everything in your initial correspondence, but make sure you give them a reason to pick up the phone.

For most new entrants, getting a foot in the door of the industry is a major challenge, often fuelled by a mixture of naivety, arrogance and desperation. That sense of frustration is natural but, as you are likely to be sending out many applications before you get your first break, you should never let your despair creep into your cover email, job application or conversations. Approach each new job application with the same enthusiastic outlook. There is a difference between saying that you are 'desperate for work' and you are 'available for work'; the person hiring you would prefer to know that you are available and interested, rather than desperate for anything.

Email Address

As previously mentioned, you should carefully consider your own email address before you start sending out professional CVs. You want a simple email address that is easy to spell and based on your own name; nothing that's embarrassing or difficult to relay.

If you are still using your .ac.uk university email address, switch to a more professional one as soon as possible. Choosing a recognised email service like Gmail or Hotmail is also a good idea: they are vigilant against hackers and so adept at getting emails past company's spam filters. Whatever email address you use, be sure it's the same on your email cover letter and CV.

Where to Send Your CV

'Entry routes into the Creative Media industries remain largely informal for many. Responding to an advertisement is the most common individual means of securing a first job in Creative Media (31% of respondents) but other more informal routes form a larger group in combination; for example, making direct contact with a company (18%), through a friend or relative (16%), direct from an employer (10%) and word of mouth (7%)'

Skillset 2010 Employment Census

At the beginning of your career, knowing where to start is a daunting prospect. Breaking into the industry can seem like an elusive and distant target, particularly if you don't have any personal contacts.

The above excerpt from the 2010 Skillset employment census highlights the fact that having a personal contact already working in the business is a major help. According to their results, there is just a 2% difference between people finding work by contacting companies directly, and by using existing industry contacts. Both of those methods are classed as 'informal recruitment' in the subsequent 2015 survey, but the point is laid out more clearly in this 2010 report. Nepotism exists in all walks of life, of course, but the familial grapevine is strong in film and TV. If you don't have any existing personal connections, it's crucial to work on building your own network from the very beginning.

One important thing to remember when approaching people for work is that the majority of crew and technicians in the business are freelance, and unencumbered by the protocols and policy of human resources departments. When you are sending your CV to someone who is also self-employed, their decision to hire you has a direct impact on their reputation. A crew member will spend more time with their team than they will with their family, so they have to carefully consider if they can get along with potential employees.

The three other methods of finding work mentioned in the excerpt above are the ones over which you have the most control: responding to job posts, contacting an employer and word of mouth.

Job Posts

When you start looking for your first job, there is no need to pay a subscription fee to access a jobs' website; most entry level job advertisements can be found online for free. Alongside *thecallsheet.co.uk*, resources like The Unit List and TV Watercooler post job adverts from production companies, and various Facebook groups do too. There are also plenty of employers posting jobs directly on their own websites.

Diary Services, Job Sites & Agents

As with most industries, there are recruitment specialists and dedicated online portals in film and drama production, but because most of the workforce is freelance and on short-term contracts, the business model does vary from other sectors.

Diary services

Formed in the days before mobile phone technology, these services ensured that a working crew member would not miss out on future job opportunities just because they were on set and not at home to take a call. Many crew members would pool their resources and hire one person to manage their diary, so all of their work calls would be directed to one number, and the diary manager would be the single point of contact. They would get paid a flat rate every month by each crew member on their roster, whether they got any work or not.

Over the years, the role of a diary manager has evolved and diary services are now used mostly in commercials. Many commercial HoDs will be registered with diary services, with companies such as Chapters, Red Diary Service, Callbox, Gems and Production Switchboard among the busiest in the market. Not all of the UK's diary services would take on a runner straight out of university, unless they had a few credits to their name and, preferably, a glowing reference from an existing diary service member.

CallTime company are the only service I know of that takes fresh graduates onto their books, running an annual runners' induction day, and has successfully placed many in paid jobs on major feature films and TV drama productions. I would urge you to take a look at the CallTime company website; details are in the resources section of this book.

The cost of a diary service can range from as little as £30 per month for newcomers to around £150 per month for HoDs, although this rate is obviously dependent on the particular company. Self-employed crew members can claim the cost of a diary service as an expense on their tax bill, so the cost is negated.

Diary services trade on their contacts and administration. If you get to the point in your career where a diary service is willing to take you on, and you are willing to pay for their services, you are effectively buying into their contacts and ability to deliver a return your investment.

Agents

Film and TV agents operate at the highest end of the industry, earning their clients more money and securing them the best work available. There are very influential agencies such as United, Independent, Curtis Brown, Casarotto and Sara Putt who have many clients in key positions, and typically take a commission of around 10% to 15% of their clients' salary. Often, there is little difference in the remuneration for their below-the-line clients, but there is a significant difference in the opportunities that are made available.

Websites

Online sites in the film and TV drama industry have traditionally failed to offer a suitable service for professional productions. Websites such as Shooting People, Film Crew Pro and Mandy.com do not offer opportunities on major feature films or TV drama; at best, they might be used by micro-budget producers looking for affordable crew. Some productions may also use these websites to find collaborators willing to work for free or for a 'deferred' payment, meaning that *if* the production makes any profit in the future you will get some return. This is, however, extremely unlikely.

Unfortunately, many new entrants are regularly duped into paying a subscription to some websites, which, as previously mentioned, is unnecessary. There is plenty of free information about entry-level opportunities out there. I would naturally recommend *thecallsheet.co.uk*, which is free for new entrants to the business and only posts paid jobs. It also has a wealth of useful information alongside job listings. There is a list of useful resources at the back of this book.

Look for a database of reputable production or post production companies (there are a number of directories listed in the resources section) and look them up online. Find out if they have a recruitment page and bookmark the link. Build up a bookmark folder with these career pages and you will be able to search them quickly and easily for any new job posts.

Applying For Jobs

A 2014 survey of film professionals undertaken by Stephen Follows with the help of *thecallsheet.co.uk*, found that industry job posts typically receive around 60 responses, with only 46 % of those being suitable for the role.

As we've seen, some people genuinely believe that because they worked as a first AD on a few university films they can walk on to the set of a professional TV drama as a first AD. In reality, however, they would be unlikely to find work as a second or even third AD. If you cannot recognise that there is a huge gulf in experience between a university film and a commercial feature, then your applications will remain ignored. There is nothing wrong with ambition, but there is a problem with a lack of awareness.

When you decide to apply for a job, you will need to do it fast. Most jobs are posted and filled very quickly, and the process does not run in the same way as in other industries. For film and TV production roles, the closing date for applications may be just a few days before the successful applicant is needed on set. The production posting the job will read the first batch of CVs that come in, and will contact any stand-out candidates for immediate interview or book them immediately. Although it may take rather longer to fill HoD roles, as the production will take the time to get the right person on the right deal, runner positions are rather more simple to fill: rate and start date will be non-negotiable, and when someone is found who fits the bill – either in the stack of CVs or through existing contacts and diary services–they will often be hired straight away. To give yourself the best chance, ensure your CV is one of the first to be seen.

Read the Advert

Before you write and send your application, read the job advert thoroughly. If start dates, contract lengths and location are given, make sure that you are able to meet these needs; if not, there's no point in applying. Location is particularly important. If senior crew need to travel, this will be accommodated by the production, but that is not always extended to runners and other junior crew. The production may also not want the responsibility of someone moving across the country to take on such a demanding role, even if the applicant says they are willing to do so. A production will always prefer local runners, particularly if they have a remit to hire a certain number of local crew to qualify for regional funding.

There is nothing more irritating, or a bigger waste of time, than job applications without any bearing to the advertised job spec. Most production companies I work with are at the higher end of the scale, and use *thecallsheet.co.uk* to control the volume of job applications. I regularly hear these companies bemoan applications that entirely miss the mark. The worst applications come from those who have no grasp of their own experience and think they can just 'give it a go'. The professional companies operating at the highest levels do not gamble on key crew positions, nor are they permitted to by the investors or broadcasters.

Before you hit send on a job application, re-read the post and put yourself in the shoes of the employer. Is this application appropriate? Do you have the right experience? Are you available when they need someone? Do you live in the area? Can you drive, if that is required? If you tick all the boxes and have triple-spell checked your cover email, then you can hit send.

Only Apply For the Specific Role Being Advertised

The other frustration many productions have about posting job adverts online is the 'open gate' trend. This is when a specific role is advertised – production assistant, for example – and the recruiter receives emails from numerous individuals fishing for other roles, along the lines of: 'Hi, I see you are looking for a production assistant. I am a cameraman, so if you need anyone to shoot this production then give me a call.' This approach rarely achieves anything other than irritating the production company and putting a black mark against your name. It also discourages production companies from advertising roles online, and may tempt them to use recruitment agencies, diary services and agents, meaning less opportunities being posted in places accessible to you.

Rates

Many companies don't post individual job rates in the advertisement, but you should only ever ask about rates if you get a response from your application, never in the application itself. Reputable production companies that are Pact & APA registered will only post adverts for paid jobs, and reputable job sites will only work with those companies. Indeed, places like *thecallsheet.co.uk* regularly reject production companies seeking free or cheap labour, as do many others listed in the back of this book.

Avoid Spamming

A large proportion of industry individuals are reluctant to post jobs online, as once their email address is made public it not only encourages inappropriate applications but also unwanted correspondence long after the event. While data protection forbids spamming emails, and companies must offer mailing list opt-outs, there is no polite way to ask an individual to stop emailing you other than to ignore them.

I know many production managers and coordinators who receive an endless supply of uninvited CVs to their personal email address from complete strangers, and they have no option other than to ignore them. They are an unwelcome distraction when you are in the thick of production.

It's crucial to treat any job advertisement contact details, be it a company or individual, with the confidence and trust you would expect yourself. Just because you know someone's email address, doesn't mean you should use it. This is particularly true within the film industry, as you will constantly bump into people you have met and worked with before and your reputation and manners will always precede you.

Direct Contact

As well as replying to specific job adverts, you also have the option of contacting employers directly on a speculative basis. (Of course, before you even consider doing this you should ensure your CV and cover email are absolutely watertight, using the tips we looked at earlier.)

Before you do so, it's important to ensure you are contacting the right companies. Distribution companies or film financiers, for example, cannot help you gain production work – you would need to contact production companies and individual heads of department/Supervisors directly.

The well-worn path of speculative applications is to play the percentages game: find a reliable directory, or reputable online database such as Creative England, Kays and The Knowledge, and send a CV to every production company from A to Z. There are currently around 450 companies registered with PACT, alongside 185 commercials production companies (currently registered with the APA) and a further 80 members of the UK Screen Association, which covers post-production, studios and assorted services companies. That's a lot of emails.

This scattergun approach, however, is not one I would necessarily recommend. Production companies come in all shapes and sizes. While some are large corporations like Working Title, who run an apprentice scheme every year, many are small enterprises without a specific HR department. A CV is easily lost in either.

It's far better to do your research and take a more targeted approach, using criteria such as an accessible location, what they do and the quality of their work. Glean as much information as you can about them from their website, including where they might advertise their jobs and what productions they are working on. If you are keen on sculpting props or making prosthetics, for example, then track down the companies doing just that. Alternatively, contact the relevant HoD of the department you are most interested in, for example an art director or gaffer. The earlier information about departments and roles will help you narrow down your best contact, and a few minutes of research can significantly improve the chances of your CV getting to the right person.

You may end up sending out hundreds of speculative CVs, so it is useful to make a spreadsheet listing their details, the date you sent your initial enquiry, the date you followed up and notes about any responses. If you are able to find out which productions they are working on, make a note of those dates so you can time the sending of your CV to coincide with when they may be looking for crew. Indeed, you can add any information to your spreadsheet you find helpful; being organised is a key element of success.

If you are interested in working in a particular discipline, such as in the camera, costume or art department, be aware that it is not always the HoD who makes the decision on which trainee will be taken on. The focus puller, supervisor or art director will often choose, so you should be looking to identify and contact them directly.

Finally, prepare yourself for getting very few responses. There are a lot of people writing a lot of speculative letters and the market is over saturated. If you make sure your CV is solid, do your research and contact the right people, you are far more likely to be successful than if you employ the haphazard approach to finding employment I so often see.

Service Companies

When you are sending out your speculative CVs, remember that the UK's film studios, such as Pinewood, Ealing, 3 Mills and Twickenham, etc, may be crucial to the film-making process but are not involved in the production process themselves. If you want to make programmes and films, they should not be your first port of call. While a production may set up shop in a studio for the duration of a project, they are simply tenants. Often, there is little contact between the studio management and the residing productions other than the discussion of spaces for hire, maintenance and telecoms requirements. Studios will be generally only be interested in site runner, receptionists, sales, security and maintenance teams, and are seeking permanent staff who know the area well and can support the studio as it plays host to production. They are not interested in your ability to hold a camera.

That being said, a job as a studio site assistant or receptionist is a potential stepping stone towards a role in production. Personally, I took a temp job on the Ealing Studios reception, which I got through a normal, high-street temp agency, and this led to me being asked to work on a Disney film. The production office team saw me working hard for the studio, liked me and found that I had the experience that they were looking for; I was in the right place at the right time with the right CV. It can, and does, happen.

If you are particularly interested in non-production roles such as camera, art department, costume or make-up, then you should research the companies that provide services to those departments, such as camera, prop and costume hire or SFX. All of these have regular and direct contact with production companies and HoDs. If, for example, you want to work in the camera department, a good place to start is by approaching camera hire companies; there are few better ways to learn about cameras than in the kit room of a rental company. You will also get a valuable insight into the process and methods of the department, as well as meeting crew members coming in to test and prep camera gear.

Once involved with a service company, you will be on the inside of the industry which means that, as well as building on your knowledge and CV, you will meet an increasing number of contacts. If you are seen to be doing your job well, and show a great attitude, you can begin to ask about work on an actual production. As I've stated before, if you can showcase a great personality, solid skills and an appetite to learn, employers (and I include more senior freelancers) will spot it a mile away.

Timing

When you are sending out your CV on a speculative basis, you are in control of its content and its destination. You have, however, less control over its timing. While it's sensible to send your CV to a production while they are crewing up in the beginning, it's still something of a game of chance.

You can have the best CV and a brilliant cover email, but you may suffer the bad luck of poor timing. Let's look at an example. Say you are an art-department assistant and you send your CV to an art director who is in pre-production on a big movie, and will need to fill their team. In order to find those crew, the art director will have several options: firstly, they will have a list of preferred crew and second choices; then they will seek recommendations from people they know; then they may look through diary services, agents and their own social media networks. Only when their personal reach is exhausted will they start to look elsewhere.

While the art director is going through this process, they have a huge amount on their plate; a workload that's seemingly insurmountable and deadlines that seems impossible. They will be working ridiculously long hours and, when they do manage to get away from their desks, the emails will pile up into the hundreds. These include important production messages – 'The director no longer wants a CGI castle for the battle scene so we have to build it' – along with spam and, of course, those speculative emails.

With all that going on, it's the important stuff that dominates their to-do list and anything that doesn't need their immediate attention is ignored; their focus is not likely to be on junior members of the crew at this stage. At this point, you need luck on your side and have your email arrive at precisely the right moment: that sweet spot where they know they need someone, have two minutes to look at the latest CV (which happens to be yours), and recognise that you have the right experience for the job.

Given the mania of the production process, it's entirely possible that you may not hear back from a single person to whom you sent a speculative CV. No one likes to be ignored and, without any feedback to go on, it can easily dampen morale and break spirits. You must try and remember not to take it too personally, and rationalise the process as it happens. Negativity breeds, and you will need to develop a thick skin if you are going to survive in this industry.

Word of Mouth

When it comes to finding work through word of mouth, it is really a form of the networking we looked at earlier in this chapter. Your contacts can either suggest you to someone else, or else inform you of a job opportunity that you can then act upon.

While you can spend many hours scouring websites, word-of-mouth jobs come due to face-to-face contact in the real world, and of being recognisably – and consistently – good at your job. This is why networking is so important. Having contacts looking out for jobs for you, or mentioning you at the right time, is invaluable in an industry that is so competitive.

Of course, many people in the business will be keen to get their family member or friend into the industry, so competition is still rife. Film and drama crew are, however, constantly putting people forward for jobs through word of mouth, and in commercials-productions companies several production managers work in the same room and regularly share details of people they are happy to endorse.

Even at entry level, good runners will find themselves in demand and regularly turning down work due to lack of availability. If a production company calls and they are not available for the job, they may be asked if they can recommend anyone else for the role, and there are some great stories in the next section about how people got their first break through their network.

Social Media

The film industry in the UK is over 100 years old, and the TV industry not far behind. It is a relatively niche industry centred in London and, historically, crew members have been sourced though personal connections. Given the inconsistent job market, highly specialised roles, the need for experience and a genial personality, it is no wonder that many people find roles through word of mouth and recommendation.

Some of the older generation working within the industry share stories of finishing one film on a Friday, walking down the corridor at Pinewood and being hired by another job starting on the Monday. It was – and still is – a small world, but the use of online websites and social media is opening up the opportunities somewhat.

Used correctly, social media is a great tool for finding jobs and acquiring knowledge. By following or liking the right groups, you can source lots of ready information. Of course, nothing beats face-to-face contact, but astute use of social media, in a professional capacity, can really help your job search. You can also use it to make valuable connections, and showcase your own work.

Generally speaking, the three main social-media platforms are Facebook, Twitter and LinkedIn. The former is personal, the latter is strictly business and Twitter is somewhere in between. Remember that every individual with whom you connect over social media will have their own way of using it: some will want to keep Facebook just for close family and friends, others will wish to remain anonymous on Twitter and, of course, many people will have an extremely limited use of social media altogether.

Below is a quick guide to each of the social media platforms and how best to use them in an industry capacity. Whichever you use, however, always take care to be polite and professional, don't say anything online that you wouldn't say to someone in person and manage your privacy settings, especially on Facebook.

Social media is an incredibly valuable tool for finding opportunities, but when you do get a job it is vital that you do not mention the production, or post any pictures, on any social media or anywhere online. Always show discretion and confidentiality.

Facebook

Since its launch in the UK in October 2005, Facebook has become one of the greatest sources of finding industry work. Much of that is still through personal connections, and groups that have been set up by individuals rather than companies.

In his 2014 survey, industry analyst Stephen Follows found that over 50% of jobs for new entrants were posted on Facebook, with over 35% of those being publicly available; the remainder were through personal connections, sharing roles

It is your responsibility to seek out those Facebook groups that are most relevant to you. I myself have seen an excellent group called 'People looking for work: TV runners'. The group lists job posts, members can share in discussions and there is also peer-review of CVs if requested. The majority of this group's members is looking for work in mainstream television, and the administrators of the group are very experienced people from that background, but it does occasionally throw up the useful lead for those interested in higher-end TV drama. Whichever group you join, and whatever your Facebook activity, it's crucial to remember that you never know who might be watching. I myself observe several groups without commenting, as I know a number of employers do also, and can see which individuals are making rude or immature comments. When that individual applies for a job, their name may already be known to the employer for all the wrong reasons.

Indeed, many employers will Google an applicant when considering a hire and, for many experienced crew, the first search result of their name will be the Internet Movie Database (IMDB): a reliable source. If you are a newcomer, however, it's likely that the first result will be your Facebook, Twitter or LinkedIn profile and, if your privacy settings are not correct, that employer will able to see every picture, status update and comment you've posted. Keep on top of your privacy settings or, better yet, refrain from posting anything you wouldn't want an employer to see.

If you are going to send a friend request to a colleague, do it at the end of the job not at the beginning. They may prefer to keep Facebook for close friends only, so judge whether it is more appropriate to connect with them via the less personal Twitter or LinkedIn.

Twitter

Unlike Facebook or LinkedIn, there are few restrictions on who you can follow on Twitter. You don't have to know someone in real life to follow and even interact with them. There are companies, organisations and individuals spewing bucket loads of information to the internet about film and television, and one of the best ways to find that info is via Twitter.

The Twitter algorithm also makes suggestions based on your recent follows, so once you have discovered a few good feeds, more and more will appear. I would suggest that you start with @thecallsheet and @unitlist for job notifications, and find publications like @moviescope, @variety and @screendaily for industry news. There is a list of publications in the Resources section that all have Twitter feeds.

Check the hashtags for #tvjobs and #filmjobs to find people and companies using the platform to recruit. There are lots of production companies on Twitter, so you can follow them and scope them out; they may even reveal details of upcoming productions. Just remember that a lot of the time, smaller production companies may leave the Twitter feed in the hands of the office runner, so the person behind the account may not have the authority to recruit.

While lots of people join Twitter to follow celebrities and actors, you should instead start tracking down all the thousands of directors, producers, cinematographers and other technicians in the UK who regularly tweet. Observe and soak up the information that is presented, and the assiduous use of re-tweeting and 'favouriting' can alert people that you are interested in and engaged with what they are saying. There's less personal information on Twitter than Facebook, and following people is less of a deal than accepting a friend request, so it's possible that line producers or cinematographers – or whatever your department – might follow you in return .

For that reason, make sure your own bio states clearly that you either want to work in film and TV, or already do so; if so, include the role you perform and the names of the shows you've worked on. HoDs will not, of course, employ you based on your profile alone, but there is now a line of communication between you, and if your CV lands on their desk in the future, they might connect the name and know who you are. This route is less likely to land you work than applying for jobs directly, but you should always be alive to opportunity.

Always think about what an employer would think if they clicked on your feed? Does it look professional? Do you really need to tweet about the delays on your bus journey? I follow one freelancer who has over 90,000 tweets to their name: a ridiculous amount. If an employer is looking at that feed, they will wonder if that person actually does ANY work or just tweets all day.

Be aware, too, that when you tweet something, it does not necessarily mean that all of your followers will have seen your posts. As a rule of thumb, expect that around 10% to 30% of your followers will read any individual post, and the peak time to post is typically between 1pm and 3pm when Twitter is at its busiest. If you have worked on a TV show or film, do try to tweet when it is broadcast or released and make sure you use the official hashtag when tweeting: it's like broadcasting your CV.

LinkedIn

LinkedIn is a social network with a corporate sensibility. Predominantly used by those at the mid management and executive level, it is primarily a form of your online CV and can be a useful tool for those in permanent positions looking for career promotions.

Connecting with someone on LinkedIn is less of a commitment than accepting a friend on Facebook, and a useful way to stay updated. Over time, your connections will spin away in all different directions as your careers progress, and LinkedIn is very useful for managing those contacts for future reference.

As with Facebook, there are lots of groups on LinkedIn to explore, but not all are useful. It is worth experimenting but you may find that you receive a stream of promotions and the occasional crackpot.

Pinterest and Instagram

Both of these are visual platforms and have a much smaller membership and reach than Facebook, Twitter or LinkedIn. Those working in the art, costume or make-up departments may, however, find it useful to explore and utilise these websites.

Pinterest is a great way to accumulate interesting images for pleasure, reference or learning, as well as uploading your own work to create a page of images that you can share through Facebook. It can be particularly useful when creating an online portfolio to send designers or for gathering images as a mood board for jobs. There is also an iPad app called 'Mood Board' which is also very useful.

Instagram is primarily used as a personal visual diary, but can also be used to showcase your work. At the time of writing, however, Instagram posts do not automatically appear in a Twitter timeline as an image, but as a link. You may want to think about posting separately if using this app.

While both of Pinterest and Instagram look good, ask yourself what the average age demographic of users is on them? Social Media expert Rose McGrory reported that 39% of Instagram users are aged between 16-24. Is it likely that the experienced designers or supervisors you want to showcase your work to, are regular users of these platforms? The answer is probably not, but those demographics may shift over time and it shouldn't stop you using them if you enjoy it.

Another useful website for those in design is Behance, which is less of a social network and more of a portfolio showcase website, and a further list can be found in the Resources section of this book

Entry-Level Schemes and Programmes

There are a variety of different routes into the business through training and educational schemes, and here we will highlight what is available, the differences between them and the relevant guidelines set out by Creative Skillset.

Each individual company will have its own take on what they expect from their schemes, as the pattern will have been repeated a number of times. While you may not be judged against previous occupants of these roles, others before you may have set a high standard that the company would like to see repeated.

Work Experience

'Work shadowing, observing, supporting someone in an existing job role in the organisation. They may perform work that classes them as a "worker"' *Creative Skillset*

Work experience should only be offered by an employer to those currently studying, and not graduates. If you are over 19, Skillset recommend you get paid the national minimum wage for any work experience undertaken: currently £5.30 per hour for 18-20 year olds, £6.70 for those 21 to 24 and £7.20 for those 25 and over. Reasonable expenses should also be met.

Work experience placements should last no longer than 160 hours in total, and should give you an insight into the various facets and inner workings of a company.

Getting appropriate work experience during your studies will certainly boost your CV and hopefully supply you with a valuable positive reference. Approach companies that you admire, and that already have existing schemes in place: the TV Watercooler website has a list of such companies, compiled by Lizzie Evans. Again, there are details in the back of the book.

Internship

'Working on one's own and with others in a job role developed from learning objectives. Often providing a service and working on a specific project.' *Creative Skillset*

Employers use internships to keep a steady flow of new talent coming into the business, offering a short term contract – usually at minimum wage – for a specific project or area of the business. Hiring someone as an intern, rather than an employee, gives the employer more flexibility and decreased costs, as well as an opportunity to evaluate an individual before offering a full-time job.

Never accept an internship that is unpaid. It is an unscrupulous practice that is skewing job opportunities in the industry for everyone.

Apprenticeship

'The apprentice learns on-the-job, supported by off-the-job learning by a training provider. Training can be at evenings and weekends, day release or in a single block of time.' *Creative Skillset*

Apprenticeships are excellent opportunities to work and train with a company, although the initial salary is quite low. Apprenticeships usually last for one year, and the typical process is to work for a company for four days a week, and spend the remaining day studying a complimentary course. Apprenticeships are aimed at those between the ages of 16 and 23, and are strongly supported by the Government.

Apprenticeships are an excellent way to enter the industry, offering a salary, on-the-job experience and a qualification. There is also a high retention rate of apprentices, with employers promoting large numbers of them to other roles within the company.

Taking Bookings For Work

After you've sent out your newly crafted CV and cover email, attended talks and network events, collaborated on some shorts and pestered everyone you know for helpful leads or contacts, you should hopefully get some interest from production companies and freelancers interested in hiring or meeting you.

At this point, it's important to remember that most production companies will want runners for a short period, perhaps just a few days. Commercial shoots, for example, tend to employ people for just a day or two at a time. In the world of mainstream TV, these people are sometimes called day runners. A common starter job is running on shows like *Britain's Got Talent* or *The X Factor*, where a large number of runners are needed at audition stage, or on touring shows like *Bargain Hunt*.

Large scale films will often use a number of runners or location marshalls for big set pieces. For example, for a speedboat sequence in the James Bond film *Spectre,* location manager Emma Pill had a team of almost 200 location marshalls dotted along a mile and half of the Thames. Those location marshalls were required for just four consecutive night shoots in June 2015, almost all of whom were found by the CallTime company and some through thecallsheet.co.uk too.

Taking a booking for a day's work on a film or TV drama is straightforward. You will usually be employed on the strength of your CV for dailies work in the office (in which case you will be hired by the production manager/coordinator) or on set (usually by the head of department or their second in command). For post-production roles, the company structure will determine who will call you to book you.

As an example of the process, we'll now look at how you would be selected and take a booking for a commercials job.

Commercials

You may receive a call from a production company asking if you are available for a certain date, and they may ask to 'put a pencil' on you. This is a common industry term, and it means to offer first refusal for your services without committing to employment. This is common practice because of the fluid nature of the production process.

The production of commercials, for example, requires the cooperation and alignment of three things: the client who wants to sell the product, the ad agency creating the campaign and the production company itself. A production company will bid for a commission and, if successful, will sign a Production Insurance Briefing Specification (PIBS) contract and invoice the ad agency for 50% of the budget to secure location and casting, etc.

The possible shoot date for the ad will be in a relatively short time frame, perhaps just a few weeks from the production company being signed, and they will be looking to line up the crew, starting with the HoDs. Things are, however, always likely to change. Huge amounts of money are being spent, and the advertising agency will want to approve everything from the casting and location to storyboards, budget, how the product will be shot etc. A few days before the shoot, the production company, advertising agency and client will hold a pre-production meeting to finalise the details. (This is different to a film and TV drama PPM, as the only crew in attendance is usually the advert's producer and director.) The PPM is usually a formality, however, and it's very unusual for a commercial to be completely derailed at this stage.

It's only at this point, once approval has been given for all of the elements of the commercial, that the production company will confirm the assistants and runners needed for the job. They will call all of the crew they previously 'pencilled in' to 'confirm' them. Once you are officially 'confirmed', the company has committed that it will employ you for labour. At the time of writing, the daily fee for a runner on an Advertising Producers Association (APA) approved advert is £182.

Given the incredibly fast turnaround on a commercial, much of the dealing is done on the phone and you are unlikely to receive a contract. The 'confirmation' is usually a verbal agreement, and you will be emailed the call sheet with your name on it. You can ask the production company for an email to outline and clarify this from the production manager of the job but, given the frantic nature of some commercials, this is unlikely to happen. In which case, you can email them with the details as you understood them, and ask them to confirm by return email

If another production company should enquire about your availability when you are on a 'pencil' with another, you can only give them a 'second pencil', meaning that the original company to contact you still have first refusal on you. The unspoken understanding is that you have given a company a 'first pencil' therefore you have entered into an unwritten agreement that they will employ you IF a production goes ahead as planned. While they have the priority booking, however, they have no obligation to employ you; runners are more dispensable than senior crew, and directors can be picky about who they work with.

It can be confusing, particularly at the beginning of your career, but you need to understand the bookings process and stick to the rules. You may not get all of the details of the job until a company calls you to confirm your booking, but when they make initial contact, even if just putting on a 'pencil' you should to ask them the following (and make notes of their answers):

NAMES

It is vitally important to get the name of the production company, and of the person booking you. If you can, also ask for the name of the director or the AD.

DATES

Write down the exact dates you will be needed. Sometimes, particularly on fast turnaround jobs, for example, a production manager may not have confirmed all details with cast or studio space. In that case, they may pencil you in for a whole week in the knowledge that you will be filming for two days, but they don't yet know on which ones. Production managers are usually upfront about this, but it's useful to know if you need to manage a second pencil. Also enquire (if it isn't obvious) if it will be a night-shoot. After all, you want to work as many days as possible, and working on a night shoot would mean you are unavailable for two days but only paid for the shoot.

If there are no confirmed dates, you may want to ask for the date of the PPM as this should give you an indication of when you will be called with confirmation of employment.

RATE

If a production company is expressing an interest in you, it's always better to ask about rates up front. One of the production manager's jobs is to talk money, so don't be shy. Once you have all the other information about the shoot and the job requirement, just politely enquire what the rate is. Instead of giving you an exact number, they may reply with something like 'its APA rates' or 'BECTU/ADA rates'. The APA rates are the standardised amounts set by that organisation, and trade union BECTU also publish their own guideline rates via the Assistant Directors Association. Companies using the APA rate will pay the uppermost limit; BECTU rates are more of a guideline so it's best to specify figures for clarity.

Runners, however, are typically paid a flat-day rate, which means no overtime. You can double check any overtime rates, but if they are available it's usually assumed that it is paid pro rata at time and a half. When charging overtime, most freelance crew give a grace period of 15 minutes, and start charging overtime from 16 minutes past the time they were contracted to finish.

As always, if you're not clear about anything ask the production manager. You should also get some friendly advice from other members of the crew.

Running Duties

Once you actually get a job as a runner, you will find that different companies will have their own needs and, crucially, their own expectations of their runners. You will be entering new environments with each new job, and will want to attune yourself to the new surroundings quickly.

There are several different types of entry-level positions under various guises. This section will give you a quick guide to some of the duties that might be expected of you, and some of the things you can do to make yourself stand out.

There are differences between an office runner, production runner, floor runner, rushes runner and other trainee roles in each department. Your head of department or office manager will have specific duties that they want you to carry out, and they will be clear and direct in asking you to complete a task. You should also show initiative in asking what they would like you to do. You may get asked to complete a lot of tasks at the same time, with seemingly impossible deadlines. Whatever happens, don't panic or get flustered; do the best you can do in a calm manner, ask for help if you need it and find out which task is a priority if it hasn't been made clear.

One piece of advice that is essential for all types of running is to make sure that you write everything down. Keep a small pad and a pen on you at all times. Runners may be given detailed directions or requests from several different people in a short space of time, so it's vital to keep a log of the tasks and the pertinent details.

If you don't perform as expected or fail to display a positive attitude, you will not be asked back. It's unlikely that you will get feedback as a runner; the clearest indication that you didn't do a good enough job is by not being called in again for work. There are lots of people going for each job and not enough jobs to go around, so you have to grab your opportunities when they arise. Knowing what is expected of you will help, but going above and beyond will keep you in work.

Office Runner

This is an in-house role where you will be supporting development, pre-production and post production needs under the instruction of the office manager or an appointed staff member. In commercials-production companies, there are likely to be several projects happening at any moment, while with film and TV drama production companies there will be one or two projects on the go.

The basic role of an office runner tends to be menial to start with: keeping the office tidy and, in particular, keeping the kitchen clean. There will also be 'front-of-house' duties such as welcoming guests, making tea and coffee for staff and visitors, and going on a lunch run, so being presentable and well-spoken is a must. Do all of these tasks without complaint.

Runners might also be expected to answer the phones in the office, especially if there isn't a receptionist, and must always remember to speak politely and clearly. The person on the other end of the line might well represent millions of pounds in business, so be sure to get as much detail as possible if taking a message or passing on a call. This entails taking the person's name, company, telephone number and reason for the call if they will give it. Be absolutely sure to deliver the message to its intended recipient, either by email or by note. It may sound simple, but this basic task demonstrates clear communication skills and will increase the company's confidence in you. And when you are considered a reliable runner, doors start opening.

A runner may be given a cash float to purchase goods for the company, and must be able to show a receipt for every single item and every penny spent. Runners will also need to keep any of the crew's personal cash from the lunch run separate to the production cash, so employ a reliable system so you know which is which. Prompt and neat reconciliation of your petty cash will win you over with the accounts department, and you definitely want them on your side. They will want you to fill out a numbered form, and list all of the receipts, numbered and stapled to a piece of A4 paper, submitted together. (There is a free, downloadable cash-float template on *thecallsheet.co.uk* if you wish to familiarise yourself with one).

At any given moment, no matter what they are doing, a runner might be required to drop everything and 'run' a document, a file, a prop, a costume or a cheque somewhere, or go and buy something for the office or the production. It's expected that a runner can get around without getting lost, so get an A to Z or use the internet to plan the quickest route to wherever you need to go. Keep your phone charged, and a charger handy. If you use pay-as-you-go, make sure you have plenty of credit; if you have run out and can't top up, make sure you have informed your superior that you can only receive calls, not make them.

Runners may also be asked to manage media files, so a solid grasp of technology is advantageous. Proficiency on both Mac and PC will be expected, as will the knowledge of software such as Microsoft Office and email. Additional knowledge of Final Cut Pro, iMovie, Photoshop and FTPs for the transfer of large files will be useful strings to your bow.

You will find some requests can be unusual; you are at the service of the production company and no two days are the same. One sunny day while I was running at a commercials company, I was asked to head down to the Thames and help a director fix his boat. It was nothing to do with production, but it improved my relationship with my boss and I now know how to fix the mast of a barge ship.

Whenever you are in the office, be alert, keen and use your initiative. Gather menus from local restaurants that offer takeaway and keep them in the kitchen. Write a note about how different people like their tea and coffee and place it in the kitchen; it will make a good impression on your colleagues and help future runners. Always keep busy, if there is nothing to do then find something – tidy up the stationary, re-do signs that are peeling, clean something that needs it. Remember that all offices are like families: they each have their own environment and dynamic. New runners need to assess and adapt to the surroundings quickly to fit the climate, and the best way to do this is to use your common sense. There is some great advice on office etiquette in the in the Pearls of Wisdom section of this book.

Production Runner

This role is similar to the office runner, with the exception that you are contracted to serve one production, usually long term if working on a film or TV drama.

The production runner is more a part of the overall team than an office runner, as there is a clear chain of command: line producer, production manager, production coordinator, assistant production coordinator, production secretary, production assistant and, finally, production runner.

The career path is geared from moving up the ranks of the production department, although doors to other departments will also open, and the learning curve is very steep. When a production office hires their runner, they will want that person to be interested in working in that department and build towards a role in production management. It may likely count against you at interview stage if you declare you want to eventually work in another department.

Most film or TV productions will be based at one of the UK's film studios and, with a few notable exceptions such as Ealing, 3 Mills and Twickenham, most are remote. Runners will usually need to drive to work, and also have access to a car to run errands such as collecting crew, ferrying props and food, and picking up and dropping various items from different locations. Most insurance companies will require any production drivers to be over the age of 21.

During prep, production runners will be mainly based in the office and will spend a lot of time photocopying essential paperwork for the crew. They are also responsible for ordering replacement toner and paper so the copier is never out of service.

When filming begins, production runners will be the link between the office and the set. There will be regular runs between the production coordinator and the second AD at unit base, ferrying paperwork and equipment. It's hard work, but that liaison role does come with the opportunity to interact with other departments.

Endurance is essential as a production runner. Typically, they join a production early on in the process, and will be working long hours for a very long period of time: often 10 or more weeks. To do so without losing your composure takes a lot of stamina and requires a positive disposition.

Floor Runner

The floor runner works exclusively on location and in the studio, and reports to the AD team. They are expected to be organised, very personable and possess a mind for logistics. They must also be able to follow orders to the letter to keep the schedule moving. Essentially, they are utility players who will be required to assist wherever necessary.

One of the more likely tasks given to a floor runner is to log, track, label and distribute the walkie-talkie radios to the crew who require them, and place spare batteries on charge ready to use when needed.

Each radio has multiple channels, and each will be a designated communications channel for a particular department. The ADs, for example, need to communicate the most so will take channel one. If they want to speak with someone directly, and not broadcast to all, they will ask that person to 'go to two', which means communication will only be between those on that channel.

Radios are one-way communication devices: if you press down your talk button while someone else is speaking, they will not hear you and you will not be able to hear them. You must wait until the person has stopped speaking, at which point you say 'copy that' and respond if asked a question. Listen to how the third AD uses the radio to pick up tips and the lingo, but here are some of the basics:

Copy That
You have received and understood the message.

'Janet' for 'John'
When you want to speak directly to someone, you state your name first (in this case 'Janet') followed by 'for' and then the name of person you need to speak to.

Go for 'John'
This is how 'John' responds to let 'Janet' know that he is awaiting their message. If there are dozens of people with radios, just saying 'Yes' doesn't answer the question, as it could be anyone.

Standby
This is when you have heard a call for you, but need to finish something else first. It buys a few seconds to finish off the other conversation or task and respond.

As a floor runner, you will spend most of your time at the beck and call of the first, second and third AD. Clear instruction will be given across the radio; this is not the start of a conversation, rather an order. When you are new on set these barked instructions can take some getting used to; don't take it personally, confirm you understand the instruction and just get on with the job.

On big-budget productions, there will be a team of dedicated location marshals but on many shoots, the role of locking off will fall to the floor runner. 'Locking off' basically means stopping members of the public – or other crew members – from wandering into shot. The first AD will instruct you to lock off, which means you ask people very nicely to halt their journey for a moment while they go for a take. Members of the public can walk wherever they wish and so it's imperative to remain polite if you want them to stop.

Floor running requires a certain level of fitness and mental stamina. As well as remaining 'switched on' and alert to the needs of the team, the physical requirements are very demanding. I asked a number of runners and third assistant directors to use a pedometer to count their steps from call time to wrap: they averaged just over 10 miles a day.

Rushes Runner

This role is primarily that of a courier but dedicated to the production. A standard courier company could be used, but insurers prefer a dedicated crew member to oversee safe passage of the rushes on a daily basis. The rushes runner is needed to collect the hard drives (or film reels) of the day's filming from the set and deliver them to the editor or storage facility. The rushes runner will only have a limited amount of time on set and their hours are different from the rest of the production team.

The rushes runner will need to arrive at the unit base or set around 30 minutes before wrap at the end of the day. Once the DIT has been safely stored and backed up the day's shoot, they will hand the drives to the rushes runner, who will take them straight the edit suite for import, safe storage and further backing up.

On occasion, the rushes runner may also be asked to bring items from the editor to the production office too. Although the primary job of the rushes runner is that of transporting, it will bring them into close contact with ADs and production office staff. Excelling in the role is effective networking for the next opportunity, which might be production runner or floor runner.

Post-Production Runner

This is an office-based role that requires great people skills and hard work. The majority of responsibilities fall into two categories: data management and general housekeeping of the office and edit suites.

Post facilities are a little like hotels: each room has a dedicated function and all the work happens behind those closed, soundproofed doors. In large post companies, edit suites are mostly 'dry' hired, which means that you are hiring the AVID and the room. Editors, directors and producers will use it for the duration of the project, and then leave. For larger productions, AVIDs are installed by specialist companies like Hireworks to the exact specification of the editor.

The runner will be required to make those present in the edit suite comfortable, without distracting them from the task of editing. This will entail making tea and coffee, taking lunch orders and running errands. There will also be some front-of-house duties as well. Whatever the task, remember that large post-production houses are big-budget operations, where customer service is integral to their success.

I once a heard a story of an unofficial 'test' that post-production runners are subjected to at one world-renowned facility and, while I don't know if it is genuinely true, I can believe it. The story goes that there is a glass-fronted fridge in the building, containing drinks. When the fridge needs restocking, they watch to see how the runner completes the task: whether they put the new room-temperature bottles in the front, or if they move the cold drinks forward and put the new ones at the back. They have seen thousands of runners come through the doors, and this one small test speaks volumes about the individual. Showing such care and attention to detail even in small tasks will surely earmark you out for more responsibility.

Working Hours On Set

Working in film and TV production means very long and unusual hours, which can take a toll on family life, health and general happiness.

In this industry, many people work 70 hours or more per week. To illustrate what this means in practical terms, let's break down these hours into a typical six-day week's work for a costume assistant. (This six-day week will be followed by a five-day week to make the eleven-day fortnight we discussed before.)

The costume assistant has a 6am call-time on location, which could be anywhere. Taking into consideration the drive to the set, as well as getting ready, this could mean setting the alarm for 4.30am every day for six continuous days.

Once on set, the assistant will have a full day dealing with issues and emergencies as they crop up, with little down time until wrap is called at 7pm. (So-called continuous days, where crew eat lunch on the run, are increasingly common and will miss the lunch hour out, so will wrap an hour earlier.) After wrap time, the assistant will disrobe the actors and re-set for the next day, leaving the location at around 7.30pm. After a drive home, dinner and a catch up with the family, it's time to fall into bed and set the alarm for the following day.

From the moment they wake up to the moment they get home, the assistant does nothing but work and is likely to have walked over 10 miles in doing so; by comparison, the UK average is just 2 miles per day. That 16-hour day equates to 96 hours of work over 6 days, and is considered entirely normal.

It's clear then that this is a physically and mentally demanding job and, considering that a standard TV drama will probably shoot for six weeks minimum, it's a marathon undertaking. And if you take into account the possibility of shooting nights, split days and 'coming back around the clock', the task becomes even more difficult.

Throughout all of this physical and mental turmoil, you have to remain calm, organised, friendly and professional and all times – even if you are a newcomer to the industry. I asked a GP to give new entrants some tips to help them cope with the workload:

Sleep: get as much as you can, even if it means shutting down your social life during the shoot. Try to avoid alcohol, as this further disrupts your sleep patterns and can leave you cranky.

Diet: eat breakfast; it really is the most important mean of the day. Don't skip meals, eat fruit and drink a lot of water. A good diet will give you fuel for the day and help you maintain concentration.

Avoid too much caffeine: it's common sense, but be sure not to drink caffeine late in the day as it will affect your sleep. Ease off on the energy drinks, too.

Pace yourself: crew spend a long time at work, so remember it's a marathon not a sprint.

Take your vitamins: some general vitamin supplements can be useful to boost your wellbeing. Zinc tablets boost your immune system if you feel illness coming on, and are easy to get hold of.

Stimulate your mind: the daily trudge of long hours can leave you isolated, so engage with something outside your everyday working life. Have a good book on the go or do a crossword, so you can think about something else other than work.

Exercise: it may be the last thing you want to do after a 96-hour week, but the benefits of exercise are huge. Could you cycle to your location, or fit in a brisk walk after lunch?

There's one more important thing to add to this list of looking after yourself and, while it may be a taboo subject, it's essential to take care of your mental health.

This industry can be demanding and appear unsympathetic, but if you are worried about depression or anxiety there is plenty of help and support available. And, if you do suffer from these, you are certainly not alone.

Here's some advice from the Mind website (www.mind.org.uk), which also contains a wealth of information and contacts.

'If you experience mental distress, it can be frightening and you may feel alone. If this is a new experience, you may not know what is happening. If you have experienced similar symptoms before then you will know what does and does not help you in such circumstances. There are a number of actions you can take:

- Visit a General Practitioner (GP), if you can, to be referred to suitable treatment.

- Talk to someone you trust, saying what has helped you in the past, if appropriate.

- Draw up a crisis card, which is a plan of action for people to follow if you start to show signs that indicate that you need help.'

Additionally, the number for the Samaritans is 08457 90 90 90. You may not need it, but someone you know might.

Work /Life Balance

Working on films and TV drama is hugely rewarding, but also incredibly demanding and very draining. Unlike most professions, it is very difficult to predict what will happen in the immediate future with any certainty. You never know what work is around the corner and even many experienced crew members have long, unexpected periods of unemployment.

When accepting work, you may find that taking a job turns your life upside down during the shooting period. You may get hardly any notice either. One day, you can be fretting about how to earn the rent this month, the next you might be on a plane bound for Morocco for a month.

This book is aimed at graduates, and new entrants tend to have a wide-eyed embrace for the industry and all it entails. As you get further into a career in film and TV, relationships with your partner, friends and family will almost certainly be put under enormous strain; particularly if they are not in the industry themselves.

Once you become entrenched in the business, it can feel like a treadmill that doesn't stop. The longer you are on it, the harder it becomes to get off and switch careers to something that does offer a work/life balance. I have encountered a number of people who quit the business for a normal 9-5 job and detest the predictability and slow pace. Such things may not concern younger people, when establishing a career is the only focus, but there are many failed relationships, divorces and lost friends as a result of these brutal hours. It is particularly tricky to balance parenthood and the irregular working regime, although many organisations like Raising Films are working to highlight the issue and help crew back into work after becoming parents.

This advice may seem irrelevant now, before you have even embarked on your career, but it might be useful to nurture an exit plan or think about keeping a side-line or secondary income from other sources, perhaps unrelated to your job.

The wealthiest people I know in the business either hit the big time or have developed a number of spin-off business deals or side lines that enable them to make money outside of their day job. These are ventures that only require occasional attention but turn over an additional revenue stream. Having 'something to fall back on' when work is scarce is an entirely sensible idea, especially if you are freelancing.

Set Etiquette

So, now you've been confirmed for a production booking and find yourself on a professional set. It can be extremely daunting, even if you've worked on student and short-film productions, so here are some key dos and don'ts for on-set behaviour.

Do

1. Be on time, which usually means being at least 15 to 20 minutes early.

2. Familiarise yourself with radio etiquette. The radios are used by all departments and you may be required to respond.

3. Dress appropriately. Wear comfortable trainers, no sandals or flip flops, even in the height of summer.

4. Treat all people with respect. If you are locking-off a location, be as polite and courteous to members of the public as you would with your director.

5. Show discretion, and keep well away from gossip and office politics.

6. Keep busy. If you find yourself at a loose end, ask your team if there's anything that needs to be done.

7. Ask. If you don't know something and the answer is not on the paperwork you have been given, query it. People would rather you ask them than make a mistake that will cost the production.

8. Show humility. Learn who is who, and value everyone's contributions to the production process. Experienced crew have seen a thousand runners, and are happy to help those who show themselves to be hard working and humble. (They have also been around the block long enough to know that today's runner might be tomorrow's producer...)

9. Learn the hierarchy of the set and show deference, respect the chain of command and always remember that you are there to do a job. It's an enjoyable and exciting job, but it is still a job.

10. Be safe. If you think there is something that might endanger you, the crew or members of the public, speak up.

Don't

1. Walk off set. Let your head of department know when you arrive on set and don't leave until expressly dismissed. Hearing the word 'wrap' doesn't mean the day is finished. Be the last to leave.

2. Touch gear or props unless specifically asked. This isn't a student production where you are expected to chip in with the heavy lifting. Offer to help if you see people in need, but never touch their stuff unless specifically asked.

3. Ask the actors for autographs. This is a big no-no. The film set is where actors need to concentrate on their job and not be distracted by fan duties, particularly from professional members of the crew.

4. Arrive hung over or anything less than fresh-faced and raring to go. I've seen careers end before they have even begun, because of one heavy night.

5. Complain about being tired. If the hours are normal, i.e. not breaking turnaround within normal limits, then don't moan to others about being exhausted. Everyone is in the same boat.

6. Snap at people. It's easy to get tetchy or angry when you are stressed and tired, but keep a cool, calm head. Those who are able to work hard without a fuss get noticed.

7. Think that you are above a menial task. Runners are there to grease the wheels of production, not call the shots.

8. Bad mouth anyone. There are only a few degrees of separation between most crew people so be careful what you say. (And remember that the sound guys have microphones and can hear more than you think.)

9. Don't call people 'mate'. Learn people's names and use them.

10. Don't forget your manners. 'Please' and 'thank you' will go a very long way.

Moving from One Genre To Another

There are lots of different genres of production, from feature film and news to entertainment and beyond, and each requires a different skill set unique to the demands of that medium. For example, a camera operator on a film is different to a camera operator for TV news; this may sound obvious but many people seem to be unaware of this fact. Not only is the content they are shooting wildly different – factual vs. fiction – but a news cameraman will generally operate alone, on a standard broadcast camera and – due to budget and advanced technology – be responsible for recording sound, while a film-camera operator works with a large team of people with a wider array of equipment.

The difference is also marked in other roles. A production coordinator on a film does not have the same responsibilities as one working in television, despite their job titles being the same. On a film, the production coordinator is responsible for orchestrating the flow of information and organising hundreds of cast, crew and companies, tasks which happen during an intense period of prep and production with constantly shifting schedules and a slew of unforeseen issues to content with. A production coordinator working in television will by contrast have fewer people and components to organise, and will generally be following a more regular formula and time frame.

Once you are established in one of field of production, such as news, entertainment or sport, it is more difficult to jump between the genres. I often hear from production staff in factual television who wish to break into the film industry. A lot of the time these people often had an initial ambition to work in drama production, but the only opportunities they could find were in television. If you are getting paid and offered consistent opportunities, it's easy to stay in the cycle.

That's not to say it's impossible to make the leap to film from TV, but if you want to move into film and high-end TV drama production you should be prepared to drop down a grade, if not two, in order to learn the new set of skills. If you are a production manager for a commercials production company, for example, it's unlikely you could walk straight in to a production manager role on a big film or TV drama. If a TV production manager wants to move across, I would suggest dropping down to assistant coordinator or production secretary; given a little time they can find their feet, shine in those roles and move quickly back up the ladder.

Changing Career

Some people who pick up this book might be older than many graduates and have already spent years working in a totally different industry. Quite a number of people reach a certain point in their career and decide they want to follow their heart into the film and TV industry, and hope they have built up some skills that can be transferred across.

Some former soldiers, for example, fit perfectly into the industry because of their skills in logistics; some early British films employed army personnel for precisely this reason. Those with over six years in the army might be eligible for a resettlement grant through the Career Transition Partnership.

It's no secret, however, that no matter what skills you have accumulated outside of the industry, in 95% of cases you will need to start again at the bottom of the ladder.

To give you an idea of how this can be done, I spoke to two members of *thecallsheet.co.uk* about their experiences. Their case studies are below, along with a story of my own. Names have been changed or removed throughout.

Case Study 1: Changing Roles

One member had spent nearly a decade working at talent agencies and in production. They had always had a love of photography and dreamt of becoming a camera assistant, but felt unable to pursue it as a viable career option until they had developed sufficient connections.

In order to make the move from production into the camera department, they pulled every favour they could and said yes to every trainee job. In doing so, they dropped down in rank and pay, and budgeted on how to survive on less money as they worked up a new ladder. They worked hard, and started getting asked back by the DoPs, focus pullers and loaders.

This person has an enviable contact list, and is working with excellent camera teams. Although they face a challenging first year, they have a head start along with the contacts and reputation they built up over the years.

If you are crossing over from one department to another, the disadvantages of starting over are balanced out by your existing contacts. You want those people to back you with recommendations and support. Let all of your contacts know what you are doing, and don't be afraid to ask for help.

Case Study 2: Changing Industry

Sarah*, another member of *thecallsheet.co.uk*, has made an even bigger career leap.

Sarah was a barrister working in London, and specialised in legal aid criminal defence and human rights representing young and vulnerable adults. In 2011, she was struck by a car while on her bicycle, and left with very serious injuries.

Unable to work while she recuperated, she spent a lot of time reflecting on her career and committed to follow her heart and break into the film and TV industry. She didn't know a single person in the industry, however, and had to start from scratch, applying for entry-level work and collaborating on short films while still consulting for law firms in the city.

Balancing her paid work as a legal consultant, Sarah's tenacity brought her success in getting initial running work and she has been able to bring with her considerable experience and a strong motivation to persevere.

Following that running work, Sarah was recommended for a role working for a major US-drama series filming in the UK, and was appointed as personal assistant to an A-list US writer/director, also on recommendation.

Despite her background and late entry into the industry, Sarah is focused on learning the ropes. With her knowledge, intelligence and desire to learn, she will almost certainly be in demand. In fact, a well-known drama production company hired Sarah through *thecallsheet.co.uk* to work as a development researcher on a new legal drama.

Case Study 3: Changing Industry Part 2

This is an example from my own book of experience, which more than proves that today's runner can easily become tomorrow's producer.

Around 15 years ago, I was working at a company when a runner turned up at the office to drop in his CV. The only production experience listed was a few short films, and he had spent 10 years as a very successful trader in the city. We booked him for a shoot immediately, impressed with his intelligence and the fact he had obviously researched the company and tracked us down in Soho. He clearly knew London very well, and as he was over 25 we could easily insure him as a runner/driver.

We had him on all of our jobs for the next six months, each time knowing we had a safe pair of hands. He learnt the ropes very quickly, and always maintained his professionalism. Once his CV began to swell with our credits, he began contacting other production companies and soon he was unavailable for us. He slipped out of view until 10 years later, when he called to try and book me for a job. He had shot up the ranks to become a producer, and a very successful one too.

That guy's previous career experience was a huge asset, as was his life experience and positive, enthusiastic attitude. He accelerated through the ranks very quickly but was willing to take the hit of that first year.

Tax and National Insurance

As a runner, you will be working on either short-term jobs of just a day or two at a time, or you may be fortunate enough to be taken on a long-term job as a production runner. Either way, you will be jumping from job to job and so would be regarded as a freelancer. There is a distinction, however, between being freelance and being self-employed.

Although you will be on a near constant search for the next running job, you will not automatically be classed as self-employed by HMRC. There are strict guidelines on the HMRC website identifying which roles in the film and TV industry can be classed as such, and the people in those roles will be responsible for paying their own taxes and Class 2 or 4 National Insurance (NI) contributions. The lowest part of the production chain, which is permitted to be self-employed in the eyes of HMRC, is production assistant.

HMRC put the burden of responsibility for correctly administering the film and TV payroll rules on to the registered employers, i.e. the production company, so ultimately it is their decision to choose how you are paid, and not yours. Most production accountants will apply the rules very strictly, as they can be fined (or worse) if they get it wrong, and it is very common on a one-off project, like a feature film, for HMRC to inspect the payroll records to make sure everything is in order.

If you are starting out as a runner, you will need to keep your P60 or P45 form on standby. Runners are always on the payroll of a company, and classed as Pay As You Earn (PAYE) staff, which is officially referred to as 'schedule E'. This means that the production will deduct your tax and National Insurance automatically before the money hits your account; your pay slip will show these deductions clearly. It is important to keep copies of all your pay slips, as they prove the production has made payments on your behalf to HMRC.

Many people in film and TV work short periods for different companies in succession, and enforcing PAYE each time you work for different companies might result in excessive taxation. HMRC's seven-day rule allows individuals to work for six consecutive days (including rest days) with the same company before PAYE needs to be applied. You are still considered an employee, and National Insurance must still be paid by the employer. This rule helps alleviate runners getting heavily taxed as they move from job to job in quick succession.

You will have a tax code on your P45 that relates to the amount of money you can earn before tax starts to be deducted, and is calculated based on previous earnings. In some cases, you may get taxed as 'week one, month one': this is an emergency tax code, and HMRC will be working to obtain more information and issue the correct one. If this happens, it can affect your pay substantially so you want to make sure that you don't get emergency taxed at each new company that employs you. If you did not receive a copy of your P45 from your previous company, either ask your new employer for a P46 or download it from HMRC website and give it to them yourself. This will help them get you on the payroll and taxed correctly.

You should have a P60 from the final project you were working on before the end of the tax year (always April 5), which will show you the cumulative pay plus tax and NI deducted for the whole year; this information transfers from production to production. If you have kept your pay slips or P45s safe, you can check if the figures tally. If they don't, then carefully organised paperwork will help you find the inconsistencies and sort out any overpayments.

There are several film- and TV-friendly tax advisors in the business, and you must decide if engaging an accountant is a viable proposition at the earliest stage in your career. I know some people who choose to pay for an accountant's services and I know many others who don't; when it comes to money, the decision is a personal one. As there is so much advice online, and HMRC offer guidance, it may not be worth employing an accountant until your career progresses and you reach the roles that are classed as self-employed. Even at that stage, you can do self-assessment online yourself.

Invoicing

Although you might be initially uncomfortable talking about money, when you start booking your first jobs it is vital that you ask for the rate before accepting. This will be a verbal agreement with the production manager or HoD, which you can also ask them to confirm in an email. They may not have the time to do so, in which case, email them before production begins and detail everything you have discussed. For example:

'I look forward to working with you next week. Just to confirm our conversation: the location is [X], the call time is [X] and the rate is [X] and adheres to the APA/BECTU terms. If you need me for anything else, my contact number is [X], and please use this email address for the call sheet.'

When the job is completed, you then supply the production an invoice containing the following information: your name, contact details, national insurance number, date of invoice, date(s) you worked, nature of work (e.g. services as a runner on [X]), the agreed rate, and the total owed. You should also include the name of the company, the contact and the reference or job number. (If you work on a commercial, there will be a job number and full invoicing instructions on your call sheet.) It's a good idea to number your own invoices too, so you can easily organise them: one useful method is to start with the last two digits of the year and then a three digit number eg.16001, 16002 and so on. This is not only good accountancy practice, but it will help you track outstanding invoices and monitor earnings for tax purposes.

If you are working for an APA company, they usually reconcile invoices within seven days. Films and TV dramas tend to run a payroll every week. If you are working in-house at a company as a runner, you are likely to go through their payroll system which is typically paid at the end of each month. If you work for one company for more than seven days, you should be put directly on the payroll.

The golden rule with pay and invoicing is to be organised. Buy a ring binder when you get your first job and keep all of your invoices and pay slips in that or, if you prefer to work digitally, store them in the cloud or a folder on your laptop. Keep everything safe and all in one place for when you need it.

All freelancers know the worry of when payments will be hitting your bank account; it can cause stress and chaos with your finances. Send your invoice promptly once the work has been completed and, if you can, confirm with the accountant when the company payroll is run. Many people open up a separate bank account just to receive invoice payments, as it is easier to manage and see when payments have been made. It's also very good practice to set up a third account for savings and try to start adding to it as soon as possible.

To combat the culture of late payment, Britain signed up to EU Directive 2011/7/EU, which states that companies should settle invoices to individuals within 30 days. If a company delays paying you, then you should email them and attach a copy of the original invoice. As new entrants to the industry you may worry about damaging your relationship with the production company, so be polite but firm and professional. In most cases, one email is sufficient to prompt the payment; it is usually due to a heavy workload rather than the avoidance of responsibility.

If the company still haven't paid your invoice after 30 days and you have sent them a reminder email, you can – thanks to that EU directive – start to charge them statutory interest on the invoice. The amount you can charge is the Bank of England's 'reference rate', plus 8%. At the time of writing, and since 2009, the reference rate has been 0.5%, so the total interest you can currently add to your invoice is 8.5% of the value.

If, in the unlikely scenario, the company are refusing to pay you, there are two courses of action you can take. Firstly, you may want to recover the money via the small-claim courts. Look online for the details, and the website is listed in the Resources section of this book. Alternatively, if you are a member of trade union BECTU you can take the issue to them.

BECTU can give you advice on how best to reclaim your money and, depending on the circumstances, contact the company directly. This is, after all, an industry built on reputations, so bad PR is often a sharper weapon than financial penalties, and BECTU publish an 'Ask First' list that names and shames companies who repeatedly don't pay their members. I would urge all new entrants to the business to look up BECTU and consider signing up.

Start Form

A start form is essentially a deal memo, used when engaging crew on long jobs like feature films and TV drama. It will be no more than a couple of pages long, but will outline the arrangement between you and the production company. It's often referred to as the 'heads and terms' of the agreement, and is signed prior to a full contract being issued.

The start form will contain the rates and dates that the production intend to hire you for, and you will be required to fill out your own details to show you agree to the terms. The form will then be signed off by the line producer, and approved for payment by the production accountant. You will now be on the payroll of the film or drama, and be paid in weekly instalments. In your first week's pay, it's possible you may be on an emergency tax code (details above), so be prepared to receive less than you anticipate.

Other Work

If you are a freelancing newcomer and are trying to build up experience, not knowing when the next job might come up is extremely difficult both emotionally and practically. If you are finding it difficult to find consistent work in the industry, you will obviously need to make ends meet. My advice is to look for short-term roles with temp agencies, such as bar work, catering, data entry and labouring. There are also several market-research companies that will pay you for your time and opinions.

If you take a long-term role outside of the industry, you are making a commitment to another company that may be difficult to wriggle out of if a good film or TV opportunity comes along. When opportunities do arise in the industry, particularly for runners, they can be filled within hours and the successful candidate expected to start almost immediately. If they can't start work on the given day, they will most likely be replaced.

Insurance

Driving is a key skill for a runner, as the production will usually want someone who is mobile for errands, collections and drop-offs. Having a member of the team who can move at a moment's notice is far less expensive and far quicker than hiring taxis and couriers. The value of having a reliable runner that can drive gives efficiency and speed to a production office, where, as the cliché goes, 'time is money'.

Being able to drive puts you at the front of the job hunting pack. You may not need your own car if the production company intend on hiring a long-term rental, so a clean licence may be sufficient. Whether you are using your own vehicle or one rented by the production, make sure you are covered by insurance. As we've already seen, most film-production insurance companies will not insure a driver under the age of at least 21.

To give you some additional insight, I asked Paul Hillier, senior film and TV broker at entertainment and media insurance brokers Integro ACJ for his thoughts:

'We would always recommend production staff using their vehicles for business purposes (i.e. shuttling people about on set, moving equipment and running general errands) should check if their own personal motor insurance includes business use cover. If vehicles are only used for getting them to work, then social, domestic and pleasure, including commuting, is probably sufficient.'

'If they are actually being paid a fee for their services, like a taxi/driving job, then that is a whole other issue, but on most productions they use unit drivers, unit vehicles and taxis.'

'Other issues arise if a crew member's vehicles are used in picture, where specific production motor insurance should be discussed.'

'If there is a problem with a production runner/manager getting business use cover – some insurers still flinch at the mention of film & TV and assume you will have A-Listers in your car – specialist film insurers can offer a solution. There does need to be some sort of hire agreement between the freelancers and the production company for use of vehicle.'

'It is sometimes a grey area, but the basics should be the same regardless of insurer and broker. We are always on hand to provide advice and assistance.'

CHAPTER 3

Industry Interviews

Up to this point, this book has given you a realistic, practical and pragmatic approach on the working of the industry, and how best to get your foot in the door. From this point onwards, I'm handing over to those who have already done it, and over the next few pages you can benefit from the wisdom, experience and advice of over 60 people currently working in the industry. Over the course of my 15-year career, I have been lucky enough to speak with a wide range of wonderfully talented individuals throughout the entire industry, listening keenly to their film-making stories, their thoughts on the process and their views on getting into the business and building a career.

For this book, I have selected and updated 11 interviews from the *thecallsheet.co.uk* archives, and I have also added the transcript from a live interview I conducted with BAFTA-winning editor Mick Audsley. These interviews should give extensive insight into what it's actually like to break into and work in the industry, and the 50-odd Pearls of Wisdom that follow will provide additional, invaluable advice.

The interviews cover a range of departments and I recommend that you read all of them; after all, it's vital to understand the ecology of the whole system and that means learning about the roles that might fall outside of your particular focus.

Enjoy!

Roopesh Parekh –   Line Producer / Co-Producer

Roopesh Parekh was line producer on the first series of the 2014 BBC comedy *Inside No. 9*

What is *Inside No. 9* and what makes it different?
INSIDE NO. 9 is a series of stories from Reece Shearsmith and Steve Pemberton. Each story is a different comedic tale, with a very dark tone. The only connecting factor is that all of the action takes place behind [a different] door number 9. We had an incredible cast, crew and facilities on this job that needed to rise to the challenge of doing six different stories with lots of characters and sets.

How did the production process happen?
I was first offered *Inside No. 9* in October 2012, when I had just come off the back of serving as production executive on *Red Dwarf X*. I've always been a fan of *The League Of Gentlemen* and *Psychoville*, and it was a really good project to move onto after *Red Dwarf*.

We shot the series in two blocks, one at the end of 2012 and the other in summer 2013. In the gap between blocks, I went off to Swansea to work on the big US drama *Da Vinci's Demons*. When I originally came aboard on *Inside No. 9*, we had five out of the six scripts, with the silent comedy 'A Quiet Night In' being a surprise package.

Although *Inside No. 9* is a mixture of drama, horror, comedy and suspense, it was commissioned out of BBC comedy so the budgets were a little tighter than if it were a BBC Drama.

Where was *Inside No. 9* filmed?
We were shooting one episode a week. The first was 'Tom & Gerri' which we shot in Wimbledon Studios. Then we went on location at a nearby house in Wimbledon for 'The Last Gasp', while the sets were turned around at the studio for the following episode, 'Sardines'. Wimbledon Studios were fantastic throughout the process, really supportive during production and positive with the marketing of the show too.

We were also very lucky that DECODE camera and lighting hire came aboard. They were hugely supportive of the show and helped us work within our budget. They were also based at Wimbledon Studios and it was a big benefit to us that they were on site, particularly for our studio sets.

What particular challenges did you face in shooting six different stories?

David Kerr was the Director for all six episodes, and Stephan Pehrsson was the DoP. They had never worked together before but they clicked straight away, setting the style, tone and look very quickly. Due to availability, we had two production designers: Tom Sayer on block one and Brian Sykes on block two.

One of the great creative challenges of *Inside No. 9* was that every episode was unique, and gave the opportunity for all departments to do something different for each one. That raises everyone's game and gives them the chance to find creative solutions for each different challenge. We did all the post at Encore [formerly Deluxe 142] with the support of Becky Start and Christopher Foster, who were exceptional and we couldn't have done it without them.

The cast is fantastic; did they sign up straight away?

When executive producer Jon Plowman, producer Adam Tandy and I started out, we had no idea of the quality of cast we would be able to attract without breaking the bank. Fortunately, the incredible scripts and the short filming window meant we were able to get all of our first-choice actors. They love and admire Steve and Reece's work and casting director Tracy Gilliam had lots of great characters to search for.

We spent a lot of time on casting and not only were we able to attract the best comedy actors such as Tamsin Greig, Julia Davis, Adam Deacon and Katherine Parkinson, but also a host of incredible film and TV actors like Gemma Arterton, Helen McCrory and Denis Lawson, as well as stage performers like Timothy West. The talent across the six episodes is remarkable.

How much input do the writers have on the production process?

They were very involved. David Kerr was able to create these worlds, and worked collaboratively with Steve and Reece. Although Steve and Reece weren't in all the episodes together, they were there every single day during production and were actively involved in the edit, the grade and everything through to delivery. Adam Tandy was also actively involved throughout the whole process and together we oversaw post production, which was fun.

Normally in comedy and drama there are lots of script changes all through production, but we only had a couple of minor tweaks over six episodes; this is very, very rare and a testament to their writing.

What have you been working on since Inside No. 9?
I was co-producer on *The Dog Thrower*, which is Jon Ronson's directorial debut for Sky's *Playhouse Presents* series. Again, we were very lucky with our cast which includes *Friends* star Matthew Perry, Tim Key, Richard Bacon and Kimberley Nixon. Executive producer was Stevie Lee of Runaway Fridge and Piers Fletcher and Olivia Aubry served as producers. I was also the Unit Production Manager on *The Hollow Crown II: The Wars of the Roses*, the Line Producer on *And Then There Were None* for the BBC and Co-Producer of *Poldark* series 2 for the BBC and Mammoth Screen.

*On the eve of publication, Roopesh was announced as the Producer of Poldark series 3 for Mammoth Screen and the BBC.

Steven Hall - Cinematographer and VFX Dop

During the course of his career, Steven has helped create stunning film sequences for directors such as Steven Spielberg, Christopher Nolan, Ridley Scott and George Lucas.

As well as having a successful career shooting VFX work on major motion pictures, Steven also films narrative work and TV drama. Steven was 2nd Unit Director / DoP on *War & Peace* (the biggest TV Drama ever produced by the BBC) and 2nd Unit DoP on *FURY* and *The Imitation Game*.

What was your role on *Jack the Giant Killer*?
Jack the Giant Killer is essentially a big budget re-telling of the classic Jack and the Beanstalk story, and it is my first stereo (3D) movie. I joined the show as the VFX DoP, shooting plates and backgrounds. I joined for two weeks and stayed for eight, also taking on the role of the splinter unit DoP.

What equipment and locations were you working with?
We used the RED Epic 3D rigs for this film, and I also did a lot of work with the Giant Simulcam system: essentially a live-action, real time pre-viz tool. We shot at Shepperton and Longcross Studios, and locations included Wells Cathedral, Norwich Cathedral and The Hampton Estate near Guildford. Most of the sets had an element of green screen work within them, so I spent a lot of time matching work that the main and second unit had already shot – or were about to shoot, which was interesting!

You also worked on *Star Wars I* and *II*; what was it like to work on such a legendary franchise?
It's nearly 120 degrees, the sun has been burning on us for hours and we're looking across the endless dunes in Tunisia. Through a megaphone the first AD screams 'Turn over!' After it seems like we've run thousands of feet of film through three VistaVision cameras, R2D2 finally appears over the dune in the foreground... ' and, cut!' That single cinematic moment made it all worthwhile.

Do you have any other particular career highlights, such as working on Spielberg's *War Horse*, for example?

I don't mind admitting that working with Spielberg has been on my wish list for a long time and standing in the middle of a field, being introduced to the great man – 'Steven, this is Steven' – is still something of a high point in my career. I was the element shoot DoP on *War Horse* – you'll see my credit some way after the goose wrangler's credit – but I also shot a lot of splinter unit material: the cavalry charge, the machine gun sequence, etc. Most of the no-man's land sequence is enhanced with elements that I shot on the stage at Longcross, and we shot the explosions in a quarry in Wiltshire.

You were also involved with the making of *Sky Captain and the World of Tomorrow*, which was a technically pioneering film...

It was shot like a massive game of Battleships; 'Gwyneth, could you move from square T3 to square G6, oh, and can you act on the way'. The whole of the massive George Lucas stage at Elstree was marked as a blue screen grid, and the actors performed everything in a pre-shot CG world. Bearing in mind that this was all shot on pre-Alexa and RED style HD cameras, it still looks pretty amazing.

On *Rush Hour 3* you were shooting the great Jackie Chan; how did his incredible stunts affect your approach?

This was great fun to do, and my work involved the sequence where the heroes jump off the Eiffel Tower, cleverly using the giant tricolour flag as a parachute. In practical terms we spent about 10 nights on the top, middle and bottom of the tower, shooting 360-degree VistaVision plates of Paris. We extended this across the Seine by matching their route from a 200ft cherry picker – terrifying!

Having worked with a wide variety of equipment on different projects, do you have a preference for particular cameras and lenses to work with?

I've shot a lot of the work that I've done on the Vista Vision system using Nikon lenses. In fact a lot of the plates in *Gladiator* were shot on my old Nikon stills system. I'm a big fan of HD now and I really love working with the ARRI Alexa and Panavision's Primo lenses.

You work both as a VFX DoP and a DoP; is the workload a challenge?

In 2012, for example, I continued to build on my credits as a conventional, narrative drama DoP and I managed to shoot a couple of shorts including an interesting film called *Belly of the Wolf*. I also shot the second unit on some really good TV dramas including *A Mother's Son*, *Ripper Street*, *Peaky Blinders* and the excellent Channel 4 drama *Utopia*. As a VFX DoP, I kicked off that same year with some enhancements for *Jack the Giant Killer* and then went off to Norway with *Thor 2* to shoot plates, textures and bubbles [which are 360-degree spheres made up of 100s of HDR still images], and I then joined the same film as the Splinter Unit DoP at the end of the year, wrapping on December. Not a bad year.

You've obviously built a successful career, but how did you get started in the industry?
I came to film and TV from being a freelance photographic assistant. Most of my work was with fashion, advertising and car photographers, so I was often around commercials and agencies and thought the world of commercials looked like a bundle of fun. One day I got a call to work with a stills photographer who was working on *The Shining*; he needed to shoot some large format pictures and I had a lot of experience of 10x8, so this became my introduction to the industry. I then drove a Winnebago and camera car for about a year or so before making enough contacts to get a job as a camera trainee.

What advice would you give those who want to break in to the camera department?
This is a tricky one. It's getting tougher and tougher to get into the business and there's no recognised way of actually getting in; unless you're the son or daughter of somebody already in it. With the advent of e-mail and websites it's now a lot easier to self-market, so it's just a question of passion, commitment... and a lot of patience! And never be without a sense of humour.

If you could change one thing about the industry, what would it be?
That all the studios would get together and shoot one film after the other throughout the whole year, rather than shooting them all at the same time during the same three months of the year.

John Higgins - Chief Lighting Technician (Gaffer)

John Higgins is one of the world's leading film-lighting technicians, and has worked alongside some of the leading cinematographers in the industry including Emmanuel Lubezki, Philippe Rousselot, Roger Deakins and Oliver Wood. His credits include *1984*, *Sid & Nancy*, *Tomorrow Never Dies*, *Children of Men*, *Mamma Mia!*, *The Bourne Ultimatum*, *Captain America: The First Avenger*, *Thor: The Dark World* and *Gravity*.

You served as Gaffer to Emmanuel Lubezki on *Gravity*, for which he won the Best Cinematography Oscar. Can you tell us about the challenges of lighting the film?
I had never worked on anything remotely like this project; it was a very fast learning curve and very experimental. It was so interesting, and there were a few different processes. In the 'lightbox' environment we used a moving light [a Robe 600 spot] which was mounted on a remote head. This lamp was fitted with a witness camera and was operated by Peter Taylor, who is a very experienced camera operator. This provided a very hard light to mimic the effect of direct sunlight.

On some of the capsule interiors we used large diffusion frames to provide the effect of the capsule being lit by Earth, with blue and green filters fixed to the diffusion frames.

You worked with Roger Deakins on *Skyfall*, which was nominated for Best Cinematography at the 2013 Oscars. How did you create the film's modern look?
Roger has a very definite vision of his requirements, and the look he wants. We did some tests and came up with some ideas and proceeded from there. He communicated his ideas to me and it was easy from his brief to put a plan into motion. I have done 14 or 15 films with Roger in the past, so I know how thorough he is in his preparation. This is great for me as I got fantastic guidance from him as to his thinking and ideas. It was he who gave me my break as a Gaffer on *1984* which was a technically challenging film and a great learning experience for me.

How did you get started in the industry in the first place?
I worked on oil rigs in the North Sea and I had a couple of months leave and saw a job advertised for electricians for a small film studio. I did an interview, got a job with them and never went back to the rigs.

Technology has transformed the film-making process; what do you think has changed most in lighting since the start of your career?

I think one of the biggest changes is the progress in electronics and the use of computers. The standard of control available now, from computer controlled dimming, LED technology and moving lights, is fantastic. It is an ever-evolving and a very exciting aspect of what we do. Also the digital cameras available are now running at 800 ASA, which produce amazing images. I think every studio film being made now has its stage lighting controlled by computer and night exteriors also rely on computerised dimming.

Over the last 15 years, you have been involved in some of the biggest movies made in the UK, including the first *Harry Potter*; how do you approach the lighting and colour palettes for those enormous sets?

I always take my brief from the cinematographer and I have been lucky enough to have worked with some of the greatest DoPs in the world. They often have a hugely different approach to lighting a set or location, and that is one of the aspects that makes the job so interesting. The approach always has to be the same: that is to listen to the brief and select some ideas of the equipment which may do the job. Testing is essential and sometimes what might appear to be ideal in theory does not work in practice. I cannot emphasise enough the value of testing.

***Mamma Mia!* was filmed in Greece and at Pinewood, how did you match the natural light in Greece when back at the studio?**

We had to match the searing sunlight of the island, and [DoP] Haris Zambarloukas had the idea of using 20-kilowatt mole-beams to provide the shafts of light supplemented with other high wattage units. We rented every mole-beam available in the UK and the result worked very well. All these lights were controlled from a dimming desk.

On *The Bourne Ultimatum*, you had the challenge of filming in Waterloo Station while it was still open to the public, and a lengthy chase sequence through the streets of Morocco. How did you approach these difficult scenarios?

It is astounding the mass of people who move through Waterloo station during the day. Consequently, the safety considerations are immense and our filming hours were tightly regulated. We were not allowed on the concourse before 10.00, and had to be off the concourse at 16.00. We considered many options of balloon lighting, 18 Kw. HMI rigs, etc. So [DoP] Oliver Wood visited and revisited the station, took lots of photographs at various times of day within our shooting window and he decided that the quality of the light was of a such that meant we only required light for the coverage. We were not allowed trailing leads in any circumstances, so the solution was to have shopping trolleys with batteries and invertors to run Kino-Flo Wall-O-Lights or small HMI units. These were held to the side and wheeled in as independent units as required. We also had floppy flags for negative fill.

Lighting in Tangier was an entirely different prospect. The Medina gets so busy during the day so the only option open to us was to prepare the sets as much as possible in advance, and get the equipment in place prior to the shooting day. We started at first light as this was the quietest time and it was possible to move pick-ups etc. with some ease until it got crowded mid-morning. We then concentrated on the individual sets. It required a lot of planning with my rigging Gaffer, Wayne Leach and location manager Emma Pill.

You worked on *Children of Men* with Alfonso Cuaron; what options for lighting did you have with those famous long takes?
We realised early on that the best way to approach this film, especially the night exteriors, was to use practical lighting which appears in the film as the main lighting source. We modified existing practical lamps to accept higher wattages and again all were controlled from a computerised dimming desk. The day exteriors were, in the main, either large bounces (ultra-bounce 20 x 12) or negative fill.

You have worked on some huge films during your career; do you feel any added pressure given the scale of the project and the worldwide audience?
I think it is only natural one would feel stress and pressure. The financial ramifications of a poorly constructed plan or a major oversight are enormous. I think that the essence of completing your brief successfully lies with planning. I think the pressure does not diminish if one is doing a low-budget project, as the responsibility is the same.

Is there one piece of advice you would give any young Gaffer or DoP who are the start of their career?
I would say to gain as much knowledge as possible as to what equipment is available, and there are a few ways of getting this knowledge. Trade shows are fantastic in this respect, as most of the equipment is under one roof it can be a day well spent. The internet is another great source of articles, and the rental companies are very accommodating with demonstrations and technical advice.

Another piece of advice is to avail yourself of the best crew around. The choice of crew is very important as a reflection of you. They should be encouraged to take on responsibility and feel part of the film-making process.

If you could change one thing about the film industry, what would it be?
The one thing would be to not have to work such long hours, but in my time in the industry it has always been the same.

Sonja Klaus - Production Designer and Set Decorator

In a career spanning over 20 years, Sonja Klaus has worked as a production designer and set decorator on a number of big- and small-screen projects, including *Robin Hood*, *Gladiator*, *American Gangster* and *Mr Selfridge*. She has collaborated many times with Director Ridley Scott, and also served as set decorator on his mega-budget *Alien* prequel *Prometheus*.

You have worked on many period films in your career, was *Prometheus* the first to be set in the future?
I have worked on science fiction before when I designed *Babylon A.D.*; that was set in the not-too-distant future and did require a lot of design work. It's always a challenge working on something that follows so much history and reference points, because we have, of course, 'seen it, done it and know it'. It's rather like reinventing the wheel.

What was the most challenging element working on *Prometheus*, and what aspects have given you the most satisfaction?
The on-screen computers. Technology is always changing, and who is to say what we will be doing in 75 years' time. To come up with a new idea was pretty difficult, so it was actually left to the graphics that were shown on the screens to indicate those changes. I had a team of brilliant people working with me, and they were constantly coming up with new ways of showing everyday information; for example when we see medical information or a message or even nutrition choices.

I thought of starting with colour, and did research into the diatoms and deep sea creatures that live in the depths of the oceans. They are the most incredible creatures, and have superb colour formations. So we took this as a colour palette for the bridge set, for example. Then the rovers needed the same treatment, so we looked at the sun and photos taken by the Hubble telescope. It was through looking at all this information that the actual imagery started to take shape; the graphics on the film are amazing and very much part of the entire design.

Prometheus is one of the high points of an incredible career, but how did you first break into the industry?
I have a degree in theatre design from Wimbledon School of Art, which led me into the theatre world, and I was fortunate to work on several West End shows. One day the phone rang and I was asked to work on a children's TV programme starring Frankie Howerd, as an art director. I had no idea what that meant, but I soon found out! I had thought I would stay in theatre, but then as the projects kept coming and I discovered more about the film and TV industry I was hooked.

You worked on *Gladiator* in 1999, and since then have worked on many of Ridley Scott's films. Why do you think you work so well together?

I have now worked with him on eight films, and we have very similar tastes and are able to understand each other. It is frustrating for some people, because we can start a conversation with one topic and by the time we are at the end we are discussing something else! Ridley is a great visionary and his portfolio of movies shows that on every level.

With both *Robin Hood* and *Kingdom of Heaven*, you need to create period decor in large scales. What were the biggest challenges on those particular films?

When working on such large-scale productions, it is really important to keep the whole film in your head; rather like a large painting. Not everyone can do that, and it is not something you can teach that easily. Good budgeting is also really important, as is having someone in the office that is on top of the budget at all times. People-management skills are a must as well. You do become rather like the Fat Controller, and spend a lot of time managing rather than set decorating. The artistic part is very small in comparison to the politics and paperwork!

On *Kingdom of Heaven* we filmed in two countries and I had a staff of 215, so you can imagine how many mistakes could be made and, as a head of department, it is your responsibility to take the flack and to sort them out. Research at the beginning is very important, but I find that part interesting and even if some of it is not right it may be for the next film. Nothing is ever wrong, you just need to learn how to make it work for you.

You also worked on *American Gangster*: how did you set about researching the locations and recreating the period?

I was at home with my bags packed ready to travel to New York to set-decorate *American Gangster* and the phone rang. It was Ridley, telling me that the union in NY has refused to let me come onto the film. We were both very disappointed. Without going into too much detail, the unions are so strong that not even Ridley Scott could help...

To cut a long story short I carried on in London and did some work here and there, then the phone rang again four weeks later and it was Ridley telling me to pack my bags and meet him in Bangkok. I did, and ended up working in Chang Mai for 13 weeks. It really was one of the best times I have had on a film, so sometimes disappointment is not always that bad.

As for the research on that film, some of the crew came from Burma and they had worked for the drug lords in the poppy fields so we recreated the scenes you see in the movie with their help. There was little time to do a lot of period research but I did find some very cool books. The main street in Chang Mai had to be completely re-dressed to look like Bangkok, so I put in 140 signs – huge neons and light boxes – and added all the street lights and building lights. Over 120 market-stall holders turned up on the day to recreate the dense markets in Bangkok; that was a bit nerve-racking, wondering if they would turn up or not.

You must be constantly looking for inspiration, where are your favourite places to do that?
I have a very big library and am a big fan of the printed word. I also like to keep up with the exhibitions in London and the UK. The internet is obviously useful, but often information can be misleading; there is nothing like the real thing in the end.

If you could change one thing about the British film industry, what would it be?
Bring back training schemes in the art department, strengthen the Guild and help the department have more of a voice in the industry; one that gets heard and acted on.

Ben Howard - Second Assistant Director

Ben Howard has worked as a first, second and third assistant director across a variety of projects, including TV shows like *The Thick of It*, *Hustle* and *Sherlock* and films such as *Gravity*, *The Grand Budapest Hotel*, *Mr Turner*, *Mortdecai*, *Tarzan* and JK Rowling's *Fantastic Beasts and Where to Find Them*.

You've worked on many award-winning productions, including as second assistant director on *Gravity*. What was your experience like on the project?

It's always good if people are talking about a film that you've been involved in, although this wasn't the most testing experience I've had as a second AD! It's rare that you only have a couple of cast to look after, and your job is made even simpler if they are as easy as Sandra [Bullock] and George [Clooney]. The success of the film owes so much to them embracing the process and the new technology. I don't think I've ever seen anybody dive in with such enthusiasm and professionalism as Sandy; not only in maintaining that incredible performance across what was basically hundreds of motion control shots but also her good humour too. She was great fun to be around. She actually invited the floor runner and me to the BAFTAs – nobody invites the ADs to anything, ever – which was a brilliant, if surreal, night out. We were also nominated as part of Alfonso's team for the 2013 DGA award, which he won for Best Director of a Motion Picture. We will be dining out on that for a while!

We know that much of *Gravity* was filmed using pioneering film-making techniques and technology. Can you describe how you manage to schedule around all of those unique elements?

The now-famous lightbox stage took up an enormous amount of main unit shooting and prep time, but it was only one piece of the jigsaw as there were many shots in the pre-viz that were never going to be achievable using that technology. Josh [Robertson, the first AD] put in place a rehearsal / prep unit that worked on other stages coming up with alternative methods of achieving the incredibly complicated shots. The process from pre-viz and early rehearsal, with stunts and wiremen determining methodology, to actually adding the actors and shooting often took days per shot, and was a highly collaborative process. Having the prep unit in place enabled filming to flow – as much as it ever could when you are faced with hundreds of VFX shots!

You also worked as second assistant director on Mike Newell's sumptuous *Great Expectations*. How was that experience?
It is an epic tale with many characters, and this production boasts a superb set of actors all the way down to the day players. Helena Bonham-Carter and Ralph Fiennes lead the line magnificently, as Miss Haversham and Magwitch. Helena's casting felt simultaneously like the most obvious choice in the world and a 'lightbulb moment' brilliant idea – she is a master at depicting emotional fragility.

Ralph was his usual impeccable self; without question the best-prepared actor I have ever encountered. He planned and prepped extensively to perfect his Magwitch, and many of his pre-fittings and pre-testing were driven by his incredible attention to detail.
Mike [Newell] is a real actors' director, brilliant to watch, and it was great to work with someone that takes full command of all aspects of his role. Combine that with this cast and the results are superb.

The department heads that the producers [Elizabeth Karlsen and Stephen Woolley] assembled were also a bit of a dream team; Jenny Shircore is a make-up magician and I've always wanted to work on a John Mathieson film, his photography captures the epic scale of the story perfectly.

What was the most challenging aspect of *Great Expectations* from an AD perspective?
It's the same for any big period job for a second AD; ludicrously early make-up calls, long drives to far flung locations in the middle of the night and very long days. But we were well supported, so it was a good experience. As with most jobs these days there never seems to be quite enough time, so the pressure is constantly on but you always get there somehow. The most enjoyable thing about being an AD for me is the team spirit that you develop under pressure, and we had a great team and always seemed to have a laugh.

You've been working a great deal since *Great Expectations*...
We were straight onto *The Invisible Woman* for Headline Pictures, which was directed by Ralph Fiennes and adapted from Clare Tomalin's book by Abi Morgan. Ralph played Charles Dickens whilst also directing, which posed its own challenges, but he's a very collaborative director.

I'll admit that I was relieved not to complete a hat-trick of period jobs when Josh [Robertson], the first AD that I work with, got his next film, an adaptation of Nick Hornby's novel *A Long Way Down* with the story firmly planted in contemporary London.

Can you explain your role as second AD in more detail?

The second AD is the first AD's right hand man. Together, we are there for the director to coordinate all his requirements for the project, and ensure he is able to carry out his artistic vision with practical and logistical ease. While the first AD runs the set, I am the person at the base running things there; often on the phone coordinating all aspects of the set's requirements, getting the actors through make-up and costume at the right time, getting them to set when required and overseeing transport etc. Depending on the nature of the job it can also be the responsibility of the second to cast all the background extras, and then coordinate getting them to set.

The main responsibility of the second AD, however, is the call sheet that is distributed to all crew and relevant cast at wrap each day. It's the filming blueprint for the shoot that everybody refers to and follows as the hours progress.

How did you get started in the industry and was there a specific breakthrough project?

I was the rehearsal runner on Mike Leigh's *Topsy-Turvy* in 1998, which was where I first met Josh Robertson, who was the second AD. We've worked together on and off ever since – me as third AD to his second AD, then as third AD to his first AD, and now as second AD to his first AD – so I was extremely lucky to have that encounter during my first job out of Guildhall.

You work very long hours and need incredible concentration; what has been the hardest day and most satisfying achievement?

It would be very hard to pick out one day, as there have been many personal highlights, but it's always satisfying when a project is particularly well received or garners some kind of award. Nicole Kidman won an Oscar for *The Hours* in 2003, which was pleasing as it was an arduous shoot. Night shoots are the hardest times spent at work. You get to base at 6pm then spend all night there, coming home in the small hours. As a second you never want to turn your phone off in case of emergencies, but it always starts ringing when the world wakes up. You spend all your time feeling constantly jet-lagged.

I've had the surreal experience of working on a couple of TV films where the subject matter of the project appears as a major news story during the shoot; on Stephen Frears' *The Deal* [about the Blair/ Brown pact made over the 1994 Labour Party leadership election] and also on the Peter Kosminsky film about David Kelly called *The Government Inspector*. It's a very exciting and rewarding experience feeling that you are involved in something so immediate and relevant.

What has been your best day at work?

Probably arriving for the first day of prep on an overseas project; either landing in Hong Kong for *Push* in 2007 or arriving for the Bali leg of *Eat Pray Love* in 2009. Very exciting times indeed!

If you could change one thing about the film industry, what would it be?
I wish that UK ADs had a strong union like the Americans do with the DGA [Director's Guild of America]. They have a rate card and set rates for overtime, which removes the need for any conversations about that vulgar subject of money, and means they pay their ADs what they are worth.

Catherine Scoble - Make-Up and Hair Designer

Catherine Scoble is a BAFTA-winning make- up designer best known for her work on films like *Lock, Stock and Two Smoking Barrels*, *This Is England* and *Complicit* and various TV dramas including *This is England '86, '88 & '90* and *Fortitude*.

What got you started in the industry, and what was your big break?
When I was doing my A- levels at school, just prior to going to Art College, I met hair and make-up designer Chrissie Baker who was a friend of the family. She told me about her career and I was incredibly inspired by her and her work, and set about gaining the training and experience needed to become a make-up artist.

My big break was being the hair and make-up designer on Guy Ritchie's first film, *Lock, Stock and Two Smoking Barrels*. This was only my second feature as head of department. It was a fantastic experience, the script was so clever and the characters were brilliant, and it was a very exciting set to be on. Also, it was a really interesting job for make-up, I remember the character of Dog, played by Frank Harper, really went through the mill. He was run over and then head butted by Vinnie Jones, who then went on to batter his head in a car door; he ended up with blood oozing out from everywhere! I've got fond memories of Lenny McLean, the Guv'nor, who was very kind and sweet to me, and Vinnie Jones was also a gentleman. It felt like the safest set I've ever been on!

You've collaborated with Shane Meadows on his *This Is England* projects; what's it like working for him and that particular group of actors.
Working with Shane Meadows is very special. We start off with a general idea of the story but things can change and you can never be totally sure of what is coming up. You have to be adaptable. It's a very exciting and inspiring way to work. I love it!

The group of actors in *This is England* are a proper family. We've all known each other for a few years now, and I love working with them because there is no room for any actor's ego or vanity. No one would allow it. It's a very refreshing way to work.

How did you evolve the look of the skinheads in the 1983-set film to the 1986-set TV show?
The 2006 film had ended in a traumatic climax; the group's rejection of skinhead culture began at that point. Any new direction had to have been a plausible step from this movement whose look was aggressive and beliefs were held passionately. Accuracy and authenticity was of paramount importance.

The process started with a long research period. I wanted to capture the look of real people during this time, and the 1980s contained many 'tribes': new romantics, mods, psychobillys, etc. There was far more diversity in youth culture than today. I immersed myself in the period, looking at all the elements of youth culture of that time.

Picture research was vital: I used Getty, PYMCA, Google and Flickr to track down 'real' images from the 1980s. I didn't want to look just at what people seem to associate with the 80s; namely big shoulder pads and big hair. I created a mood book for the series which contained several hundred images, with sketches and plans for each actor. Shane and I collaborated on the look for each character; we then discussed it with the actors, who had to be happy and confident with those looks. I based my final designs on those discussions and drawings.

How did you create the various tattoos seen on screen?
I spent a long time at Diamond Jacks, one of the oldest tattooists in Soho, who had records of tattoos going back to the 50s. For the character of Combo, played by Stephen Graham, some of the tattoos had to be older than others, as some were meant to be from borstal and some from prison. I then used a combination of transfer and hand drawn tattoos.

There was a scene in *TIE '86* where Combo was in the bath and cleaning blood and mud from his head. This was challenging for me, because the mixture of hot water and sweat meant I had to retouch all of the tattoos between each take.

As a make-up artist, you are often the last person an actor will see before stepping on set. How do you help them prepare?
At that point, as a make-up artist, you do what is absolutely essential and you leave the actor to prepare. It's not a time to chat about what they want for lunch. You want them to know that you are there, but you don't get in the way.

What's been your best day at work?
Flying to Monaco to make up Roger Moore, at his mansion overlooking the sea, was pretty special.

How did it feel to win your BAFTA for *This is England '86*?
It was overwhelming, and I'm still in shock! I never expected to win and being nominated was an honour in itself. I feel incredibly lucky to have won for something I enjoyed doing so much.
The evening itself was wonderful; our table had Shane Meadows, costume designer Charlotte Walters and Roberto Troni from Channel 4. Peta Dunstall was also there, she worked with me on the series, and not only is she an exceptional hairdresser but she is also a great friend. When my name was read out, I couldn't move. I was so shocked; I forgot to thank my assistants Lily Beckett and Nadia Stacey.

If you could change one thing about the UK film industry, what would it be?
That's easy. Shorter working hours and more money. At the moment, we seem to be going backwards.

James Graham – Film Production and Finance

Co-Founder, Galileo Media and Finance Group

Having been in film production and finance for over 20 years, James began his career as a small-budget documentary maker, and progressed to become Vice President at Amblin Entertainment and co-founder of the Lumiere Group. In 2005 he helped set up Galileo Media and Finance, helping to guide banks and insurance companies through film finance.

Despite your long career in the industry, you've worked hard to keep a low profile...
It's interesting about keeping a low profile. If you work in-house at a large production company, you don't usually get a credit; or you didn't when I first started working. Increasingly, the ranks of producers have been enlarged by sales agents, lawyers and financiers, all jockeying for position with each other in being producers, or executive producers. Normally if you are a staff member you still don't get a credit. I've mostly been a staff person and that sits fine with me; I'm a supporter of the current movement for truthful credits, which has been heightened by the fact that when there is an Academy nomination for best film, there's often 10-15 people with the word 'producer' in their title. This is clearly ridiculous, and the Academy has to winnow this down to who actually did the job. There are only one, two or three people at most that you could realistically call the producer of a project.

How did you start out?
My background was in documentary and a stint at film school, so going from an $80,000 documentary back in the 1980s to a $50m feature film was quite a jump. But what I learnt very quickly was that if you kept your common sense, most things were the same in principle. The people I found myself working with were so used to handling large budgets that their sense of calmness rubbed off on me. Also, of course, I was very junior, which fortunately limited my ability to make major mistakes!

In terms of how I got the opportunity... one comment I remember from that time was that the people who hired me were so used to hearing from film-school graduates who expected to swan in at the top as producers, but few who were interested in learning the nuts and bolts from those who had basically evolved the business. I wasn't without ambition, but I figured that if the average cost of a British film at the time was £2 million, not so different to that of today, which is a little worrying maybe, in America it was 10 to 20 times that amount, and there had to be more to learn over there than over here. Just in terms of sheer logistics.

How did you arrive at Amblin?

Quite fortuitously! I had begun in documentaries, and in those days you had an idea of what you were going to film but you didn't know how it was going to work out. You filmed a bit, edited it and worked out what you had got. After a while, I found that instead of filming what was in front of me, I began to join the dots in advance, thinking in terms of what I wanted to find and constructing what I wanted in terms of narrative before filming. If you are going to do that, you might as well be honest and say this is fiction, or at least part construction. So after a while I thought I better learn how to make feature films and not call them documentaries.

As I left film school I was fortunate to come across someone who was one of the great producers of his era, a Brit called Robert Watts, who was well known in Hollywood. He was central to the team, which made not only the first *Star Wars* films but also the *Indiana Jones* movies for George Lucas. I approached him – I'm not sure with what in mind – and he in turn put me in contact with Frank Marshall, his contemporary at Amblin, though, much to my shame, I had not heard of Frank Marshall nor Amblin – they were well beyond my radar. My hope at that time was just to get any work anywhere. This was probably in about 1985, and I owe a great deal to Robert Watts; not only a fine producer but a thoughtful and kind man.

Frank Marshall and Kathleen Kennedy, who were Steven Spielberg's producing partners, came over to the UK and based themselves at Elstree for the making of Empire *of the Sun*, so I started working with Kathleen and the rest of the production team. Also on this film were people like Norman Reynolds, the production designer, and Allen Daviau, the cinematographer: magical people to observe at work. All the heads of departments were legends already, with multiple Academy Award nominations behind them, and now I found myself working with them. I can't put over adequately how exciting that was. We filmed in England and in Shanghai and then a lengthy stint in Spain, near Jerez; and then at the end of the film, much to my surprise, I was asked to go back with them to Los Angeles. A bit like winning the lottery.

That must have been an overwhelming feeling.

It was astonishing, and I was overwhelmed. But I took stock of what I could do, or where my strengths were, and was determined not to blow it. It had been hard enough to get accepted into the UK film union that existed back then, the Association of Cinematograph Television and Allied Technicians (ACTT) – which should have given me membership by right from having attended one of the approved film schools on their list – but getting the appropriate work visa to allow me to work at Amblin was a challenge of a different order. They took care of it, which made me feel that if they were prepared to go to that length to get me working for them, I must have been doing something right.

I knew that I was a hard-working individual, and happy to work 20 hours a day using whatever intelligence or learning I had. I was first and foremost a good listener, I must have had ears like Dumbo the elephant, not only listening to what they asked me to do, but also trying to listen through the task and anticipate what they really wanted a day or a week from now. That was probably the thing that helped me a lot, thinking around the problem.

What was your initial role at Amblin?
On *Empire of the Sun*, I was lower than low; I was production associate, which is not production assistant and not associate producer, but somewhere in between, a nebulous role. There were the three partners, a head of development, a head of merchandising and head of post production if I remember correctly, and about six or seven executives in total and about 30 production assistants. It was a life within a life. I did suffer from a fair jolt of culture shock in Los Angeles; nothing can prepare you for it.

I remember sitting in meetings with Steven Spielberg and watching him go through the scripts in minute detail. It was fascinating to sit through those meetings with such talented people: a bit like a fly on the wall – I thought very hard before opening my mouth – and hearing them construct or break down the constituent parts of a film.

It was certainly an exciting place to be. Spielberg's career since then is well known, but Kathleen Kennedy and Frank Marshall have also gone on to be probably the most successful producing partnership of the modern era.

What was it like moving from England to LA?
It was a bit like joining the circus; a surreal dream, especially when you came to LA from parochial England. And when you go to a phenomenally successful place like Amblin, it's especially hard to compare it to anything you've ever done before. The place had a relaxed atmosphere, people were open and friendly but they also worked hard, and were very focused, which is not something you always see in the UK film business. Surface appearance and the way business was conducted in LA were very different. From the outside, LA can seem flamboyant but don't let it fool you.

Do you miss it?
I was in my 20s and it was the 1980s; I don't remember the UK being much fun during that decade. It was an interesting experience, not only being in LA but also at one of the highest profile production companies of the time. But no, I don't miss it. I prefer what I do today in many ways. They have a saying over there that the trick is to be as successful at 40 as you were at 30; I think LA would be a tough town to live in without being visibly successful. That may sound shallow but it's a competitive place. I think that long term I was a little too quiet to have pushed my way to the top over there. Los Angeles definitely rewards some temperaments more than others. By contrast, I know exactly where I fit in anywhere from London to Beijing.

Were Amblin and, in later years, Lumière, competitive places and were you swamped with speculative scripts?

Each company that I've worked at have had very strict policies about accepting scripts. All the big companies do. You just can't take the risk of someone claiming you stole their idea from a script you don't remember but were supposed to have read 10 years ago. The only scripts that were allowed in the door were from accredited sources, though I do remember one notable director trying to get around this by faxing his 150-page script through in the dead of the night. Come morning there was paper everywhere, like a snow storm! I also remember another writer, an accomplished stand-up comedian, waiting in reception until someone had read his script. I can't remember whether this ploy worked or not, but the film was eventually made elsewhere.

There are, and were, so many scripts written and so few places to take them, so the high profile companies get an enormous amount of attention. At Lumière, for example, we received somewhere between 20 to 30 scripts per week – and turned down many more unseen – so you would just be bricked in if you tried to read them all. If you figure it takes three hours to read a script, that's a ninety-hour week by itself. And it's not as if you can sit in the office during the working day reading; it's strictly an evening and weekend task, so script readers became a bit of a necessity. I don't think any exec feels completely comfortable about using them; after all, a writer submits a script hoping the head of the department is going to read it, not an unknown script reader.

Do you enjoy reading scripts?

In general, I found the script development part of production too labour intensive and not a particularly enjoyable part of the job. If there is one thing I am definitely happy about it's that I don't have to read so many scripts nowadays. My rule of thumb was that I 'found' – maybe 'recognised' is a better word – one great script in every two hundred I looked at; not an encouraging statistic if you happen to be a writer, and not particularly encouraging if you happen to be working your way through all those scripts. That judgement also involved other factors, and whether the script could be developed further with the team that owned it. Some producers and writers were more amenable to collaborating than others. There are quite a few competent writers out there but – forgive me for seeming harsh – fewer actually talented writers. If you liked a project, admired the writer, but didn't see eye to eye with them and couldn't work out how to communicate mutually, the development process could be very tricky.

On the whole, I think it's better for a production company not to get too waylaid by the scripts that are offered to them, but to concentrate on what films they want to make and who they want to make them with. Otherwise you risk becoming a passive script-reading service for anybody who wants to send in a script. And once you've read someone's script, there is an implicit sense of obligation to report back to them your impressions and thoughts, if constructive. Rather than start with a script, I found it more efficient to concentrate on a handful of directors and find out what they wanted to do next.

How did you develop your career after Amblin and Lumière?

Both of these were reasonably sized companies, and both achieved – in differing degrees – artistic and commercial success. Even Lumière, the lesser known of the two, had its share of success: for instance, *Leaving Las Vegas*, a project I found for the company, went on to win Oscars and earn significant financial rewards for Lumière. Moving on from these, I really felt that I had had my fill of working in an overly corporate environment, and was determined to move in a different direction. I was head of production for Lumière in England but we had another of those in France and one in Los Angeles too, and occasionally I think our likes and dislikes cancelled each other out!

For a while I worked independently, behind the scenes, with various productions that had got quagmired. At any time, in any year, there are productions that have good teams who mostly, through no fault of their own, have been hit with a series of problems: anything from hurricanes, earthquakes, death of an actor or a military coup. In these situations, they can benefit from someone objective fresh from the outside, who can come in and help bolster their activities. Each time I got involved in a production – however peripherally – I came back thinking that I'd met people I'd like to work with again. I guess that's one of the main attractions of working in the film business: you're always learning, or you should have that feeling.

At the same time, I worked with a few leading European banks on their media banking. It was like trying to protect yourself in a hail storm, with projects hitting you from all angles, and the impetus at the banks was to do business at any cost. Myself and my partner at the time spent most of our day trying to talk the banks out of one scheme after another.

Over the last few years, I've been working with a group of former bankers and fund managers at Galileo. On my side of things, we've been looking at ways in which the film industry can meet investors' requirements, without weaving through loopholes, tax structures and the like, and also about how to make investing in films a sensible, long-term, medium-risk investment. Something that's repeatable, something that breaks the 'use and burn' model that has marked the film business' way of treating its financial partners over the past few years. There's also strong institutional interest in the areas we're focusing on; indeed there's more money available than appropriate projects for investment. Galileo does much more besides this, but my area is media in general. As a group we're growing exponentially, and we have some exciting years ahead.

Philippa Broadhurst - Standby Art Director

Philippa Broadhurst is a standby art director and graphic designer working in feature films and TV drama in the UK. Her big-screen credits include *An Education* and *Made in Dagenham*, and she has also worked on small-screen projects including *Downton Abbey*, *Peep Show* and *Game of Thrones*.

Game of Thrones is a mammoth production with many huge sets; how do you prep for such a job?
The size and number of the sets doesn't really alter the way in which I prep; a standby always has to break down the script in the same way, whether it is a huge scene involving 900 extras or one involving only two key characters. Some of the larger scenes obviously require you to be conscious of the number of extras and scope of background action you will have to populate with appropriate props and action. Most importantly, each set is meticulously designed, so staying in touch with the designer to ensure I understand the look and atmosphere we're trying to achieve with each one is vital.

What's the most challenging aspect when doing a series like Game of Thrones?
For me, the main challenge is that we have two main units shooting all the time, so as a standby I have to break down the entire script yet I'll only be filming roughly half of the scenes. Sequences that alternate between the two units present the biggest challenge: in terms of which unit establishes character props or locations, and maintaining the continuity between us.

You worked on the first two series of Downton Abbey; what are the particular challenges of a period drama?
You have to know so much about the life of the period: what people do in their spare time, what inventions are around or yet to come, and basic everyday details such as what size paper is in use. You also need a thorough understanding of period styles to ensure you're creating a true visual narrative, and also because there will always be a change on the day that requires you to know if some aspect of architecture of furnishing is appropriate or not.

It is also easy to fall into the mistake of assuming that since a style was around at the time, it can be used extensively. Just because you're filming a 1980's drama, for example, does not mean all aspects of the design should be from the 1980s; it is actually the 1970's style that will likely be dominant, because people don't rush out and pepper their houses with every latest thing. You also have to be mindful of what your modern audience perceives that period to look like, whether it actually does or not. Details are all choices based on what is accurate, what your audience believes to be accurate, and what serves the story best visually.

What has been your greatest day at work?
My greatest day at work has to be my first day on my first film, just walking through Pinewood and feeling all that history was magical. I've always been a big fan of British films, especially of the 1940s to 1960s, so just seeing the 'reserved for Peter Rogers' sign was ridiculously exciting.

Chris Munro - Production Sound Mixer

During a career spanning over 40 years, Chris Munro has worked in film and TV sound for productions as diverse as A Fish Called Wanda, *United 93*, *Casino Royale*, *Captain Phillips*, *Gravity*, *Mission Impossible: Rogue Nation* and *Wonder Woman*. Together with his colleagues, he's won two Oscars, for *Black Hawk Down* and *Gravity*, and two BAFTAs, for *Casino Royale* and *Gravity*.

You've had a truly stellar career, but can you tell us how you got started in the industry? I started at Elstree Studios as a trainee, aged 16. One of my many interests then was electronics, and my great passion was films and the cinema. I was so desperate to work in films I would write to all the studios, only to be told that they only employed union members and, of course, you could only join the union if you had a job. So when by chance I met someone who worked at the studio and he told me there may be a job for a trainee, I was straight on to it.

My knowledge of electronics got me the job, particularly as modern electronics were a mystery to some of the older technicians who were more used to valve technology. It was bit like a few years ago, when people were moving over to computer editing and experienced editors needed a kid to work with them because they would be the technical experts. I took the job and told my parents it was just a summer job during the school holidays, which worked fine until September when the school called to ask where I was. The rest is history, but needless to say I kept the job!

What sort of equipment did you use in your early work?
It was the start of recording on Nagra. In the studio we recorded directly to 35mm magnetic, but used Perfectone and then Nagra recorders when we went on location. Microphones were made by RCA and were those really heavy ones that you sometimes see on old TV broadcasts. But of course we mainly used Fisher booms, so only occasionally had to hold them on a boom pole.

What was your breakthrough moment in sound? Was it a particular project or technological advancement?
I left Elstree and went freelance to work on a TV series at Pinewood, and then freelanced as a sound maintenance engineer and as a boom operator. Then I had a call to mix second unit on a Sam Peckinpah film called *Cross of Iron*; I was about 25 years old and didn't look back! I have remained fascinated by technology, but wouldn't say I am a geek. I have always been amongst the first to adopt new technology, like digital recording and computer based recording. Nevertheless I would still describe myself as a film-maker specialising in sound rather than a soundman specialising in film.

Of course I'm proud of *Gravity but I'm also* proud of *United 93*. This was equally a technically challenging film, but also the most professionally satisfying. It was great to get a BAFTA nomination for it, and there were mixed emotions when I actually won for *Casino Royale,* which was also nominated the same year. As far as I know this is the only Bond film to win a BAFTA for sound. Another is *Captain Phillips*, also directed by Paul Greengrass. The challenges were similar to *United 93* with the addition of the problems of working at sea.

You worked with John Cleese on *A Fish Called Wanda*, *Clockwise* and *Fierce Creatures*. Did you do anything different to capture his often explosive delivery?
John Cleese hated ADR, and felt confident that I would do my best to get all usable sound on location. *A Fish Called Wanda* was a great experience, directed by Charles Crichton, who had directed *The Lavender Hill Mob* and several of the Ealing classics. He was a master of comedy and, as an ex-editor, had a great sense of timing. We had no idea that this fairly low budget film would be the success it ultimately became.

You also worked on *A Muppet Christmas Carol*; was it particularly challenging collaborating with puppets?
I always enjoy working on very technical films like, *United 93* and *Gravity*, but this was something else! Before this I had no idea that the puppeteers were also the voices of the characters and that it was all recorded live. I somehow imagined it would be done to playback, but they all needed to be able to improvise. This almost caught me out on the very first day of shooting when we were shooting a sequence on a camera crane, with a fruit and vegetable cart crossing the foreground. The director, Brian Henson, shouted cut and said, "I couldn't hear the melons – I've given them each a line". I was prepared for anything to talk from then on, even fruit and veg. It wasn't until I later found myself asking Kermit to speak up that I realised I was a total believer.

Tomorrow Never Dies was your first Bond; how have they developed since then?
I have recorded five Bond films: *Tomorrow Never Dies* was my first, and the first Bond to be recorded digitally. It was a technical milestone as it was also the first to be edited non-linear, all of the others were cut on film. We were able to develop a lot of technical innovations, which are commonplace today. Each subsequent Bond bought a new challenge and a solution, particularly in regard to digital multi track recording and developing processes to enable such a short post-production schedule. They usually start shooting from January to July for a November release. Unfortunately, I've fallen out of sync with Bond films and did not work on Skyfall or Spectre but Stuart Wilson continued to push the boundaries and did a great job.

You won one of your two Oscars for *Black Hawk Down*, which tells of a battle between the US Air Force and Somali soldiers during the Battle of Mogadishu. How did you capture these difficult sequences?
Black Hawk Down was another of those very technical films. It was a challenge, but very satisfying. Ridley Scott is an amazing director and one of the few that can use multiple cameras so effectively. I think that at times we had up to 14 cameras, including aerial shots. Not many people were using multitrack recorders at that time and we were recording to digital multitracks which allowed me to record all of the isolated tracks and to create different mixes for each camera. This

was also the first time I had been able to use live ammo for sound FX recording, which gave some great results and sounds very different to some of the gun FX in libraries. I have since done this on many subsequent films with results that I have been very happy with.

Two of your recent projects, *John Carter* and *Gravity*, have been set in space. Did you do anything different to capture those other worldly locations?
John Carter was another of those very complicated pictures for sound. I seem to always get the complicated jobs! Many of the characters are animated but were performed by actors working on stilts and with headcams capturing their facial expressions. The Director, Andrew Stanton, particularly wanted to get usable dialogue as he felt that though he would be animating the actors' faces he wanted to be able to remain true to the original performance.

Gravity was a totally different kind of film. The important part of this was not only to be able to record dialogue from Sandra Bullock and George Clooney, without hearing the noise of the motion-control robots that had cameras on, but we also had to be able to run a complete communications system for them to be able to hear the various radio voices that they interact with, in addition to atmospheric sounds and even some music. So we became all of the other actors in the scene when we played back their radio dialogue. We pe-recorded several versions of the interactive radio conversations and made them in to loops so that we could trigger them from a keyboard. That way we were able to send a variation to both of the actors that felt more like they were interacting with a live voice. We had quite a lot of fun doing this and during long re-sets I would try to play music or anything that may keep them entertained. On one occasion I was playing Rapper's Delight and was amazed when both George and Sandra started to sing along knowing every word.

As with all technical departments, sound workflow has changed significantly over the last 15 Years. What are the biggest changes you've witnessed?
There was a point where workflows were changing so quickly that it was different on every film. That seems to be settling down a bit or perhaps we're just getting used to new challenges on every film. The things that currently cause problems are that many cameras and even some lighting equipment have noisy fans in It's as if the designers have no idea that the equipment would be used on a film set where sound may be an issue, and I'm often surprised that these problems are not recognised before going on set at the same time ADR has become less popular with directors wanting to use much more original dialogue. What is interesting is how we draw on past experiences for example when I worked on Captain Phillips I had to find ways to record dialogue over large distances at sea and also just overcome the challenges of working at sea. This experience came to good use when some time later I worked on Heart of the Sea with Ron Howard. I spoke earlier about John Carter. I am about to start Ready Player One with Steven Spielberg where some of the same techniques will be used. It seems we never stop learning with every film that we do.

Frazer Churchill - VFX Supervisor

VFX supervisor Frazer Churchill was nominated for a BAFTA for *Children of Men*, and was also Oscar shortlisted for his work on *Scott Pilgrim vs the World*. Other projects he has worked on include *Pitch Black*, *Bridget Jones's Diary*, *The World's End* and *Miss Peregrine's Home for Peculiar Children*.

How did you prepare to create the apocalypse for Edgar Wright's *The World's End*, and did you look at anything in particular for inspiration?
The great thing about VFX design is you to get to draw on the numerous WTF moments you've experienced in your life and I've had a few of those. I got my inspiration mainly from a trip to Formentera, a volcanic eruption and some biblical paintings.

Can you tell us about any particular challenges you faced on this production?
I started talking to Edgar [Wright] about the film around two years before it was made. It was pretty clear then that the trick would be getting his quite expansive vision realised with a smallish budget. 'Michael Bay scale shots with a Mike Leigh budget' So we had to be very selective and smart about how we shot and produced the VFX. We couldn't have too much CG, it's simply too expensive.

We all liked the physicality of prosthetics but wanted to push them a little further than you could with straight in-camera prosthetics. So we made a decision to shoot lots of practical elements and prosthetics, and rely heavily on a VFX technique called 're-projection'. This is where you take photographed elements and their geometric form, and composite them in a way that's more sophisticated than straight 2D work but simpler than full CG. Put simply, it allows you to photograph an element and put it convincingly into any moving camera shot.
Re-projection is cheaper and less labour intensive than creating pure CG, and relies wholly on good on-set reference photography shot in the same lighting conditions as the live-action photography.

It's a technique which requires an investment from everyone involved and, although it's cheaper in the long run, it will take up more time on set. We had to plan and make sure we shot all our references and elements, largely on the same sets and at the same time as principal photography, because we couldn't rely on CGI-ing our way out of trouble later. There simply wasn't the budget for that. Obviously shooting elements and references takes time so we had to make sure everyone knew what was required on the day. For some shots we'd need to shoot an additional four or five passes.

Edgar will support me in anything that makes the VFX more impressive, so having his support and the support of first AD Jack Ravenscroft was invaluable in getting everything we needed.

Most of the filming for *World's End* took place in one town over a lot of night shoots; was that single environment easier to work with?
Most of the film's exteriors are shot in Letchworth at night. I've worked with production designer Marcus Rowland before [on *Scott Pilgrim vs the World*] and we had a fantastic locations' manager, Camilla Stephenson. The collaboration with those two was invaluable in getting what we needed. I did a lot of stills photography in central London to make some of the concepts work; again working with the art department and locations was essential to making this work.

How did you get your start in the industry?
When I left university I had a part-time job as a graphic designer. I thought I'd like to get into video games, as that seemed like a realistic goal. Saying you wanted to work in film in England in the early nineties was a bit like saying 'I want to be an astronaut'. Anyhow I got a job as a runner at MPC and after three months was lucky enough to get promoted into their digital film department, FilmTel.

In FilmTel, we transferred completed commercials from video to film for cinema release. We had a Matador Paintbox for retouching and adding high resolution graphics and captions, and that's kind of how I learned to be a digital artist. From doing Matador Paint, I learned Kodak's Cineon compositing software. In those days we were using SGIs, silicon graphics workstations, which cost a billion pounds and are obsolete now. I think my iPhone has a faster processor than the machines I used back then.

What makes a good post artist, and how do you manage the teams that work for you?
A good post artist needs to add something special to the shot they're working on. They need to think, 'How can I make this better'. They also need to have the confidence in their choices. When you are starting out and your eye is maybe not so developed, you spend a lot of time thinking, 'Does that look right?' and 'Is this good?' The ability to make good choices and stand by them tends to come with experience. When I go into dailies sessions I have to assess and critique up to 80 shots in 2 hours. If I make bad choices, the director tells me off.

I will see strengths or weaknesses in artists' work and will assign shots accordingly. It's very important that people feel they have input in the creative process. Films get made by people from differing perspectives offering ideas, and a good VFX supervisor will always be open to ideas. That's how good films become great.

Can you talk us through your process once you get the edit? How much consultation will you have with a director?

It's really rather laborious. We get sent a cut by the editor; he's cut the sequences with raw blue-screen footage or 'temps' [temporary versions of the VFX shots]. We drop in the work in progress shots, at which point it may become clear that a shot needs to be extended or trimmed to make the effect work. I'll make a recommendation to the editor, who may or may not take the advice. On a large production there'll be a VFX editor who manages the editorial process.

It's a long and drawn out process, and daily communication with the cutting room is vital. I'll be by the director's side throughout the shoot, and speak to him every day in post.

Which effect or sequence are you proudest of and why?

I'm very proud of *Children of Men* and *Scott Pilgrim vs the World*. People are still talking about and emulating the long takes from *Children*, and *Scott Pilgrim* will be copied for years to come.

What tips have you got for producers using VFX for the first time?

Plan and prep. VFX are cheaper when you plan them and stick to the plan. And make sure every dollar you spend is on the screen.

And what can technicians and audiences expect in the future of VFX?

Visual Effects Departments on mid to high budget movies have already become Digital Production Departments. We scan every prop, set & character in order that we can make digital versions of everything. With the advent of Image Based Lighting and HDRI we can create exact digital copies of everything, all lit completely photorealistcally, so that no one would ever be able to distinguish it from the real photography.

We have achieved complete photorealism to the point that VFX professionals often can't tell what's real & what isn't. Look at MAD MAX : FURY ROAD and how everyone was praising the practical effects with no idea that there were 1200 VFX shots in the film. So expect more effects that you can't detect (if that's possible!) There are already hundreds of shots in movies every year that people have no idea are digital, which is why the whole "CGI is rubbish" backlash is a nonsense. You can't detect our CGI because it's so good now. Basically, the future is VFX everywhere, we're into the age of pure creativity in VFX craft. There are no more limits.

If you could change one thing about the UK film industry, what would it be?

More money for independent film and more genre film-making.

David Allcock - Storyboard Artist

As a storyboard artist, David Allcock has worked on big screen projects including *The Wolfman*, *Anna Karenina, Hummingbird, Edge of Tomorrow, The Man from U.N.C.L.E, Pan* and *Star Wars: Episode VIII* as well as TV shows like *Merlin* and *The Deep*.

***Anna Karenina* was nominated for four Oscars in 2012, three of them being in the design categories. Did that feel like a huge achievement?**
I think the nominations were well deserved. The whole team worked tirelessly to create what I think is a totally unique and bold interpretation of the material. Sarah Greenwood's art department is one of the best in the world and they embraced [director] Joe Wright's unorthodox vision and really brought it to life. It was a daunting task, re-interpreting and re-imagining the whole scenario within this theatre set-up, but the concept worked and we all pulled it off. It was brave and challenging but often the best things are. Joe was right in not doing another traditional adaptation. I love the artistry and creativity, all created with practical FX and some stunning set design.

***Anna Karenina* is set almost entirely in a theatre, how did you set about the storyboarding process for the film?**
The storyboard process was one of the most involved and complicated I have ever had. A lot of the scenes had to be carefully planned out, as the transitions from one scene or set to the other often took place in the same shot and had to be seamless. We were meticulous. Joe used every trick in the book and it was all carefully choreographed with a minimum of CGI. That is what I'm most proud of. We came up with some beautiful set-ups utilising all in-camera techniques; it was literally smoke and mirrors.

I'd spend days at Joe's house, sketching away as we went through scene by scene. We had the set designs pinned up on the wall, with all the reference material, and we'd plot it out shot by shot with the DP, brainstorming ideas of how to make it all flow and serve the story in the most effective and dramatic way. It was pure cinema, and I was in my element. Joe had me work very closely with him and I'd often be working as they were shooting. He was, and always is, extremely well prepared but things were constantly being refined on the fly as it was a relatively tight budget and schedule. This forced us to think 'outside the box' and come up with even more inventive ways to communicate with the audience. Joe is collaborative, and I'm flattered that he let me have so much creative input.

Anna Karenina **is obviously a career highlight, but what got you started in the industry?**
I have always wanted to work in film and TV since a very young age. I grew up with *Star Wars*, Indiana Jones and James Bond; a friend and I used to steal his Dad's camcorder and make our own mini-epics in the back garden. We dragged everyone we knew into it. We'd make dummies and throw them out of windows and splash fake blood everywhere. We'd do car chases by shooting each other in close-ups sat in our parents' cars in the driveway then splicing this together with wide shots and stunts from Hollywood movies. I'd edit by plugging two VCRs together, plus a microphone for sound effects, and my Dad's record player to lay music over the top. My parents tried to dissuade me from actually working in film though. They believed I should keep it as a hobby but not a career choice. They didn't think I could make a living at it, but since breaking into the industry they have been extremely supportive.

I left secondary school with some decent A-levels and then did a degree in film and video at the Surrey Institute of Art and Design in Farnham. I told them I wanted to be an editor. They liked the sound of this and let me in because everyone else had come in saying they wanted to direct and thought they were the next Tarantino. Along the way I saw what the editorial life was like and decided that I didn't want to be stuck in a dark room 24/7. But I think like an editor, and I have a huge admiration for what editors do. They are massively under-appreciated sometimes but I couldn't do it for a living. I would have turned into Jack Nicholson in *The Shining*!

After graduating I managed to get some work experience at a commercials production company as a runner. I ended up staying with them and working for a long time unpaid before becoming a full-time production assistant. This was my initiation into film and advertising; it was a crash course and a real eye opener. A million miles away from the cosy world of student filmmaking! Vadim Jean was one of the directors at the company and he let me get involved in all aspects of the process. My main job was putting together the show reels and distributing them around town. I was a gopher, but I also helped out the production manager with organising shoots, I got to go out on location, did some AD-ing, sound recording, casting, went along to the editing; every part of the process. I saw how it was really done and got an invaluable insight into the entire process.

One day a storyboard artist had come in to do some boards for a commercial, and after leaving they decided some changes were needed. A big video conference call was set up with the American clients, but the artist couldn't get back in time. The office manager must have seen me doodling away in a lunch break and she told them I could draw. So I put myself forward and offered to sketch the changes for them. They liked what I did, we made the deadline for the meeting and from then on I sort of became an in-house storyboard artist between doing the show reels and making cups of tea.

I continued as a PA and travelled with Vadim on commercials and feature films as his assistant, but also did the storyboards. I started to get requests from other people outside the company for drawings and reached the point where I could go freelance as a fully-fledged board artist. This was far more my cup of tea; it combined my love of film-making and my strengths as an illustrator perfectly. I fully admit I was not a great PA, but it was a brilliant foot in the door.

Which other artists inspire you?
As far as other artists go, I have always been a comic book fan and an avid reader of graphic novels; sequential art has always been a part of my life. I never read superhero stuff. I used to like *Tintin*, *Asterix* and 2000 AD when I was young, then when I was a teenager I loved crime and horror comics: *The Punisher* and *Tales from the Crypt* were my favourites.

When I learnt about storyboarding, I discovered Martin Asbury's work through behind-the-scenes books and making-of documentaries. He came from a comics background, and he's been the number one storyboard artist in the UK since the early 80s. I absolutely love his work. I used to hunt down everything he did and study them meticulously: the way he broke down the shots, indicated camera movement, pacing, editing, notes on FX and stunts.

Another favourite storyboard artist and major inspiration is Mike Ploog, who also started in comics and moved into film. I got to hang out with him at Comic Con in San Diego a couple of years ago, which was a dream come true; a great guy and a great artist. He showed me some of his original pencil storyboards for John Carpenter's *The Thing* and my head nearly exploded.

What was your first paid job, and how did you get it?
My first job as a professional freelance storyboard artist was a movie called *White Noise*, for Director Geoff Sax and Gold Circle Films. I had been out in Vancouver with Vadim doing another movie for Gold Circle, and they had seen me boarding away while I was there. This was my last job as a full-time PA and, just as I went freelance, Gold Circle said they had this horror movie starting up and the director was based in London; could I meet him and do some boards? The budget was fairly tight and they needed to plan out the more complex stuff as best as possible for budgeting and scheduling. I boarded all the main action/FX sequences with Geoff, and thoroughly enjoyed it.

The movie turned out great and Geoff is a very good friend to this day. I worked with him on his fantastic Christopher Isherwood biopic for the BBC, *Christopher and His Kind*.

When you started freelancing as a storyboard artist, what sort of work was available?

When I started it was mainly small stuff. *White Noise* was a diamond in the rough, and I was very lucky to be in the right place at the right time and get a feature film as my first gig. Apart from that it was all little things. I did numerous short films, low-budget music videos, corporate stuff, development work as favours for directors: anything I could to build a portfolio. It was my second initiation. I had to build from scratch again, carving my niche and creating a reputation, working for no money round the clock just to gain experience. This led to more high-profile commercials, then TV drama and feature films. I grafted 'til my fingers bled!

What research will you do before you take a job?

I will try and do as much as possible, and be as prepared as I can. You should always do your homework. I find out who the director is, and the other HoD's, and get a sense of their style and the tone of the project, adapting myself to the environment as best I can. I watch the director's previous films and see what shots he likes and how he tends to cut a sequence. Some directors love Dutch angles, others hate it. Some like tight, handheld long lenses, others prefer wide-angle tracking. For example Guy Ritchie likes to mix things up a bit, using slow motion mixed with fast cuts. He likes to push the technology and get quite stylised and dynamic. He lets me do my own pass on scenes and think outside the box before we go in and refine things. On the other hand, Joe Wright likes longer takes and sweeping camera moves; every composition is carefully considered and he likes to play with symbolism. I know these preferences going into the project, and I apply it.

If it's a period film or based on existing property I try and immerse myself in that time or that world and get 'in the zone'. I also make little notes and thumbnails on the script when I first read it. On the big studio movies nowadays there will be a researcher and a central computer network with all kinds of reference material stored up. When I'm actually in the office or studio I will often have access to all this reference, plus books, set designs, costume drawings that are specific to the project. I like to do my homework.

I also value my time in production and seeing all aspects of the process. I try to get on set when I can and learn about new technology and techniques, particularly with stunts and visual effects. The more background knowledge I have and sense of exactly what goes into achieving a shot the better informed my storyboards will be.

Do you use any software for your work, or is it all traditional method?

Everything is digital nowadays. All departments now have a digital workflow and I have had to follow suit. I still draw pencil on paper to begin with, though; I always have and I always will. It's the fastest and purest process for me, and I hope I never lose that. But I then continue my work on computer. I often scan my drawings and clean them up in Photoshop, rendering them, labelling, re-organising, layout, etc.

Storyboards are constantly changing and I will do numerous different versions of the same scene. The digital process has made this part a lot easier; no more cutting and pasting with Sellotape and scissors! Now and then I do some digital painting in Photoshop and Corel Painter as well, for full colour concept art and key frames. Biro thumbnails are my pre-production, neat pencils on paper is my production and Photoshop is like my post production. I then have the ability to save my artwork in any format, which is usually as separate jpegs for printouts and sending to the editor if they want to play around with a scene early on, or PDF's for a whole sequence, which is good for distributing to other departments. The digital content then also allows me to cut animatics if that is required. They are fairly crude but when you add some music and sound effects it can help with pacing and get a sense of actual screen time for a sequence.

When do you typically come on board and leave a production?
I am usually one of the very first people hired on a project, and I have the luxury of seeing it grow and develop. If I come on really early in prep, or even in development, then I get some great one-on-one time with the director, and sometimes DoP and production designer. As the project gains momentum you see them less and less as things get busier and their time is limited. The storyboards are then used to inform the prep process as schedules are drawn up and budgets made.

On large-scale features I will usually work all through pre-production and maybe a few weeks into shooting, but then I'm gone and onto the next thing while the rest of the crew slave away. On smaller scale projects I might only be hired for a couple of weeks to work on one scene. Nowadays, though, projects are constantly evolving all through shooting and well into post production, as so much is done with CGI and reshoots are built into budgets to tweak things after test screenings. I will sometimes be re-hired during post to help figure out stuff that didn't exist initially, or to help plan new scenes that have been added at the last minute and decided upon during the editing and test-screening process.

How much consultation will you have with a director, and what's it like trying to interpret their vision?
In a perfect world I would get lots of time face to face with the director, and have constant access to them and a hotline to their brain! In the real world this simply never happens; they are just too busy. I have to use my time with them as efficiently as possible, and make the most of the brief meetings I get to stay one step ahead and fill in the gaps as best I can. If I can gain the director's trust I can keep pumping ideas through and making suggestions.

I also work with the second unit director, stunt co-ordinator, DoP and production designer. Often I have to talk on the phone or Skype with them and email stuff back and forth as they are off at other meetings, scouting locations or on set shooting. I work remotely more and more, and the technology allows this nowadays. I have worked on projects based in the US and all over Europe without ever leaving home.

Some directors like to go into great detail during storyboarding, and are very specific and board everything. Others like a bit more freedom and like to keep things looser, allowing for more experimentation on the day. Good storyboarding should bridge those two worlds: providing enough information clearly so everyone knows what's going on but not getting bogged down. They should suggest not dictate. And it isn't about pretty pictures, it's about information.

Action sequences need to follow the storyboard tightly, is your imagination at the mercy of the budget?
The big action scenes are often the priority as they are the most complex. Time is money, and they take a long time to shoot and involve lots of special equipment and crew. They are dangerous and expensive, so the more it can be figured out ahead of time the better prepared everyone will be. I will usually end up re-drafting an action scene many times over a period of weeks as more and more information is fed in and the sequence is shaped and refined. The board becomes a visual script; we often start bigger and whittle it down as the days are scheduled.

There is never enough time or enough money, so the budget is always a concern. Sometimes the storyboard informs the budgeting process and other times the board must fit the budget. It depends on the production. Nowadays there are lots of VFX involved, and the storyboard will be handed over to a pre-viz team to construct an animation factoring in precise lenses and all the live action elements and CGI elements. On the big movies, a lot is figured out way ahead of the game to avoid those frantic last-minute changes. There is so much at stake, it has to run like a military operation. Of course, you still get the occasions where you're re-drafting the night before because even if one small thing changes it has a knock-on effect. It's a house of cards.

Which sequence from your career are you particularly proud of?
I'm very fond of the Tower Bridge finale in *Sherlock Holmes*. That was very heavily storyboarded. When I started on the movie it was the first thing I did. I met the producers and they said, 'Hi, nice to meet you, thanks for coming in, here's the script, now go and figure out the ending'. I was given a lot of freedom. I worked quite closely with the VFX team as there is so much green screen in that sequence. A lot of my shots are in there and it ended up very close to what I boarded; that is always satisfying.

I am also extremely proud of all my work on *Hanna*. I really enjoyed working with Joe Wright and the DoP Alwin Kuchler on that in Berlin, just the three of us sitting round a table being creative. Joe is a true visionary and a master film-maker. I loved the approach to the action, and we tried to make it as beautiful and fluid as it is brutal and thrilling. I think it elevates action cinema to another level; it's art

And if you could change one thing about the UK film industry, what would it be?
Better films! Honestly, a lot of our home-grown product is severely lacking. Maybe it's the scripts, maybe it's the type of projects that are gaining the funding but I think we have fallen way behind within the international market. Most of the large-scale movies made over here are funded by the US studios and the smaller films, which are often UK developed, are so limited in their ambition and appeal. We have Bond and Potter. We make some great period costume dramas, a ton of gangster movies and countless kitchen sink dramas… but what else? That's an extremely limited repertoire.

Take a look at the Asian market: they are making some of the most eclectic and ground-breaking cinema in the world. I am a huge fan of Korean and Japanese films. They vary in quality but they are brave, bold, complex, experimental, thrilling, entertaining and technically amazing. They cover so many genres and subjects, it's mind-boggling. They also get a lot of international recognition nowadays. Many Hollywood movies are remakes of Asian films, or they are copying their style and techniques. Asian films are winning awards at ceremonies all over the world and conquering festivals left, right and centre, because they are unique and bold! UK film should take note.

Mick Audsley - Editor

BAFTA-winning editor Mick Audlsey has worked with directors including Mike Newell, Terry Gilliam and Stephen Frears on a variety of films such as *Twelve Monkeys, Dangerous Liaisons, My Beautiful Launderette, The Grifters, Dirty Pretty Things, Tamara Drewe, High Fidelity* and *Harry Potter and the Goblet of Fire*.

As we speak, you've just complete Baltasar Kormakur's *Everest* for Universal and Working Title Films. How did you find that experience?
It has occupied just over a year of my life! We started shooting on January 16, 2014 and we finished the last bits of the mix updates and finalisation of the Dolby ATMOS mix in June 2015, and I'll be completing more 3D and VFX shots before release in September.
The film is set in 1996 and is the story is of two companies in a competitive adventure to climb Everest, one from New Zealand and one from California. They join forces and become involved in a tragedy. There is a lot of supposition and objective opinion as to exactly what happened; there were different accounts and none them quite matched although they correlated in certain areas. It's the nature of recall when at high altitude. So there has been a great deal of effort involved in getting things as accurate as we can. We've still got to make a movie that works, and the spirit of the movie and the participation of the relatives of the survivors have been applauded.

The filming unit went overseas, did you go with them?
The shoot broke down to be filmed in Kathmandu, Nepal and the journey up to Everest base camp. We then shot in a place called Val Senales in Italy, which was used for the proper snow and rock stuff, and then they went to Cinecittà Studios in Rome to do all the base camp material, using green screen backing. And then the rest was interiors for exteriors, shot in Pinewood. The cutting room went to Italy for approximately six weeks of that shoot; there's helicopter stuff and climbing foregrounds, so we had to paint out the ski-lifts.

Is it beneficial to be near your director when shooting and editing?
I really prefer to be close if I can, but not so close as to be in the way. As it was, we were all very busy and I wasn't able to spend too much with my boss really. He was very busy. I think it's very good if you can be on site and people can visit you. It was a very tough shoot, being on the mountains in winter. We were constantly having to check what we thought was necessary to make things work and see how it was going to read.

As the film progressed and you start to see the background [VFX] go in, you start to get a sense of the movie. Then if I go back and look at the early cuts before any of the information was put in, it can be really hard to gauge. You might even only have an eighth of a frame perhaps, just two figures. We had this thing called the 'Magic Mountain', which maps out Everest virtually and you can explore it in three dimensions, which was very useful. There's a night sequence and they actually found out exactly the arrangement of the stars as they would have been in 1996. That's detail for you!

The interesting editorial issue with *Everest* is that you know there's a calamity coming. It's based on a true story, and if people know the rudiments of the facts then the question is how long can you keep the audience in the set-up period, before you start throwing in the problems? If you've a complex number of characters, it always takes that bit longer to get them all in place and to care about them sufficiently. There's always a balance between how long it takes to set it all up and to let it go. We reduced and reduced that until we felt we got that balance correct.

You have always had great relationships with your directors: how often do you communicate with them?
In the case of *Everest*, I've never worked with Baltasar before so we had to sort of learn about each other. Certainly by the time we finished shooting, we were meeting every day for two or three hours. I would show him a reel and we would take notes and talk it through and he would have ideas, then I would show them to him the next day. That worked really well. I did the bulk of my work in private. I would work on my own for most of the day, and then we would have a couple of hours together.

You really want someone else to keep you fresh, as you get blind to the material. Someone might come along and say 'why have you done that?', and they give you a new perspective. I think a technique of having some distance yourself is useful; working on something and then putting it aside for three or four days. I'm much better in the mornings, getting in early and watch what I've made from a few days before. Then it speaks to you about what is wrong. By the end of the day, when I've had your nose to the windscreen, refashioning and re-cutting everything, my critical ability falls off by 6 o'clock. I'd love to hear about how other people do it and steal their techniques!

Do the studios ever insist that you keep a film within a certain length?
It has happened. I do remember with *Twelve Monkeys* that if the film came in under two hours, then Terry retained his final cut. We were filming it in Philadelphia and Baltimore, and I was in the realms of two hours for that cut. So I said to him that I could get it down to 119 minutes if he didn't mind me nipping a few bits out, and nobody will ever witness a film that he didn't have sole control over. He said 'Go for it!'.

In the case of *Everest*, it's more the evolution of telling the story that brings the film down in length. It wasn't a case of 'let's cut this out to get the time down' like it was a TV slot, it was a case of articulating this material as best we can and making the story work as coherently as possible. I was very keen for it not to be overly long, because it's a harrowing subject and I just didn't think you'd get through it in the cinema.

When you are editing, you have input from the studio, the director and producer. How do you deal with all that input?

You need to be a diplomat. I think the skill, if I can call it that, is finding a balance between what you feel the film should be, your own internal narrative mechanism and your belief in that, and an openness to listen to everyone else around you. You are going to hear what might be unhelpful suggestions, and you've got to take them on board and try them for longer than you may do if you are left to your own devices. So it's a question of receiving all this information and direction from the director, the producer, the exec producer, all of the people that surround you, and hanging on to what you feel the film should be yourself. It's a bit of a high-wire act to get through that.

And editors can spend a lot of time in their chair with so much material...

We spent a lot of man hours on [*Everest*]. There's a complexity to the story and you've got to give everything their hour in court, as it were. Obviously, it takes two seconds to lift something out so, in a way, the answer is to let the film live and see how things juxtapose. Don't be too greedy to take stuff out; let it live a bit because you will find things, you discover things about it. Even if you think a scene may go in the end, keep exploring it until you are sure.

Do you have a secret bin where you hide things?

Yes, definitely! I have a very private bin that largely holds things that are unwatchable because I don't think I've done them quite right. I like to keep copies of things and keep scrupulous notes. The answer is to not close your mind. I've made some really bad errors of judgement and taken something out, and then someone's had a different point of view. You have to be prepared to shift your ground gracefully and admit that you got it wrong.

***Everest* is the latest film in a very illustrious career. How did you make your first steps in the industry, and did you always want to be an editor?**

No, I actually came from an arts school background of graphics, and animation was the first area of film that I was interested in. I was a graduate at the Hornsey College of Art, made a short animation and managed to get into the Royal College of Art film School on an MA post-grad course. It was sort of the beginning of when the national film school was about to be born, in the early 70s. I was attracted to film-making but I didn't know what side, and I realised quite quickly that professional animation was quite a lonely business and was then drawn to drama.

I did work in a cutting room at the film school as an assistant but [editing] wasn't really on my map at all. I was interested in sound, and I did a lot of sound editing for the BFI production board. There were lots of union issues at the time; you could only work in non-unionised film-making. So when I left the RCOA, the only places I could legitimately go were the BFI production board, the Arts Council and the BBC. I worked as a recordist and as a sound editor.

Coincidentally, after going out and shooting stuff, I was asked to cut a pilot that we shot. Those days you need to make three-minute pilots to get a grant to make a production board film. We shot a test of a theatre production of *King Lear* in Leeds; there was nobody to cut the pilot and my colleague suggested I do it. The minute I started, I thought 'Ah, this is what I want to do'. It was literally overnight. I just found it incredible that you could stick things together and get this visceral excitement from it all. I realised that that was where the power of it all was.

I was lucky because, at that time, the BFI production board had a good group of people like Bill Douglas, Mamoun Hassan, Charles Reese, Kevin Brownlow, Peter Smith and Peter Greenaway. There was a nice convivial sharing thing going on and, looking back, I think I absorbed a lot from them. I got that pilot, then I got the whole film and I never stopped after that.

The business with the union was critical, because it was a closed shop, which meant there wasn't a legitimate way in; you needed a job to get a card and you needed a card to get a job. The nature of it was really stultifying. Eventually I had started editing pictures and a wonderful sound mixer named Doug Turner helped me get an ACCT sound-editors card. Eventually I became 'legitimised' and went from there. It was very tough in those days and it felt like a very exclusive club that you were not invited to join.

Most of today's newcomers will start off as trainees or assistants; what qualities do you feel are the most important for those roles?

If a trainee or a second comes under the jurisdiction of my chosen first assistant editor, I leave that to them to make the right choice. The quality that they look for is not only for someone who has got all the technical knowledge required to run the complexities of a feature film cutting room, which are now immense, but somebody is who is a good team member and is going to fit in. Someone who has got a strong sense of themselves in relation to the team. People know that if they know their jobs very well then we don't have to police each other in any way.

I'm entirely reliant on the assistant editors running the material and the whole technical side of it. It's a huge job now; the workflows from camera to delivery are changing and they're complicated. The equipment, the uploading, the security and so on, it's all changing all the time. Nothing is standard. They have to run that in order to free us up to worry about the content and the rhythm of the movie.

In terms of young film-makers and people coming through the ranks, you're the head of the team, can you describe who is in your department?

In a pretty standard department for a film, in my experience, there would be myself, a first assistant editor, a second assistant editor and, possibly, a trainee. Bigger films require a larger number of personnel. If it's very heavily biased towards visual effects, early on you are going to need a VFX editor responsible for the circulation of the shots as they progress through their developing stages, in relation to the changing cut. So they are chasing the cut the whole time, and working with the VFX houses or supervisors. That again is an interface between a first assistant editor and the job of VFX editor. It's a hugely time-consuming and labour-intensive job. It tends to start in the latter part of shooting as the mass of material and the cut is starting to form.

The core of the team is three of us, four if you are lucky. There's always a lot of work to be done. If it's a VFX film, then that might expand according to the size of the project and the time demands.

What qualities that you see in people that are definite no-no's?

I don't think you necessarily need to want to be an editor as such, to be a good assistant editor. They are in many ways quite different. I think it helps if you don't get a sense from your assistant that they are about to jump into your shoes, or that they really want to be directors. They should understand what the world of editorial is, celebrate and enjoy it. It's a sort of humbleness with a great deal of curiosity. You just find people you like working with that are also very good at their jobs and I've been incredibly lucky working with the best people in London.

How do newcomers come to you, or how do you find them?

I don't know, really! I've just have an extremely good flow of people come to work with me for five to six years at a stretch. On my last few films, I've worked with Pani [Ahmadi-Moore], and it seems to work very well. I have nothing but praise for the people I've ended up working with and I would find it very hard to go into projects the size of *Everest* without that sort of cohesion. It's a team business and I need their support, judgement and guidance.

There was a time when the wonderful Dan Roberts leafleted me for many years before he worked with me, we did about four or five films together. I had a stack of his CVs and eventually we met and he was free. It was great, and he's gone on to become an editor in his own right. So people sort of come to me, I've never really had someone phone up and say, 'can I have a job please?' It's always through people you know.

Do you feel experienced professionals like yourself should be actively helping today's newcomers?

I'm passionate about helping younger people get a smoother entry into the business and am hoping to organise future events with something called 'Sprocket Rocket Soho'. It is really a way of bringing people together. The digital world is rather isolated, and this will allow younger film-makers and more experienced ones to trade thoughts, and also make older film-makers accessible to the young. To show them that we are real people with the same worries and the same difficulties when making movies. We will have three or four gatherings a year and some side events, teaching and things. This was born out of the feeling that the digital film-making world has put us into more and more isolation; we're not getting together in the same way we did as I remember it, in analogue cutting rooms where the doors were a bit more open.

And this ability to interact on a personal level is an important skill to take into editing jobs...

The nature of the work we do in the editorial side of film-making is, by its nature, intimate. You're in a room, or two rooms, and you're going spend a big part of the week banging in to each other. So I think it's very important that you have an empathy and affection for one another that allows you to work well. Everybody's job is very difficult and they've got huge responsibilities in their work day. If we all understand what our roles are well enough and we divide that, hopefully correctly, then we all understand each other's needs and demands. Generally, if people feel relaxed and secure and that you look after each other, then people work well.

I like it to be kind of open; I don't believe in the sense of a hierarchy as such. That hierarchy exists anyway, and I don't need to overstate it with the people I've chosen. They're supportive and respectful, and hopefully I can return that from the other point of view.

What other advice would you give to aspiring editors?

I think the best advice is to start doing that job, however big or small. If you've got a friend who's making a film and they allow you to edit it, start doing it. Start working with people, start cutting movie.

Also, try and understand as much about screenplay writing and film structure. Try and see as wide a range of movies as you can. You can learn a lot from big £200m Hollywood films, or something shot on somebody's phone. If you are open to it all, it's a visual and audio language, and there's always a lot to learn. As an editor, you're essentially making somebody else's film. You may possess it, ingest it and put it out again, but it's a collaborative medium. You're going to have some great ideas and you're going to have some terrible ones but in the end, you don't have a final say in cutting a film; you have a very big say, but you're making it for other people. I think that the sooner that young people adopt that sort of humility and that sort of diplomacy that you need in the cutting room, you can go pretty far.

Going back to your films, you edited Stephen Frears' adaptation of Nick Hornby's *High Fidelity*. Did you have a lot of material to work with there?

It wasn't a huge amount by today's standards, because Stephen is very economical in his shooting and knows what he wants. I also think in those days we used to get selected takes, so if you shot 16 takes then you probably only got three or four. It wasn't huge at all in the way in which it is now. I was probably getting between 40 minutes and about an hour a day, for 10 weeks, which is not the same as getting six hours rushes a day for a year.

It's a hugely funny film; did that come through in the edit suite?

I did laugh all the time. I adored that film from the get-go, and I don't remember having to cut it for laughs or anything because it was so intrinsically funny. What was interesting, there was a legacy of affection for Nick's book about the record shop in Camden Town. The idea of making it in Chicago... some people were a bit sniffy about that, claiming that it would compromise Nick's book. Of course, it was brilliant and, Chicago being what it is, it transposed, but that was as much to do with those wonderful actors and Stephen.

Everyone did such a great job, but I can't say it was effortless. Deciding on the music was the trickiest thing. It was a tortuous process, choosing what we as a group wanted to put in and to then get the clearances and then the financial side of clearing them. It went on for weeks, I think. I remember the dubbing theatre being like the floor of the stock market: 'we could afford that one [song] if we get rid of that one'. It was all trading. I can't emphasise it enough, though, Steven did a brilliant job, it was beautifully shot, beautifully played, the writing is heaven. What more do you want as an editor?

Is it a particular challenge to edit comedy? You've said before that you have to consciously leave in time to accommodate the laughs?

If you are making a film for the cinema, there's a sort of chemistry that goes on where laughter promotes laughter. So, if there are 300 people laughing around you, you're going to miss the next line, so you need to loosen it up a little bit, give it time to die down.

[With *High Fidelity*], we realised that there were certain things that were pretty much going to give a guaranteed reaction on that scale, so needed a little bit more time. It's not so good if you are on your own in the living room, watching it on a DVD, because bits of it feel a bit slacker, but we decided to go with the 300 people having a good time in the cinema. They need a bit more because they are not going to hear the next line.

Comedic values also need an absolute precision in communication terms. You've got to make sure all the things are in the right place; if you miss a line you are shooting yourself in the foot. So you've got to make sure all of the building blocks are set up the situation are perfectly placed and communicated so that you get the pay off. And that's the editor's job really, to orchestrate that correctly.

You also edited *Harry Potter and the Goblet of Fire*, what is it like to be involved with such a juggernaut of a franchise?

I'd had a brief involvement with the second one [*Harry Potter and the Chamber of Secrets*], I did a sort of uncredited guest appearance. Chris Columbus, the Director, was finishing the first one and that overlapped with beginning of part two and David [Heyman, producer] and Chris asked me to stand in for Peter Honess, who was the editor they wanted to do the whole of the film. So I did the first two months of *Chamber of* Secrets, the sequence where the cars fly over Kings Cross, working quite closely with the second unit director Peter MacDonald.

So, I'd had two months in Potterland when I came back for number four [*Goblet of Fire*]. I remember we were sat down to watch the outgoing third film [*Prisoner of Azkaban*] directed by Alfonso [Cuaron]; I thought it was great, and remember feeling slightly queasy afterwards thinking, 'OK, now we've got to pull the next one off!' The franchise was starting to really explode and there's the feeling of are we going to be the ones who trip up?

A year into that project, we previewed it at a secret screening in Chicago before it was complete; there were bits of blue screen and green screen. I saw all these kids and their parents and realised the scale of the whole thing. When you sit in a theatre and these kids are absolutely spellbound, in many ways it makes the job easier. Our one [*Goblet of Fire*] was quite dark and quite long; I thought perhaps it was too long for kids, but Tanya Seghatchian, who was one of the producers, said, 'Don't worry about it, they love the [Potter] world, they just want to be there', and she was absolutely right. Warner Bros. were immensely supportive of us, so they really just let us get on and finish it. There were notes that came along, but they were just how to make it better really. There was never a sense of them wanting us to push it off in some other direction. We were encouraged to carry on to get to where we were going to; a great feeling.
Goblet of Fire also had all the underwater photography, which Peter MacDonald did very well. We had a tank built and divers in there for weeks on end, and the kids being chucked in the water. It was incredible! Post production was heaven as well, once we started seeing the film we were going to have and the visual effects started to come in. It was a very happy experience. I was on that for 70- plus weeks, and I think we had something like nine AVIDs at one stage.

Finally, if anybody who reads this ends up in your team one day, what's the one thing you would like them to know about the way you work?

Always have a sense of humour and remember that making a film is a privilege. It's a crazy alchemy that brings together the ability to spend money and make films at that sort of level, and we consider ourselves to be lucky in the respect that we've landed there. It's such a precarious business nowadays; we've never made the film before, each one is a prototype, an exploration, and there's a lot of stress and strain on everybody involved. It's unpredictable, and sometimes people go a bit nuts on the way.

We're lucky enough in the editorial department to come in pretty early on in the process, so we get to meet everybody involved. And you're going to be there, fingers crossed, to the bitter end, and have the pleasure of finishing the thing, of seeing it through. It's an exciting exploration. That to me is what counteracts the enormous amount of hard work and grind. Once you get to the end, it's very rewarding. If you hear people talking fondly of a film, that gives me enormous pleasure. Film brings people together in a common endeavour; you talk about it over lunch, get excited about it, and you share it with everybody.

CHAPTER 4

Pearls of Wisdom

The following inspirational comments and exclusive advice have been given to me from a wide range of industry professionals, specifically for this book.

Carola Ash
Director of Europe, Academy of Motion Picture Arts and Sciences (AMPAS)

I would say that persistence and clarity as to what you want to do are the two main factors to take into account when wanting to break into film or TV. You may get rejected the first time you apply, but you really do have to keep trying as it does eventually pay off. Self- belief is very important, and don't let anyone put you off your ultimate goal.

I have also found that a lot of people trying to break into the industry often want to be a writer/director/producer, but the skills that are most needed in the industry are the crafts. Making a film is a collaborative process and each person is equally important, so think carefully of what ultimately is the best route to take. Each year there are more and more Oscars being won by British craft members.

Amanda Berry
Chief Executive, British Academy of Film and Television Arts (BAFTA)

Find out as much as you can about the industry you want to get into. At BAFTA we want to make it easier for career starters from all backgrounds to get their foot in the door in the creative industries, and help talented people starting out in film, television and games, with events, scholarships, mentoring schemes. People can also find tips and advice for career-starters on BAFTA Guru.

Don't expect to start at the place you want to get to! Looking back at my career, every job I have done has given me the experience I needed to do the job I do at BAFTA. And don't be afraid to ask for guidance. Most people will support you, and if you aren't helped, move on and ask someone else. I got into the industry through a work placement, and we now do a number of paid internships at BAFTA. Make sure to surround yourself with like-minded people, as this will support you as your career develops.

Prepare for interviews and research the company as thoroughly as you can. Look at their websites and watch their TV programmes and/or films before the interview and have a constructive opinion on them. Also expect to be asked about your favourite film or TV programme.

Throughout it all, 'believe and achieve, doubt and live without'; in other words, don't give up and keep believing you will find the right job for you.

Lord David Puttnam
Producer (*The Mission, The Killing Fields, Chariots of Fire, Midnight Express, Bugsy Malone*)

Someone once asked me, 'How does a movie get made?' and I replied that you reach a point where you're so in love with the idea you refuse to allow it *not* to get made. If you want to succeed in this industry, you must fundamentally believe in the value of what you have to offer. If you don't believe it, no one else will! In your career you will need a combination of teamwork, serendipity and hunch but, most importantly, you must have the sheer will-power and tenacity to drive your idea forward.

I would say that networking among your peers early in your career, and then carrying on doing so, is incredibly important. It enables you to start building a 'web of trust' to figure out who you can genuinely learn from, and who you can seek advice and support from in a crisis.
You must be prepared to share your learning, your experiences and your mistakes at every possible opportunity; this is the very best way to ensure that you remain equipped to deal with a rapidly changing environment.

Finally, I'd like to share a quote from the play *Man and Superman* by George Bernard Shaw: 'Be true to the dreams of your youth'.

Alison Small
CEO, the Production Guild

Don't ever give up. Self-belief and determination are key to succeeding in the industry. Getting your first foot in the door can involve quite a bit of knocking; do your research by finding the details of production companies, broadcasters and studios. A personal approach always works, so contact the relevant people directly and outline why you'd be an asset to their team.

Networking is also essential when working in film and TV. Have the confidence to approach a variety of people; you never know who they might know. It's a very collaborative industry and no one succeeds alone.

When you find that job, always use your initiative. It might be asking the crew whether they need some water, or the DoP and director whether they would like a cup of tea. Always have a professional can-do attitude and actively look to help solve problems. Doing it with a smile also goes a long way.

Make the most of every opportunity. One of the best things you can do to help you move forward is to volunteer for tasks, no matter how small. This may lead to you meeting someone who will remember you and take you onto their next project. It's a great way to build contacts and show people what you are capable of. And, as we now live in an age of social media where information can be distributed very quickly, it's essential that you honour the confidentially of any production on which you work.

Film and TV are fast-moving industries, so it's essential that you learn as much about the industry as possible and keep your skills up to date. Try to gain useful skills, particularly when starting out, which might help you stand out from the crowd. Health and safety management qualifications for example, will not only help keep you and your colleagues safe, but will look great on your CV. At the Production Guild we run a variety of courses from runner training to production management to help people. We also run a series of seminars and events for our members, which helps keep them up to date with all the latest financial, fiscal, and commercial developments within the US, UK and European production environments. People can find tips and advice on our YouTube channel.

Dinah Caine CBE
Chair of the Board, Creative Skillset

I'll let you into a secret; no one really enjoys networking, but in the creative industries it's a must. Working in film and TV can involve long hours over a long period, intense working and risky projects, so employers want to hire people they know and trust.

That doesn't mean, however, that if you don't have contacts already the doors are closed to you: seek out opportunities to network at festivals and events; set up your own projects and look for collaborators; stay in touch with the people you train with. You never know when someone might open up an opportunity to you.

If you're looking at a higher education course, make sure it has good links to industry; Creative Skillset's Tick accreditation is a sure sign that it does. There's also Hiive (*www.hiive.co.uk*), the free-to-join professional network for creative people, which will help you to connect with like-minded individuals as well as showing you some of the best events, courses and job vacancies in the creative industries.

Getting your foot on the ladder can be tough, so be prepared to be adaptable. Your first job may not be your dream job but if you have the right attitude you can always learn from any experience, develop your skills and move your career onwards. Make yourself valuable and memorable; the people you work for will notice and appreciate if you are enthusiastic, willing and proactive so always attack every job with your best effort and you will be rewarded.

Throughout your career you will never stop learning, so if you can keep that thirst for knowledge and an open mind, it will stand you in good stead. Creative Skillset's website has loads of resources, job profiles and real life stories to get you started. There is also Trainee Finder (*www.traineefinder.co.uk*) which matches Ticked-course graduates and recommended industry newcomers with productions looking for trainees in film, TV (high-end drama and children's), games, animation and VFX.

The creative industries are a brilliant place to work, where you'll be surrounded by passionate, talented people making some of the best creative output in the world so make sure you enjoy what you do and good luck!

Roy Button
Executive Vice President, Warner Bros. Productions Ltd.

Never sit back and think you've made it, and always try to better your last work and improve yourself. There's always more to learn and more to do.

Amma Asante
Director, Screenwriter (*Belle, A Way of Life, A United Kingdom*)

We each have a champion out there. For every 20 rejections, there is someone out there who will get your brand of creativity and will champion you. It's about not giving up before you reach that person. There's one at every stage; just keep plugging away, banging on doors and honing your talent.

John Yorke
Former MD of Company Pictures; former BBC Controller of Drama Production; author: *Into the Woods: How Stories Work and Why We Tell Them* (Penguin, 2014). Now Managing Director of Angel Station TV and Drama Consultant to King Bert Productions

How do you break into the industry as a writer? You just have to be persistent. It took me three years of unemployment! In the meantime, enter every single writing competition you can. Send great specs, befriend people who know the people commissioning, and get writers to recommend you to their agents. Get your work put on in pubs. Write for theatre and radio: it's much easier to get your work developed there and they are brilliant training grounds. Having a few great spec scripts ready to send out is especially important – they are your calling card in the industry.

Above all, you just have to be very tenacious because it's really competitive. But if your work is good, you will get there. We want to be sent scripts that keep us gripped from beginning to end. Work on that and your writing will get commissioned.

John has developed his book on storytelling for TV and film into a practical how-to online course: www.johnyorkestory.com

Rebecca O'Brien
Producer (*The Wind That Shakes the Barley, Looking for Eric, My Name is Joe, I, Daniel Blake*)

When I started out in film a long time ago, I thought a producer was a big fat man with a cigar hanging out the side of his mouth and his feet on the desk. It never occurred to me that I could be that person (albeit without the cigar, and my feet are on the windowsill). I just loved being involved in film, and was happy to do anything to make it work and to learn about the different elements. I think it was the keenness to muck in and be useful which kept the jobs coming. Being able to drive was essential – it also helped in finding temporary jobs when there wasn't any film work – and persistence in following leads and not being put off by rejection was also key.

The people who come to work with us often think they want to be a director or producer, but when they leave with the reality of the business ringing in their ears they've usually discovered a career that suits them. We've had people who've become a casting director, a comedy writer, a post-production supervisor, a media lawyer, a company manager, a production manager, a documentary director and a producer: all great jobs. So keep your eyes open and choose to specialise in the thing you like doing best.

Jed Mercurio
Writer/Director (*Line of Duty, Critical, Lady Chatterley's Lover*)

I took the traditional route into TV, by starting as a junior hospital doctor! There are plenty of people who study media or film as a route into the industry, but I'd caution against believing they're the only gateways. Many successful careers have begun in unexpected places, and having an unusual CV can sometimes work to your advantage.

Contrary to popular opinion, ours is a very open industry. You can go from watching a programme on TV to working on it in a matter of days. If you work hard and have ability, you'll succeed in the end. But no one succeeds by their own endeavour alone, so seek out the people who can enable you. They are the ones who've done work you admire that you intend to aspire to. Make contact with them; chances are, like most of us, they'll respond to flattery.

My beginning was as a scriptwriter. I was exceedingly fortunate that my clumsy efforts were taken seriously and developed by mentors. Some of these working relationships are ones I still depend on to this day. But not all relationships with more experienced professionals are supportive. If you find you can't do your best work if you follow the guidance of a certain producer or executive, you should have the courage to leave that relationship behind. When you do find the right champion, you'll know it, because you'll be proud of your work, whether it succeeds or not.

I'm very fortunate to have acquired a great deal of influence over how my scripts are realised; whether I produce or direct them is now largely my own choice. Before I reached that stage, I had to challenge for a say in how actors delivered my lines (or didn't) and how directors shot my scenes (or didn't). Confrontation rarely works, and in the long term it's far too damaging to creative relationships. Recruit people to your point of view. There are directors and actors I worked with nearly twenty years ago whom I'm still delighted to collaborate with.

Think long and hard if this is the right career for you. If it is, give it your all. Take-offs are optional; landings are mandatory. Everyone makes mistakes. You can't play the shot you just missed, only the one in front of you. Experience is the quality you've gained just after you most needed it. You'll only get the benefit if you keep going.

Jacqui Taunton Fenton
Head of Production Talent, BBC Drama

If you are thinking of a career in broadcast media you need to be prepared for hard work, but most of all you will need the following characteristics: passion, enthusiasm, determination, creativity and flexibility.

The first step is to try and spend as much time as possible working in a TV environment, so get some work experience with media organisations, production companies, or broadcasters. Having this on your CV will show enthusiasm and determination.

You should always explore all the options when trying to add to your skills and experience. Does your university or college have a radio station or TV channel where you can volunteer? Companies specialising in corporate videos can be great places to learn camera and production skills. Networking is key to getting on in the industry, so have the confidence to speak to people, make yourself known, ask for contact details – most people are willing to offer help and advice but you need to make the first move. Contacts are vital!

When applying for a job or placement, you need to maximise your chances of securing a placement against hundreds of other applicants by preparing for the interview carefully. Watch lots of television! Get to know as much as you can about the programmes you love; watch the credits and familiarise yourself with different production companies and the various roles in television. Think about the things you like and dislike about a programme or the characters.

It's relatively easy to find production companies and broadcasters' contact details on the internet, so once you've got an idea of who you'd like to approach, write to them directly. Show them how passionate you are about TV, but back it up by telling them how much you know about their output. Nothing annoys me more than someone who doesn't know anything about the programmes they're applying for, or says they haven't had time to watch recent episodes. TV is an oversubscribed industry, so not having time to prepare properly is not an option.

However difficult it may be in the beginning, if you are determined to work in the industry don't give up! Most people working in the industry will tell you that it took a lot of blood, sweat and tears to get a foot in the door. Keep up to date with what's going on, keep networking and continue to work towards your goal; with hard work and determination you will get there.

Gillian Berrie
Producer, Sigma Films (*Under The Skin, Starred Up, Red Road*)

Get to really understand the business side of the market. So often, we filmmakers are strong on the creative aspect of drama but it isn't enough. One has to know the market trends, the aspects of your project that have value, what your project is worth internationally and how you are going to reach your audience. Think about how to create a sustainable business, and create a long-term strategy that transcends the typical hand-to-mouth existence

Debbie Vertue
Head of Production, Hartswood Films (*Sherlock, Edge of Heaven, Lady Chatterley's Lover*)

It's quite incredible that we have so many different jobs in one industry: from writers and drivers to caterers and creative leaders in the form of directors and producers; the list is endless. I started as a runner. As a runner, generally, you're looking to move on up as quickly as possible, and I was no different. It took me four-and-a-half years, as the unions made it frustratingly difficult. Starting out there again though, I wouldn't rush. It's a perfect place to meet people who can help you at the beginning, and who you'll probably meet again years on.

It's also a brilliant position to observe from, watching other crew do their job and deciding whether it could be the right one for you. Don't be afraid to ask questions, but pick your timing and don't be too opinionated. You'll probably make assumptions in your head as to how you might do something differently, but keep this to yourself as, 9 times out of 10, you'll see there's a reason it's done that way. It will show you how hard everyone has to work, how long the hours are, what great camaraderie a crew has, how creative each and every department is and how good they are at their job. It will teach you how rigorously we observe the clock, how terrific we are at problem solving, what a fantastic industry it is to work in and how you're only as good as your last job – so make an impression!

Sue Greenleaves
Agent, Independent Talent

Loyalty is rare in the film industry, so honour it when you can. And always be nice to the runner.

Sarah Greenwood
Production Designer (*Atonement, Pride & Prejudice, Sherlock Holmes, Anna Karenina*)

Production designers never know what they'll be asked to do next. Period, contemporary, futuristic; it could be anything, so you have to keep your eyes and ears open all the time, drinking in the world around you. It's also important to study human nature and human relationships, and how they manifest themselves visually. The characters and the story are the baseline of what you're trying to convey and, within that story, you aspire to create a complete world by taking risks and being brave.

You need to have enormous self-belief and the courage of your convictions, but equally you've got to be able to listen to others and admit your mistakes.
It's important to build relationships with people that inspire you to better yourself. I was lucky to meet Joe Wright who was like a mad fizzing animal, just brilliant! We have a totally collaborative relationship; I push him and he pushes me as we try to better each other's ideas. I've also gathered a great team around me. There are four or five key people who are with me on every project and then others who come and go depending on scale and style of project, but it's a pool of such talent and creative energy that together we are far bigger and better than the sum of our parts. Our approach allows for creative freedom without fear. Fear, laziness and sloppiness are the enemy. If you're going to fail, it's better to have had a damn good try.

When I start to design, I immerse myself in imagery – anything that's relevant – and then it's a process of refinement and simplification, boiling it all down until you find a key that unlocks the whole film. The key might be a simple colour-contrast, or a multi-layer philosophy that gives you rules and a structure to follow.

Starting a film, you have to rationalise everything and understand which sets are designed for very specific shots and which have to sustain days of filming. Then you can add depth, drama, angles, scale and tone where it's most needed to sustain the action. Above all else, it's pointless cutting corners because in the long run it never saves anything: not time, not money, not creativity. Do it properly or don't do it at all. And the thing is, when design is working really well, the audience won't even be aware of it!

There are many paths to the job that's right for you so if one route doesn't suit, try another. I started in theatre design before moving into television and eventually film. What I love about film is that every shot is a point of view, and your set can be something as small as a pinhead or as massive as a universe.

Tom Rye
Second Assistant Director (*War Horse, World War Z, Pan, In the Heart of the Sea*)

No matter where you start, aim high and stick to your principles. I started on a soap opera and always said I wanted to work on feature films. I then moved up to TV drama and eventually, after years of doing major TV, I made a conscious decision I wanted to do films. So I did what goes against every freelancer's instinct when unemployed; I turned down the first offer of work I got, because it was a TV drama. Two weeks passed and I had the feeling of 'never working again' doom. Then the phone rang and it was the production manager from *War Horse.* Needless to say I've never looked back.

I've nothing against smaller projects at all. In fact they are often more enjoyable to work on, and I'm sure I will work on them again. But I made a decision and stuck to it. Aim high.

Lauren Dark
Producer (*War Book, Mediastan*)

I think making work in any way that you can is probably the best way to get a foot in the door and feel like you're moving forward. When I was a student, I used to help on any short film advertised on Shooting People that would have me. If you can't find work on other peoples' short films, generate your own!

I still found it really difficult to get in the room with people who could give me a job when I graduated, and didn't have a lot to put on my CV. Even if the short film doesn't feel like it's leading anywhere at the time, you might be surprised at the contacts or opportunities that come out of it later on. That's why I think that even though it's nice when you have the opportunity to talk to experienced film-makers on set, the people who can often really help are your peers. When we're looking for additional crew generally we'll ask the relevant department who else they like to work with, and then get in touch with them. So you might have been a runner with someone on a short film who is then going to do some dailies on a film the week after and can recommend you.

Most of the interviews or jobs I have got have been friends I've made along the way, mainly as a runner, putting me forward or mentioning my name. In fact I got a job at Sixteen Films, where I worked for nearly five years, because of a friend I made when I was a runner on a film. She's still one of my closest friends, and I still ask her advice and share most ideas and projects with her.

Holly Pullinger
Production Manager (*Fortitude, The Smoke, Dr Who*)

If I'm in the lovely lull in between jobs, full of kindness, sympathy and gentle wisdom to those coming up, I would say things like: always be honest about what you know and don't know and ask for help when you're in a jam. Everyone around you knows more than you and will want to help rather than have you struggle on your own, possibly making the wrong decision; never forget we're a team. Listen to everything that's happening in the production office, read what passes through your hands to the photocopier, always be positive, commit to the job you have, and always be willing, every single day, to go above and beyond what is asked of you.

If, however, I have a coffee cup stapled to my right thumb, a phone in each ear and am typing furiously with my feet, before you ask me any question... READ... THE... CALL SHEET!

Jude Campbell
First Assistant Director (*Monsters: Dark Continent, Mr Stink, Utopia, The Gunman*)

Have your own car, even if it's the standard AD Golf. Find out quick what's considered to be good as a runner, and then be 10-times better in every way. You move fast in this industry if you impress and to impress, break the rulebook slightly. Offer to work extra hours, offer to pick up crew or drop them home even if it's out of your way. The small things count, even making lots of good tea all day. Crew will notice and remember.

Always be upbeat but not annoying, and don't step on others to better yourself. Be sharp and aware on set, so that when somebody suddenly throws you some bigger responsibility you don't get flustered. Never be late, arrive extra early if necessary, and your second and third AD will learn to trust you; there is always something they need assistance with, especially at 6am in the morning in the middle of a car park in the pitch dark. And finally, it always helps to know where the good coffee shops are!

Gwen Gorst
Former Production Supervisor, World Productions (*The Bletchly Circle, Line of Duty*) & Script Editor, Mainstreet Pictures (*Unforgotten, I Want My Wife Back*)

My biggest bone of contention is when we get CVs, letters or emails from individuals who have recently graduated from film school or university introducing themselves as directors or DoPs, just on the back of having directed or produced their student films.

More than often they are doing themselves a huge disservice because that is never going to be something that we can offer them; even if they were the most talented individual in the world, it would never be approved by a broadcaster! If they were explaining their experience and saying that they were looking for jobs as a camera trainee or a runner, however, they would often be really successful and would speed their career on by finding the relevant on-set experience.

Once people have been given a job on a production, as a runner, for example, they should look like they actually want to be there. In the past it has driven me nuts when you know how many people want the opportunity to work on a production and yet you have someone who looks completely disinterested and bored. It often *is* boring and tiring, but showing willingness and enthusiasm – even if it's fake – is far more likely to make people ask you back.

Emma Lawson
Producer/Production Executive, Roughcut TV (*Cuckoo, Count Arthur Strong, People Just Do Nothing*)

Don't be narrow minded, or snobbish; you will learn something from every job that you do. When you are trying to get a foot in the door, take every opportunity that comes your way, regardless of whether you want to end up in the field in the long run. I did everything, from casting, locations, news research, floor running, office running... basically, as much as I could get my hands on. I always wanted to work in production, but wanted to gather as much experience as possible before choosing my field. Every job gives you something new, and you meet so many new people. Having the opportunity to see more of individual departments from the ground up has given me a good, rounded view on production, which has helped shape how I manage productions today.

When you are working, don't sit down or look bored; always be ready for action. There is always something that you can be doing: making tea, washing up, watching through company back catalogues, filing, office tidying, making more tea, reading proposals. Even if it is boring, when people see you being proactive they see potential in you, and will start to consider you for more work. And if someone asks you to do something, do it right away; learn to prioritise and manage your time, and maintain a can-do attitude.

Throughout your career, be tenacious and never give up. The runners I have employed are the ones who kept getting in touch. Runners' CVs often get lost in a mass of other emails, and time doesn't always permit for reading and responding to individual letters. So being persistent pays. I have one girl, for example, who very politely emailed every couple of months, updating me on her progress, and her ambitions. As soon as I had an opportunity she was the first person I got in touch with as I had admired her tenacity and general manner. She started with us doing work experience, and then did dailies running work and I am about to employ her for the first time as a full-time production runner on a long-running studio sitcom.

Always respect the people who have gone before you; everyone started somewhere, and most people can empathise with how hard it is to get a foot in the door. Do your research, and find the people at the top of their game in the field you would like to be in. Email them, express an interest in their work, show respect for them, ask if they have advice for you or if you could shadow them at any point. Building relationships with people is key to surviving in the industry. Keep in touch with the people that help you, and work hard for them if they do offer you an opportunity.

Finally, always remember that you are replaceable. There are a million people who want to be runners, so make sure you do it for the right reasons, and if you get it right, you will never 'work' a day in your life. Cheesy, I know, but true. I will never make a million doing what I do, and the hours that I work do compromise my family and social life, but it gives me huge satisfaction. I still bounce out of bed and look forward to getting in to work, as I love my job and I know how lucky I am to be doing it. Never get complacent, as there will always be someone waiting in the wings ready to take your coveted spot.

Yuen-Wai Liu
Assistant Production Coordinator (*The Dark Knight Rises, Kingsman: The Secret Service, Now You See Me 2*)

People coming into this industry need to have a full grasp of what it is they're signing up for: hard work, long hours and no appreciation for what they go through! They will have to come in first and leave last, make the tea, clean the kitchen and do all the rubbish jobs that no one wants to do without complaint. The jobs may seem unimportant but it's a reflection on the team and the production that they are organised and tidy, so you can't be lazy, huff about coming in early or argue back. Usually the person asking you to do something has more experience and knows how to run things. It's great to have fresh new ideas but you also need to know your place and when your opinion isn't required.

You must be committed to the job, and understand the hours and effort that you will have to put in. There is a new generation of coordinators and production managers who actually do believe that life is more important, and that production isn't the be all and end all, but you are generally not able to have days off or leave early during a production. You still find a lot of old-school production managers who do not think you should take a day off to go to a funeral, but it's slowly changing and hopefully you get to work with people who are sympathetic to the fact you'd like to go to your best friend's wedding.

While you are working, make yourself indispensable. Runners are incredibly important to the team but, whereas other members of the team are relied upon for their knowledge of the production and the contacts, the runner can be replaced. Remember, you're only as good as your last job; the industry is small and word gets around! So smile, make the tea, jump up to help when someone you don't know walks into the office and make friends with all the suppliers, couriers, security and delivery guys because they will be the ones to help you when things go tits up, and they also talk to other production people...

Always be as organised as possible and learn to prioritise. It's difficult when everyone is throwing things at you which all seem equally as important, so if you are ever unsure of anything, ask. Similarly, if things go wrong, don't stay quiet and try to hide it if it's happened under your watch; it's human nature and it's better to just own up to it and work out how to fix it together.

Nicky Ball
National Crew & Facilities Manager, Creative England

When applying for a job always make sure you tailor your cover email and CV for the role you are applying for; don't just send a standard email and CV that are generic and unfocused. I have read too many CVs from people applying for, say, a floor runner role, but the profile on their CV tells me they want to work in the camera department

If you're passionate about working in a particular department, be prepared to have an opinion. What films or directors inspire you? What do you like? What film would you have loved to work on? So many people get to interview stage, say they are passionate about something but are unable to back it up with examples

Even if you've just completed a university course and been working in a team as a DoP, producer or first AD, when you get out into the industry you need to be realistic about the level you pitch yourself at: camera trainee, floor runner, production runner. But think outside the box; everyone wants to do those roles, but not many people think about working as a location assistant, grip trainee, accounts assistant or production office runner and this is where more opportunities may lie.

Don't be set back by companies who never respond to your emails; keep on plugging away, do your research as to what companies are out there and remember all opportunities are springboards to other work including time spent working at film festivals, on short films and on corporate shoots

Finally, pass your driving test and save up for a car. And remember that please and thank you go a long way as does being on time, using your initiative and being prepared to muck in.

Nick Ferguson
Production Manager - commercials, Ridley Scott Associates

There are ways to behave in a production office and although it might sound militant, my advice would be to keep your head down and to understand that you are in a professional working environment. Someone who goes around the office talking out of turn isn't going to get asked back. Work out the dynamic, take half a step back and actually listen to what's going on. It will pay dividends.

Vicki Allen and Tamana Bleasdale
The Call Time Company (*calltimecompany.com*)

It's a tough industry to break into and it's very competitive, so try and make a good impression so you get the next call. Here are our top tips on what will make you stand out from the rest, based on the qualities demonstrated by the most successful runners on our books.
Firstly, try and say yes to every paid job you get offered; contacts and opportunities can often come from surprising sources.

When you have been booked for a job, buy *two* alarm clocks, and always try and be 10 minutes early for your call time. While a car is pretty much essential, don't use not having one as an excuse for being late or for not taking a job. Don't turn up for work drunk, on drugs or smelling of alcohol, and always be prepared to work late.

When on set, have a note-pad permanently to hand to write everything down, and try to learn everyone's name. Always listen to what is being asked of you; don't try and do what you think is being asked of you half way through it being explained to you. Never assume anything, and if you don't know something, ask. Never be afraid to say 'I don't know', but always follow it up with 'I will try and find out for you'. Even if you can't get the information that person needs let them know that you have tried. (But always make sure you know where the nearest toilet is; it's the most asked question, and people will expect you to know!) If you make a mistake, own it; don't pass the buck, and you will be respected a lot more for holding your hands up.

If you are asked to do a boring job, don't pull a face. Approach every job with enthusiasm, as it all needs to be completed to make the production work. And always befriend your fellow runners; don't forget you are all working together to produce a final product. Being overly competitive only makes your job and theirs harder, and remember that your fellow runner could be giving you your next job. Smile, be polite, confident and friendly, and treat everyone exactly how you would like to be treated, no matter their role.

Lucy McCutcheon
Former Sales Manager, Twickenham Studios & Former Commercials Manager, Pinewood Studios

We at Twickenham offer general work experience programmes, which involve joining our runners' pool on a paid basis, assisting productions and the running of the studios, and we also provide short internships into our audio sound post-production facilities.

Although we tend to take a relaxed and informal approach to the interview process, we still expect the right candidates to stand out through their initiative, enthusiasm, achievements and merit. If you know what it is that you want to do in your future career, be clear and specific and highlight the skills you possess which make you a stand-out candidate. If you are not entirely sure – and once upon a time I wasn't – then be clear on what it is that interests you and have some well-researched examples. Who is your favourite writer or director? One of my personal favourites is Anthony Minghella, and I have listed this on my CV under interests along with various workshops I have attended about him. It's slightly more relevant than scuba diving; unless of course you want to be an underwater camera operator! Blog and websites are becoming popular, and a good way of showcasing your creative talents so be sure to include a link on your CV and covering letter.

I am always very impressed when people have done their research about the studios. It sounds obvious, but it's surprising how ill-prepared people often are or they get us mixed up with another studio. One woman told me that Twickenham Studios was once an ice-skating rink, I had no idea! She was able to tell me all about it, and followed up by emailing me some pictures. I have also been very impressed when someone sent us a clip of an old commercial that was shot with us and suggested we tweeted it; we now tweet clips or images from past projects on a weekly basis.

Leda Shawyer
Principal, Delamar Academy of Make-Up & Hair

The industry has become so competitive to get into and, with so many courses trying to recruit you, there is the feeling the students are being sold a dream. This leads to unrealistic expectations which can only result in disappointment. Although people often believe that it is their make-up and hair skills which are going to get them the work, it is actually good manners and a positive attitude which will take them further. In a climate of increasingly entitled young people, being humble and showing respect will also go a long way. If you have passion and determination, you will get there in the end.

Flora Moody
Make-Up & Hair Artist (*The Hobbit, Into the Woods, Avengers: Age of Ultron, Star Wars VIII*)

Early on in my career, I became aware of a few key words that would either get me into trouble or help me avoid it. When I wrote them down, I realised that not only did they all begin with the letter 'P', but they are the backbone to any healthy career.

Patience

I am a sucker when it comes to patience. Luckily, the hair and make-up industry changes on a daily basis, especially in film: different scenes, characters, locations, wigs, sets, crew. But that isn't to say we don't have weeks, sometimes months, of the same scene. On *Wrath of the Titans*, for example, we spent over four weeks shooting in a Welsh quarry with mud up to our knees; it was cold and uncomfortable, the days were long and the extras grew to dislike being smeared with dirt and blood. But I got to see one of the biggest explosions I have ever experienced! In front of us, hundreds of soldiers stood behind sharpened wooden stakes, their weapons glinting. Fires raged all over the battlefield and smoke covered everything, forcing a lot of the crew to wear breathing masks. On a countdown from the first AD, the extras roared and seconds later a HUGE fireball erupted in front of us, followed by many smaller ones. Hot air rushed past me, and I can safely say I had the biggest smile on my face.

Persistence

Any industry is going to be hard to 'crack', but the film industry does seem to have its own set of rules when it comes to gaining entry. The main thing to remember is that you are only going to get out what you put in. Use down time to research what films are happening in the studios, trawl the internet for information and get your CV out there. I have heard so many stories about 'right time/ right place', but it really is true. I happened to get my job on *The World's End* by texting the designer Jane Walker on the very day she was struggling to find someone to fill the third position on her team. I had already worked with Jane about five years previously but, had I not texted her then I probably wouldn't have been at the forefront of her mind.

Presumption

Simply put, don't presume. Although I have heard myself say on quite a few occasions, 'but I thought…' never, ever assume. This is one of the most important pieces of advice anyone can give.

Perception

Be perceptive: allow yourself to assess a situation, be sensitive to those around you and act accordingly. With such a melting pot of personalities on a film, it is wise to develop quite a sensitive awareness of how people are feeling. For some people this ability comes naturally but for others they have to work on it.

Passion

Passion is something that cannot be extinguished. It will help you through the tough times and remind you of how lucky you are when things are going well. Don't be afraid to be childishly excited about something once in a while.

I still have to pinch myself when working on a set that is particularly mind blowing. On *Prince of Persia*, for example, the sets were absolutely incredible; the attention to detail was phenomenal. Built into a deserted ruin there were streets of market stalls laden with fruits and nuts, houses that you could walk into and huge open market places hung with drapes of the most amazing colours.

Perseverance

Ask yourself where you want to be in five or 10 years' time. Set yourself goals and think about them regularly. Not only will this help you appear as someone with direction, but it will help you climb the career ladder. Be aware that a hair and make-up trainee within film can expect to stay at that level for approximately three years, then become a junior for a year or more, before qualifying as an experienced artist, particularly in the eyes of those who have been in the industry for a great deal longer. Enjoy being a trainee; make mistakes, be a sponge and enjoy the lack of responsibility.

Politeness

Being polite to everyone will get you further than you can imagine. It is a well known fact that hair and make-up designers will work dailies in between jobs, so you never know who you might be talking to. On long jobs that may run over a few months, small favours and a polite demeanour are an essential to making everyday life run smoothly. It is key to making you an indispensable part of the team. And a smile goes a hell of a long way.

Alf Tramontin
Freelance Steadicam Operator (*Harry Potter, Cinderella, Gravity*)

Never think that you know it all. I have been in this business since 1978, and I'm still learning.

Nigel Heath

Re-Recording Mixer, Hackenbacker Studios (*Downton Abbey, The Double, Submarine, Four Lions*)

Don't be afraid to make your CV stand out from the rest; take time writing it, and be sure to clearly and succinctly express your 'passion'. For me, passion is much more important than what version of ProTools you're brilliant at. Given time almost anyone can learn how to operate kit, but the passion from within is what can make the ultimate difference.

Learn from everything around you; remember there's always someone around better than you no matter how far up the ladder one may climb, so we can never afford to stop learning. And fall in love with any project you are fortunate to work on, no matter how humble. Do your best at all times to look after the project to the utmost degree.

Don't even think about pulling a face when confronted by often unexpected long hours; no fellow member of your team, let alone a client, ever wants to see that. Always remember that no matter how tired we may be in the studio, the producers and directors have probably been working on their project for weeks, months and, in some cases, years; we owe it to them to work hard but with a smile and with a glad heart in the industry we love.

Iain Mackenzie

Production Manager (*Kingsman: The Secret Service, Kick-Ass, Eddie the Eagle*)

Work hard, never be late, don't be afraid to ask questions and put yourself out there because you can't always be lucky enough to wait for a phone call.

Jonathan Paul Green

Production Designer (*The Wrong Mans, Episodes, Brass Eye, Stag*)

When putting together a department, it's easy to go for familiarity and to use people you know and trust. I'm after hard-working people with a passion for what they do and a commitment to the job.

I also look for people that will work well together as a team, and people that are proactive; people that will spot a potential problem without me having to point it out to them. I'm a very fair person, but if people take advantage, I tend to lose faith in them. It's a tough demanding job, so being personable and friendly is vital.

Simon Rogers
Production Designer (*Broadchurch (Series 2), Tyrannosaur, Stewart Lee's Comedy Vehicle*)

If you are starting out in the industry, you have to work hard and learn the ropes. Spend a bit of time developing your contacts, and focus on the areas of work that you enjoy the most. It's very useful to have as many strings to your bow as possible. You need to make yourself a useful and indispensable member of any team.

Andrew Daniel
Senior Colourist, Molinare (*The Wrong Mans, Virunga, Banished*)

When I started out in the film and TV industry I was, as many people are, a runner. This involved taking care of clients and making enough tea to not only sink a ship but to also swamp a small island. It was, however, invaluable, as it gives you real exposure to clients and also to the different elements of post production. Indeed, when I first started I wasn't even aware that the role of colourist was a job. The idea that sitting in a dark room manipulating light and colour to create the mood of a film or TV drama was beyond me, but here I am.

Like anything in this industry the journey wasn't easy and I had to slowly edge my way closer to my ultimate goal by doing a lot of other jobs in other areas along the way. Ultimately all of these jobs helped me without me fully realising it; think of *Karate Kid* waxing the car. I worked incredibly long hours and then spent time with the in-house colourist in my spare time. In fact, he gave me some advice which has stayed with me: 'There is nothing like learning in the job and remember that 95 percent of what we do is people skills.' That's not to say that being a colourist is easy, as there are a lot of different technical aspects to it, but you will often find yourself locked in a dark room with a director, a cameraman and a producer so it helps to be affable.

Starting out you are never just handed the keys to the kingdom, and it's not always easy to find time to sit in and learn. That being said, there are opportunities; know when to ask and when to leave well alone. Join in, but know when to step back. Look at the existing infrastructure in the company- data management, for example – and push to go that route. The skills you learn will serve you well moving forward. Lastly and most importantly, never give up

David Worley
Camera Operator/Second Unit DoP (*Game of Thrones Seasons II – V, The Girl with the Dragon Tattoo (US), V for Vendetta*)

Shortly after I started as a trainee assistant cameraman with a documentary unit, I was told by an old hand that being in the film business was the nearest thing in civvy street to being in the army. I never forgot that, nor the sentiment behind it. You could never be late, took instructions from superiors and would be sent all over London on errands; as one embittered martinet barked, 'You're only here to obey orders!'

Things eased off considerably, however, and have become more enlightened during the intervening years. Young people entering the business now have almost certainly acquired a high standard of education – film schools, media courses, A-levels and university degrees – and have similarly high expectations for their future careers.

Nevertheless, the self-discipline that was instilled in me still holds sway. Don't be afraid to start at the bottom – the very best place to start, to go through the ranks, so there are no gaps in your knowledge – be a good timekeeper, learn from your mistakes and those of others. Be willing and helpful to all crew members, and only make suggestions where appropriate. Become the best tea and coffee maker and, above all, be kind, pleasant and have a smile on your face. You may be in an industry where 'creativity, innovation, talent and genius' are buzz words, but it doesn't stop you being courteous whoever they are.

Movie-making is a collaborative process, and being a team player is essential to have a successful career. Not everyone is suited to this way of working, in which case, you'd be better off painting pictures or writing a worthy tome. Make no mistake; a film director may be multi-talented but he or she still needs a lot of assistance to realise their vision. This is where you and the rest of the crew come in; be helpful and inspire each other and do your utmost to be as caring and professional as it is possible to be. And try to have a bit of fun while you're doing it!

Andy Lowe
Gaffer (*Paddington, Suffragette, Four Lions, Black Mirror, The Crown*)

One of the best bits of advice I was given when I was starting out was from Barry Ryan, now head of production at Warp Films. I'd been gaffering and sparking on a lot of student films and short films, and was working on a low-budget feature Barry was producing. He suggested on each job I order one extra piece of kit I'd never used before to really learn how that item worked. This was brilliant advice; a well as playing with something new, it also helped me develop relationships with the lighting hire companies that I still work with today.

The other thing I did when starting out was regularly phoning around DoPs, Gaffers and the rental houses, asking if they needed anyone to help out or knew of any film shoots that were coming up. I kept a list of who I'd phoned and I'd try and phone them back once a month or so. I'm sure a few people only told me about things to stop my annoying phone calls!

Another bit of advice I remember reading somewhere is that there isn't anything in the film industry that can't be explained in 20 minutes. I really believe that's true. There's no big secret to how it all works; it's just lots and lots of crumbs of knowledge. Eventually you feel you have an idea of how it all goes together, but it never stops changing and it's important to keep learning.

It's also important to understand how other departments work as each department is set up slightly differently. Working on a film is about being part of a bigger team, so it's necessary to realise that other people's priorities might not be the same as your department's, but they are as equally important.

Neil Corbould
Special Effects Supervisor (2 x Oscar Winner and 4 x Bafta Winner)
Gladiator, Gravity, The Fifth Element, Saving Private Ryan, The Day After Tomorrow.

Breaking into the movie business can be very hard. It means working long hours with little in return to begin with, but once you are in, it's a truly amazing business. When I am looking for new talent I look for enthusiasm and a knowledge of film. It's great if you have qualification in engineering, prop making, plumbing, electrical, etc. but it is just as important to have dedication, enthusiasm and people skills. I have been in this business for nearly 40 years and I still love getting up in the morning and going to work with some of the most talented people in the world of film. I get such a buzz in seeing new talent evolve.

Yvonne Grace

TV Drama Producer (*My Dad's a Boring Nerd, Holby City, Crossroads*) Script Editor (*EastEnders, The Ward*); Script Consultant (*www.scriptadvice.co.uk*); Author (*Writing for Television - Series, Serials and Soaps* – available on Amazon http://amzn.to/SSUUWG)

Read a lot of good books. Surprisingly, this is the first must-do for all good script editors. You need to be fascinated, and not a little obsessed, with the written word. Read the classics, read contemporary Brit literature, read international works and have opinions on all of it. Talk about stories and books and share your thoughts with those that will stay in the room long enough with you.

Watch a lot of television. When I was starting out I would keep a notebook next to my chair when watching my favourite TV dramas and jot down the names of the writers and producers that came up on the credits. As well as forming strong opinions about why certain dramas work and what you like about them, also note the opposite. What makes a potentially good drama not deliver in your eyes? Have more opinions than is probably good for you, and be prepared to back up all your creative findings.

Become obsessed with writers. Don't stalk; but do get to know your favourite writers' work. Study why you think they write like they do, and then share your opinions with people who may listen. Network, and use social media. The best thing about the internet is that you can mix with like-minded people without having to buy a train ticket or drink an acidic wine. But do that too, because going to media events is another great way of finding people you may ultimately work with some way along the line. Twitter is great for surrounding yourself with people you admire, whose work has influenced you and with whom you could potentially forge a working relationship. Be tenacious but polite, be witty. Never be boring and self-serving. Join writers' groups and media friendly groups on Facebook, LinkedIn and Twitter, and get talking.

Read as many scripts as you can. Approach companies that run script competitions, and offer your services as a reader. Contact theatre groups and production companies that accept unsolicited material and generally get yourself out there, offering your skills. Reading scripts from the internet will get you used to working through a story scene by scene. Again, form constructive and clear opinions about how the script is written and how it works. If it doesn't in your opinion, ask yourself why.

A strong script editor needs to be: instinctive in your creative reactions to the written word on the page; visually articulate so you can 'see' scenes unfolding in your mind's eye; verbally articulate that you can translate your findings from the page to the mind of the writer; democratic and thoughtful, as receiving notes can be really hard for creative people.
Be all this and then read some more...

Kate Kinninmont, MBE
CEO of Women in Film and Television (UK)

The first pearl is in your hands: this book is a treasure trove of great advice and information. Use it to the full. Read it, make notes, don't skip the bits that you think don't apply to you. There's so much good advice here that you won't take it all in with one reading. Read the book again. Actors and directors know they have to really mine a script to truly understand it. But the same is true for every role in this industry.

Watch, listen and learn. Study everything you can, solicit advice from anyone who seems inclined to give it. Take any role you can find to be on a film set or in a production office. And when you get your chance, don't waste energy competing with your fellow workers. Spend every waking moment figuring out how to help them.

There are great tips about networking in this book. Here are a few more: go to any industry event that will let you in. Force yourself to smile and approach anyone who looks approachable. BUT: don't interrupt other people in mid-conversation; don't buttonhole people who clearly want to get away; be sensitive to whether your pitch is going down well or not. If it's not, smile, thank the person and move on. Sometimes it's like speed dating. Ask other people about them – it's not all about you. And if you're young and just starting out, don't shy away from other people in the same boat. Often you can help each other. These days you can make a film on your smartphone, but a few talented beginners working together will make a better film than you will working alone.

Lots of people do their jobs competently. You finish working with them and have nothing to complain about. Then there are people – at every level – who do their job superbly. They are efficient, cheerful, thoughtful, and collegiate. They think about the project, not just their own job – but they always do their own job first. They anticipate problems and have solutions to suggest. They don't become huffy if their suggestions aren't accepted. They smile, often make us laugh, and contribute to making the project as good as it can be. We like them. Those are the people we can't wait to work with again. Whether you're hoping to work as a runner or as a producer – or anything in between – you should aspire to be that indispensable colleague: the person with whom everyone wants to work.

Finally, relax. Don't be too intense. It scares people away. Everybody – *everybody* – would rather work with people they like; people they can trust, people who make them feel secure – and who are quietly committed to making the project absolutely wonderful.

David Jones
Production Accountant (24: Live Another Day, Sherlock, The Selfish Giant, Life of Pi)

The accounts department is one of the few that get to experience the whole production cycle and see something of the inner workings of all departments. The hours can be very long and some of the working environments challenging, and you may frequently be working away from home or even overseas, so having a real interest in film and TV will really help. When starting out in the industry I think it is better to work on smaller shows with a small accounts team rather than the big studio films. The blockbuster shows tend to divide the accountancy function into distinct focussed elements such as purchase order processing or managing travel movement orders. You might find you become an expert at say processing purchase orders but don't gain a knowledge of expense payments or payroll. On the smaller shows you will be able to diversify and develop a broader set of skills quicker. It is also usually much easier to get an overview of the production process on a smaller show, which can give you a really good grounding when you move to bigger shows and take on those specialised tasks as you will have an idea of how your element fits in to the whole.

If you can get hold of a film or TV show budget and read it through thoroughly, you most likely won't understand it at this point but then read the script and start relating the elements of the script to the budget, gradually the words on the page will start making sense in terms of the budget, which will really help in building an understanding of the cost drivers of a film project.

A very large part of the job is about good communication both in listening to people to glean information and in explaining financial information to people with creative craft skills rather than a financial background. Work at building good communication skills as they are really essential to successfully tackling any job within the production accounts team

Jody Knight
Grip (The Man from Uncle, Fast & Furious 6, Mamma Mia, Harry Potter and the Order of the Phoenix)

The best advice I can give for anyone who wants to break into the film and TV industry is patience. You will gain far more respect in the industry if you take your time to learn your craft. If you are passionate about the job and enjoy the job there should be no rush to jump in at the deep end. I worked at a rental house for around 6yrs. In that time I learnt about grip equipment and the way in which it was used on set. During this time I got the opportunity to meet a lot of Grips that I could ask questions and gain valuable advice. It was only when I felt enough confidence with my abilities that I could progress onto a trainee role.

Grip trainees should register with the Grips Branch (the union for grips and crane technicians). They can then be contacted from the trainee list by grips who require a trainee for their job. It is also the first stepping stone to working towards there NVQ qualification, which is an essential qualification.

Laurajane Miles
Script Supervisor *(Gravity, Paddington, Mission Impossible: Rogue Nation, The Danish Girl)*

Be determined – never stop sending your CV, emailing and getting in touch, and offer to work in any department if needs be. I can certainly remember how difficult, and at times disheartening, that stage was. But it will pay off and you will get your foot in the door. And that's all you need.

Once you are there, turn up early, go home late and when you are there, listen. Listen to everything that happens and keep learning – we are all still learning. I would say that 90% of my job is listening – knowing when to speak up and more importantly, when not to.

I had no idea what a Script Supervisor was. But when I was a runner I took a look at the shooting floor, saw a lady doing what I thought was 'just admin' (it wasn't) and thought 'I can do that' (I couldn't) but she was at the centre of all the action and creativity and it was then I realised, that that was where I wanted to be. I didn't have a clue what she was doing, but I kept asking questions and if she needed anything. In the end, she let me help her and on all my subsequent running jobs, I always sought out the Script Supervisor and asked how I could help her and her advice on how I could start a career in it myself. It was that original Script Supervisor, nearly a year later, who called and offered me my first Script Assistant role on *Harry Potter*… we still remain friends and now she does my second units from time to time… all because I offered to help her when she was busy.

I guess that's the most helpful piece of advice I can offer. If there is a department you are interested in or a role that you feel you warm to, pursue it, offer to help, ask questions when the time suits – we all love to talk about our departments – and we all need help (or a good cup of tea)

Be courteous and respectful to all crew and their roles. In the years preceding my training to be a Script Supervisor, I worked in any department I could – including Locations – now when I am in an hour or more before call and leaving hours after wrap, feeling exhausted – I remember that someone was there 2 hours before me – and will leave after me at the end of the day too.

I believe there is a role for everyone in the film industry if they want it enough. Those who are not necessarily suited to academia; those that are, people from all types of backgrounds, beginnings and stories, with all levels of talent in many areas – there is a job for everyone on set.

That said, this is not an industry for everyone – you will probably miss weddings, holidays, birthdays and celebrations. You might not know when you are getting paid next, and that certainly doesn't suit some – but if you find your role, and stick with it, I think it's one of the funniest, most satisfying, exciting and ridiculous worlds you will ever work in. I hope our paths cross soon.

James Cox
Stunt Performer *(Star Wars: The Force Awakens, Avengers: The Age of Ultron, Skyfall)*

While working in the film and television industry as a member of the JISC stunt register I've been given the opportunity to double some brilliant actors, experience some quite unbelievable situations and live out a whole host of childhood dreams.

Like many of my colleagues, coming to work each day presents a vast array of challenges and possible risks. From a one-on-one fight, to a huge futuristic battle scene (involving a large stunt team, hundreds of supporting artists, practical effects, rain machines, action vehicles etc) safety should always be the number one priority.

No film, commercial, photoshoot or TV programme is worth anyone getting hurt or unnecessarily injured for.

If you see something unsafe, or you yourself feel endangered then try to have the confidence to speak to either a member of the stunt team or the appropriate crew member.

As well as keeping safe, having a professional demeanour will always leave you in good standing for any line of work you hope to go into.

Beyond that, treat people with respect and have fun (where appropriate!) it's a wonderful industry to have the privilege to work in

---

Mike Baldock
Location Manager (Over 300 commercials for campaigns including Apple, Sainsburys, VW, Fosters, H&M)

Work hard and be nice to people!

With that sentence I don't think you can go too far wrong in any walk of life. But it's particularly true for the film industry – it's a freelance world, and people will naturally choose to work again with people that are good at their job and are nice to work with.

Getting that first break can seem daunting, but stick to that motto again and keep persisting, and you will get a break. Take advantage of that opportunity – and show people how hard you can work and how nice you can be! Do the hours, go the extra mile, and do it all with a smile on your face!!!

Enjoy being a runner! Sure it's the bottom rung, and it can be a frustrating job, and at times pretty thankless. But you get the opportunity to see how everything works –it's the runners who work hard and take an active interest in all the departments who will succeed in the end. There is no structured route through a career in film, so working as a runner not only provides valuable experience, but also will help you decide how you shape that course.

And if you're really insane you might like to consider locations! As I mentor once said to me, we're a little bit like the marines – first in, last out! Early starts, late finishes, logistical headaches and disgruntled residents are off-set by scouting beautiful locations, meeting all manner of people, and the opportunity to be at the real sharp end of the creative process way before the actual filming begins. As a location manager you're the link between the real world and the film world, and through the scouting you are able to give a real steer to the creative. It's most often the job that other crew members would least like to do, but in my opinion one of the most challenging and rewarding of departments to be in.

It's hard to get in to the film industry, and at times it's a challenge once you get there... but it's also a hugely varied, rewarding industry to be in – decide you're going to do it and then go for it! Good luck! Keep smiling!

Ros Little
Costume Designer (*The Last Kingdom, The Crimson Field, The Bible, In The Loop, Horrible Histories,* currently working on *Poldark series 2)*

Make the most of every work experience and trainee job you secure.
See every project as a learning opportunity, a chance to observe and understand the various roles and responsibilities within the costume department and to collaborate closely with other departments.

Be prepared to work very long and unsociable hours and accept that you may be asked to do seemingly menial tasks to begin with. Always present a positive, can–do attitude, be patient, and in time you will be given the chance to show what you are capable of.

As part of the costume team, take on board instructions and follow them carefully. Ask questions at an appropriate moment. Make sure you are never late and are always well prepared for the day ahead. View any advice as useful and do not take criticism to heart.

Be aware that the new contacts you are making are the people most likely to recommend you for future work.

Kate McLaughlin
Co-Founder and CEO of We Got POP (*Star Wars: The Force Awakens, Spectre, Everest*)

Contacts and credits are the key to getting gigs in the film industry. But how do you get credits if you don't have any contacts? And how do you get contacts if you can't get that elusive first credit?

The answer for me was short films. Teams making shorts are always looking for runners or runner drivers to help them out. Offer your services and be willing to muck in and do whatever is needed: organise the breakfast rolls, pick up random props from miles away, clean up tea tables, lock off alleyways, persuade your friends to be extras; be there first in the morning and be the last to leave. On a short you will get the feel for a film set, have the opportunity to see the different departments in action and meet people who work in the industry. Try and get work on a short backed by an institution: Film London, Film4, the Irish Film Board. These shorts tend to attract great people who already work in the industry and you may well meet someone who will take you onto their next big project.

In the meantime, start doing your research: find out what films or TV shows have been made in your area, find out who worked in the department you're interested in, and work out who is making the hiring decision - usually the co-ordinator or one below the head of department. Research those people, find out what they've worked on and who they've worked with, and make a shortlist of your dream teams. Then get in touch with them - if you can work out who has just started a new project, that is the best time to connect, as that's when they'll be putting their team together and might be interviewing. Make sure your cover letter is bespoke and concise and your CV focuses only on relevant experience: ideally credits.

If you get an opportunity on a big film or TV show, be prepared to make lots of tea and focus on doing the tasks you are given, to the best of your ability. Entry level positions generally include a proportion of boring tasks, but you should stay focused on being valuable. You will learn so much from being part of a film crew and working with great people. And if you do a good job, you'll be offered other opportunities. The hard step is getting that first credit.

Bob Bridges
Video Assist Coordinator (*Harry Potter, Edge of Tomorrow, X-Men: First Class*)

I have two pieces of advice that I offer to anybody coming into the Industry:

The first is that, whatever position you may aspire to; Director, Producer, Cameraman, Production Designer, you must do the very best work you can in the jobs you do on the path to achieving that ambition. I have seen too many fail because they think those first trainee or Runner jobs are below them and just an unnecessary barrier to achieving their goal. There is no clear, regulated career path with automatic progression and promotion - progression comes by invitation from those who recognise enthusiasm, diligence and conscientiousness. If you can't be trusted to do the job at hand with those attributes, no-one is going to trust you on the next rung up the ladder.

The second 'pearl' is to not be blinkered by your ambition. Use the opportunity that working on a production gives to look around at the many different departments and trades that make up the Crew. You may find that one of those interests you more than your original aspiration.

Chris Burdon
Re-recording mixer, Warner Bros. De Lane Lea. *(Children of Men, X-Men: First Class, Captain Phillips, Edge of Tomorrow)*

The people I have seen making the greatest progress in our industry are typically hard working, enthusiastic and personable. Raw talent is obviously helpful, but that plus good inter-personal skills is a winning combination.

If opportunities are not materialising, be patient, retain your focus and there is every chance something will turn up. If a colleague is chosen ahead of you for a job or promotion, use this to motivate yourself and try not to get down about it. A positive response will really impress your employer.

Make the most of every chance to learn about your work and any potential roles, it will become apparent that you are ready and willing to take responsibility. Develop your relationships with those above and below you in the food chain and you will soon gain their trust. This will put you in good stead for your whole career. To this day I and the team I work with are doing as much as we can to gain the trust of our clients. That trust once attained will provide you with long-term, loyal working relationships.

Mark Sanger
Editor (Gravity*, The Jungle Book) *Oscar winner alongside Co-Editor Alfonso Cuaron

I've had the privilege of having worked with many great crew members in my time. Although each of us have our own unique stories of career inception and perseverance, I would say there is one common thread among those of us with enough luck to linger.

You can have bundles of creative talent, a solid technical education and an encyclopaedic knowledge of the language of cinema, but without an understanding of the industry hierarchies, politics and diplomacies, I would argue that it is difficult to flourish.

There are no specific lessons to be learnt because these factors are unique to the DNA of every single project you will work on. It's like rafting a ferocious white water rapid. The creative egos, wild personalities, financial restrictions and personal agendas create a dynamic that is often as tricky to negotiate as it is exciting to ride.

Every day is slightly different and though experience will teach you some tricks, you can never simply coast through it. Saying the right thing at the right time is rarely as important as not speaking at all if the moment is misjudged.

There is no film school course that will teach you these skills, but having the patience and awareness to accumulate the experience is not only essential to carving a career, but also part of the mystique that makes our industry such a thrill ride.

Adrian Wootton
Chief Executive of Film London and the British Film Commission

Knowledge, skills, talent and experience are the combination we're all looking for. Whether you have talent is largely determined by other people's judgments (although healthy self-belief – not arrogance – is essential to developing talent) and experience can only really be gained from time doing a job. This means starting out is very much about gaining as much knowledge and skill as you can. Learning about film, television and animation formally or informally is therefore pivotal: watch lots and often, from classic to contemporary; grab any training or mentoring opportunities that come your way and research not just the kind of job you think you want but also the companies and the people that work within the industry. Networking, making contacts and trying to get placements or internships is really important, but only if you've already done your homework about the organisation you're trying to work for and the key individuals who work there.

To get any prospective employer to be interested in you – whether it's a commission, a freelance contract or a permanent job – you have to show real interest in them and what they do and demonstrate it in a straightforward, self effacing way. It's a key part of becoming a team member in the creative industries to know your stuff without being overbearing, to listen to and learn from others (something which should never, ever stop!) and being as useful as possible. You have to do all this right from the beginning, because first impressions mean so much.

Ultimately, if you have ability, are ludicrously hard-working, really, really dedicated and enthusiastic then you'll have a great headstart!

CHAPTER 5

Resources

Glossary

Above the line
On the front page of a production budget, there is an imaginary line. Anything above that reflects the expected cost of any official 'above-the-line' member: actors, director, producer and writer. These above-the-line costs can fluctuate wildly depending on the individuals involved, and can be double, triple or quadruple the costs of below-the-line crew members and equipment (see below).

Action vehicle
A vehicle that appears on screen that requires management and maintenance. Action vehicles are often not driven to set, but delivered by an individual car transporter to ensure they remain in perfect condition.

Action prop
A prop that is involved in the story and used by the actors, not just used as set dressing.

AD: Assistant Director
The AD team usually consists of first, second and third AD and a floor runner, and they are responsible for scheduling the production, managing the cast and organising the shooting day.

The first AD is the person who calls 'action', and interprets and relays the wishes of the director to the rest of the crew. If you are starting out as a runner on set, it is likely that the first AD will be your head of department.

The second AD can be found at the unit base, looking after cast and preparing the schedule for the next day, and has responsibility for writing up the daily call sheet. The third AD is on set helping to organise cast and crew, and takes instruction directly from the 1st AD. The floor runner will work on set and at unit base as is required.

Additional Photography

Filming that takes place after the main unit has completed the original schedule, usually after the first edit assembly has revealed a clear need to add or replace scenes to alter and improve the story.

ADR

Additional dialogue recording or automatic dialog recording. This is when actors' lines are re-recorded in a post-production studio, most likely because the location sound has collected unwanted interference or noise.

Agency

May refer to either the advertising agency behind a commercials shoot, which if present on set will usually consist of TV producer, creatives, art director and/or copywriter; or talent agents.

Akela Crane

An 85ft crane that supports a three-axis head and takes at least three hours to set up with a recommended crew of four grips. It's a large undertaking, but yields some stunning results.

Alexa

Ubiquitous digital camera from Arri. Achieves similar results to 35mm camera and can send to multiple outputs, including on-board memory and has a PL mount.

Animatic

Quick and rough animations, normally based on storyboard images with added sound, typically used to show advertising agency clients how a commercial will look. It's less costly to make any changes after the animatic than after the final cut.

APA

Advertising Producers Association. The body for commercials production in the UK since 1978, with over 200 company members mostly based in central London.

APA rate

The standard terms and freelance rate for crew working in commercials. Current terms and conditions can be found on the BECTU website.

Apple box

A solid wooden box used by grips for camera stability.

Art department:
Normally tackled after a script negative check and during the course of clearances ongoing filming. During prep, the art department will begin to assemble a list of wanted items that may require clearance, and will either set about those clearances themselves or will employ a specialist to work for them. Each clearance should have a paper trail of documented evidence to show that it has been approved; the production's lawyer should provide standard forms.

Aspect ratio
There are several aspects ratios used in film and TV. The standard shape is 4:3, and the ratio gets increasingly wider to 14:9 and 16:9. The numbers represent the scale, i.e. 16:9 is 16 bits across by 9 bits high, all in the same measurement. The ratio is set prior to filming.

ATMOS
Dolby sound system comprising of a complete surround mix in cinema.

Available light
The absence of electrically powered lamps: reflectors, practical lamps, sunlight and a DoP's expertise is all that is available.

AVID
AVID is the most commonly used offline-editing software. Daily rushes are delivered and transferred into AVID, where the editor can view them and begin to make an assembly on the timeline.

Ballast
Lighting department equipment that controls or limits the amount of electricity going into a lamp. If a lamp is hooked up directly into a generator, it will absorb an increasing amount of electricity until it pops; the ballast controls that flow and ensures there are no power surges.

Barn Doors
The metal flaps on the side of most lamps that can guide, beam or block light according to the production's needs.

Barney
An insulating jacket that helps muffle the sound of the 35mm and 16mm film cameras

'Based as local'

This phrase is used in job postings, and indicates that the applicant must be prepared to accommodate themselves for the duration of filming at no expense to the production. It discourages speculative, inappropriate applications from non- locals and opens opportunities for those who live in the area of filming. Lots of crew members have bases in different parts of the country, such as friends or relatives, which means they have more options to work as local.

Baselight

Colour-grading system by Filmlight.

Bazooka

A 'bazooka' arm is found in the grip department, and comes in sections that hold the camera at a distance from a tripod or dolly. So-called because it resembles a slightly larger version of the missile launcher.

BECTU

Broadcasting, Entertainment, Cinematograph and Theatre Union. Founded in 1991, it has around 25,000 members in the UK.

BECTU Rates

BECTU publish guideline rates, terms and conditions for all roles, on their website.

Below the line

On a production budget, these are the expected costs for any 'below-the-line' expenses, including most crew members who come with a locked-in cost and will be hired according to the budget. In contrast, the cost of 'above-the-line' elements, including director, producer, writer or on-screen talent can vary hugely, ranging in cost from mega blockbuster to shoestring indie.

Best boy

Second in command of the lighting department. Actions and manages the lighting plans as set out by the Gaffer.

Block

A portion of the overall shoot. TV Drama is usually filmed over a long period of time and may require several directors to complete. As an example, a six part series might use 3 directors taking 2 episodes each. The first director would shoot their episodes together in one block, then go into the edit suite and director would then step in to shoot their two episodes in the second block, and so on. The same crew would cover the entire shoot to retain continuity. There is typically a week off between blocks in order for the unit to refresh and prepare for the next episodes.

Blocking

The movement of characters on screen. The director and first assistant will map out the starting positions and subsequent movements of the actors during a take.

Body rig

A body mounted rig (sometimes known as the doggy rig) that attaches straight onto an actor. The rig consists of a jacket with four long poles that extend directly in front of the wearer, where a lightweight camera is mounted. The actor can then walk freely, with the camera pointed directly at their face. A wireless playback connection is usually required.

Bolex

A brand of 16mm and 8mm camera, made by the Swiss company of the same name. Small, boxy and mostly handheld, they originated in the 1930s for domestic use and are now collectors' items. Due to the great craftsmanship, older Bolex cameras have stood the test of time, but the company are still making new models.

Bowser

A portable liquid container, used to carry a supply of either water or fuel. A bowser can be towed along behind a larger truck, and can be used by catering, the art department (for rain effects) and for the facilities vehicles.

Box Rental

Payment made to crew members for the use of their kit on the production in addition to their salary, usually for consumable items, for example, the art deparment or make-up materials. Box money is paid weekly along with and on top of the payment to the crew member. Only applicable to crew members who bring their own kit for jobs, and with prior agreement with the production manager.

Breakdown

The deconstruction of a script or schedule to identify what component parts might be required. An assistant director will, for example, breakdown a script to work out the schedule.

Call time

The time you are due to start work, which could be different every day. Breakfast is usually available at least 30 minutes before your call time. It's important that you are never late for the unit call, and enquire with the person booking you if you need to be present at a specific time for your department. (The costume and make-up teams, for example, are usually called in one-to-two hours before the main unit to prepare the cast, and runners are sometimes required to assist the second AD when the cast start arriving.)

Cannes

French city that is not only home to the famous film festival, but also hosts festivals for advertising (Cannes Lions in July) and content markets for TV (MIPTV in April and MIPCOM in October). New entrants are not taken to Cannes for festivals or markets, but if you are working for a company that is attending one of them, you may find yourself helping them prepare for the event.

Carnet

'Carnet de passage'. An internationally recognised term for the transport of items between countries. Typically refers to the freight of camera and lighting kit, where a full inventory is required before shipping can take place.

Cast & crew screening

This is the first screening of the film, usually before the premiere, exclusively for the cast and crew of the film. Quite often, Cast and Crew screenings take place on a Sunday morning when Large cinemas have availability for private hire.

Casting headsheet

Form filled in by actors prior to a casting session, containing name and contact details as well as details of their agent and their personal measurements. A photograph or screenshot from the casting camera will also be attached to the form. For commercials, actors are also asked to list if they have appeared in any other adverts in the last two years. When casting dozens of people, the headsheet is a quick visual reference to identify your favourites.

Chimera

A soft, collapsible frame and cover used by the lighting department to diffuse and distribute light evenly over a target. It looks like a tent and attaches directly onto a lighting stand, and comes in various sizes and grades of diffusion.

Chippie

Carpenter.

Chit

A voucher that confirms the working hours for background artists for budgeting and invoicing purposes. Each chit will be signed off by the assistant directors after wrap. Traditionally, this has been a paper voucher, but software company We Got POP have introduced a paperless version that can be accessed via phone and tablet. This software is likely to make the paper-version redundant in the coming years.

Chroma-key

Another term for blue screen or green screen. A single colour background has an image or footage 'keyed' onto it.

Cinesync
Software that allows multiple people, anywhere in the world to review footage in precise sync. Essentially a conference call where all parties can be sure that they are looking at the exact frame of footage at the same time.

Clearances
Clearances can fall into three key categories: script clearances, visual clearances (known as art department clearances) and music clearances. All three require a production to seek either approval or permission to use something on screen. Script clearances require a neg check, while art department clearances require a mixture of permissions, contracts and clearing names for use. Music clearances require patience and paperwork; certain music can cost far more than others but every piece of music in the final edit must be cleared for use.

Completion Guarantors
Ensure the financiers that filming will complete, akin to an insurance policy. A guarantor is set in place by the financiers to support the production in delivering what is agreed. The guarantor will approve key staff and crew, and keep a vigilant watch over the production via daily reports. Should a problem arise, the guarantor is there to assist the production and guide it to a conclusion. In the very worst-case scenarios, when a film cannot continue, the guarantor usually ensures that the financiers will get their money returned.

Conform
The final part of the post-production process, where all of the locked elements of audio and visual are synched together using the highest resolution file sizes. As this point, an off-line becomes an on-line and results in a master version.

Coning
The act of placing parking cones out, usually overnight, to block off an area for filming or parking.

Consumables
Materials that are used for the production that cannot be used again such as batteries, aerosols, gaffa tape, make-up etc.

Continuity report
The script supervisor compiles a meticulous and detailed account of the scenes shot, and their notes are sent to the editor. The notes help the post-production department identify the contents of the rushes, the impact on the continuity of other scenes and the director's favoured takes. There are typically two parts to the paperwork: a report of the daily activity and marked-up script pages identifying the length of takes for each set up.

Continuity, character
Costume and make-up departments track the continuity of characters as they progress through the story. Films are not shot in chronological order, and so monitoring such continuity is vital. Departments use photographs as a visual reference, allowing teams to consult with the head of department to ensure the design is correct for each upcoming scene. The visual references also help dailies crew when arriving on a project for a short time.

Correx
A lightweight plastic board, normally 8ft by 4ft and in a range of thicknesses, used to protect floors on location.

Coverage
Shooting a scene from a variety of angles and lengths in order to give the editor the requisite footage to cut a scene with.

Covert kit
In- ear and microphone piece that connects to walkie-talkie.

Croc clip
A small metal spring-loaded clip, shaped like a crocodile's jaw. Primarily used by electricians to clip a coloured gel to a lamp, they have multiple other uses.

Cue sheet
A music cue sheet is used to log the audio in a production, and provides the title, author and in-and-out points for every track used in a TV show or film. The broadcaster can then pay the rights' holder of the track, via the MCPS/PRS alliance: the collection service for musicians, composers and record companies.

Cutting room
Otherwise known as the edit suite, this is a room where the editor and their department work on the AVID, away from the set.

Cyc
Short for cyclorama (or infinity curve), the smooth black wall that surrounds some studios. It's curved in the corners and at the floor, so if you are using a green screen there are no edges or lines, giving the impression of infinity. The Cyc can also be painted, usually at a cost.

Dailies (i)
Individual crew who are brought in by a department head for specific, busy days such as large crowd or action sequences.

Dailies (ii)
Reviewing the previous day's rushes.

Day for night
When shooting a night time scene during daylight hours, the DoP will usually require blackout drapes or film for windows to block out sunlight.

Day out of Days
Also known as 'the doods', this document shows which actors are working, and on what days. It is a chart that contains each character name, along with their cast number, along with a 'W' denoting the days they are scheduled to be working. Department heads can then figure out who is due in for what days, and prepare around the schedule accordingly.
Other terms are used to indicate first ('SW'; start work) and last ('WF'; work finish) days of work for particular cast members. Actors who are scheduled for one day only will be indicated by 'SWF' (start work finish), while 'R' indicates a rehearsal day and 'T' stands for travel day

DCP
Digital cinema package: the files issued to cinemas and screening rooms containing the film to be digitally projected.

Deal memo
A one-page summary of a supplier contract. Generally distributed to crew as a summary of the terms of contract, it covers such things as salary, period of engagement, holiday pay and job title.

Deliverables
The collective name for the final film, paperwork and any supplementary materials that a production is required to hand over on the scheduled delivery date to the production company and distribution.

DIT
When shooting on HD or Red, the digital imaging technician (DIT) aids the DoP to ensure that the optimum image is captured and stored. The DITs are also responsible for the storage, file management and data distribution on set, and will liaise with the post-production facilities.

Dolly
A small yet heavy vehicle that holds the camera steady, and runs on tracks, pushed or pulled by the dolly grip. Dollies allow the smooth movement of the camera to move closer to, further away from or alongside the action. The DoP or camera operator will be able to sit on the dolly as it travels, follow-focus is normally used and end boards are often employed, depending on the shot.

Double Banking
Two units filming different episodes/storylines of a TV Drama at the same time.

Drone
A small remote-controlled aerial filming device, using rotor blades and a steady gimbal head to get shots. It is cheaper than hiring a helicopter, has no downdraft from the blades and is nimbler in tight areas.

Dub
Post-production recording and overlay, particularly for voice recording.

Dutch head
A head acts as a lock between the tripod, arm, crane and the camera itself. While the tripod is static, the head allows smooth movement of the camera for panning and tilting. The Dutch head allows the camera to roll sideways into a Dutch tilt, and requires a tight lock on the camera and a balanced centre of gravity.

EDL
Edit decision list is a precise breakdown of all the in-and-out points of the final 'locked' feature film. The EDL will be used to start the conform.

EIS
Enterprise Investment Scheme set up by HMRC to encourage investors to put money into small, high-risk companies (such as film production). Investments made under the EIS offer several tax benefits, including rebates and Capital Gains exemption.

Eleven-day fortnight
This is a working pattern often found in TV drama and film. Individuals are contracted to work for 11 days out of 14, which usually means working every Sunday regardless of the rate. Over the course of production, those extra 'free' days amount to an additional week of filming compressed into the shooting schedule.

Employers' liability
Insurance cover for any claim made following injury caused to an employee while engaged in the company's business.

End board
Occasionally, the clapper board needs to be used at the end of a take rather than the beginning, if the shot is particularly tight or the camera is in a difficult spot. In this case, the board is held upside down and 'end board' is clearly stated for sound (and the editing department). The board is essential for the editor, providing a visual reference to enable them to track takes with ease.

EPK

The electronic press kit (EPK) crew are responsible for capturing behind-the-scenes footage and key interviews during the production process for use in the press materials for the film launch or broadcast TX date.

Equity

The actors and performers' union, which sets the terms and conditions for engaging all performers to appear on screen. Fees range from background artist standard rate to the variable lead actor ('above-the-line') fee.

EZ up

An 'easy-up is a mini pop-up marquee/gazebo normally used for covering food and keeping crew and equipment protected from rain. It can also come with 'sides', making it ideal for costume changes next to set, rather than having to return to unit base.

Final checks

A term called before the camera starts to roll for a take, giving departments, primarily costume and make-up, a final chance to check for continuity before another take.

First Positions

The starting spot for an actor at the beginning of a scene. At the end of a take, they will be asked to return to first positions, ready for another take.

Fitting

Costume tests with actors. Typically held at costume houses or studios prior to filming.

Flag

Used in the lighting department, this is a black square of thick, lightweight material stretched around a metal frame and used to block or diffuse light. It's also effective at blocking paparazzi from getting shots of talent when filming in public.

Flame

Post-production visual effects and finishing system from Autodesk.

Fluid head

A camera that is mounted on a fluid head can pan and tilt smoothly, as the head uses viscous oils for sleek movement.

Foley

Post-production sound effects, recorded in a studio. A Foley artist uses a sound studio and a selection of tools and props to match the audio in any given scene.

Follow focus

A special geared device that is attached to the outside of the lens and operated by the focus puller via remote control. Essential for hand-held filming and in tight spaces.

Fresnel

A lens that enhances the output of a lamp and gives a soft beam. Most Fresnel lamps allow users to move the lens towards and away from the light source, meaning you change the focal length of the beam.

Gate

The window inside the camera that sits between the shutter, where the negative passes through. Any imperfections, dust or breakages in that window during filming will appear on the negative. At the end of a set-up, the first AD will usually call to 'check the gate', removing any debris with canned air.

Genny

A power generator to supply the lights with electricity. Mobile generators come in various sizes but all make considerable noise, so long cables are used to keep them away from the action.

Gimbal

A specialist camera mount for a helicopter. It's normally within a sphere that is placed on the nose of the helicopter and protects the camera and mount from poor weather and absent-minded birds. The gimbal can move on its line of axis to capture the ground below, and is operated from inside the helicopter

Gladiator stand

Large lamp stand with an extendable upright arm on lockable wheels.

Going over

Running behind schedule. At the end of the day the first AD will inform the crew that they are going over, the crew then allow 15 minutes grace after the scheduled wrap before overtime kicks in. (See the BECTU website for overtime rates.)

Grade
During post production, the telecine op or colour grade op will use specialist equipment to manipulate the colour palette of the offline to create a 'grade' for the film. Some grades are very subtle and others, particularly in effects-laden projects, use a lot of colour enhancement to create atmosphere.

Guide Track
A piece of music temporarily placed within an edit assembly, to indicate the tone and feel for a scene. This music guide may be removed or replaced with another recorded song, original composition and in some cases, left in place.

Handles
Extra footage captured before and after the main action of a take, allowing the editor flexibility to cut in or out of a scene. If an actor needs to deliver a line that take 5 seconds to say, the camera will roll for at least 5 seconds before and 5 seconds after the line read. This gives the editor flexibility.

Hiatus
A brief stop in production. This could be for financing reasons, casting issues or other problems during filming. Projects that are filming through December and January will also stop for a Christmas hiatus.

HMI
A Hydrargyrum medium-arc iodide lamp, which is efficient, reliable and gives a warm colour temperature.

HoD
Head of department. Each department needs a chief, and each has its own path to the top; experience and skill is always crucial.

Holding area
Background artists are often given dining buses or rooms near the location so they remain grouped together before they are needed for make-up and costume, or required on set.

Holiday pay
Workers in the film and TV industry are entitled to 5.6 paid holiday days every year. As most workers in the industry are engaged for short periods of time, it means that their employers must pay them for those days that they are not able to take a holiday while working for them. Usually, on long form productions, this paid in a lump sum at the end of the contract.

Honeywagon
A lovely (misleading) name for a mobile toilet.

Hot in the hand
Catering expression for a lunch that can be eaten on the move, without sitting down. Normally used during a continuous working day.

Inferno
Autodesk post-production system. More expensive than Flame or Smoke, this is mainly used in features because of its powerful 3D compositing.

JIGS
The Joint Industry Grading Scheme was set up by the BBC, ITV, C4, Sky and BECTU to form a coherent and standardised approach to health and safety. JIGS oversee the Production Safety Passport (PSP).

Jimmy jib
A simple, easy-to-use crane with a long extension, up to 40ft.

Kino
A brand of fluorescent lighting systems. Typically a series of flo' tubes in varying length. There is always more than one tube in a kino, so they are referred to as 'banks', for example, two bank or four bank. When ordering different lengths and banks, it becomes known as 'two-by-two' (two tubes of two feet) or 'two-by-four', etc. There are also mini versions used to light close interiors, for example filming characters inside vehicles.

Legs
Tripod. Comes in short or tall versions, also known as 'sticks'; with short 'legs' sometimes referred to 'baby legs'. Always check the head of the tripod matches the fitting to the camera.

LLB
Late lunch break. A financial penalty for going over schedule, if stopping for lunch. Not required on a continuous working day.

Locked: script
While scripts are regularly being rewritten, even during filming, there is a point between script development and pre-production when the script becomes a shooting script. The producers will sign off on this draft being the script they intend to shoot. Using Final Draft, scenes and characters will then be assigned numbers, and all technical information will be included so that all departments can plan their requirements. From the moment a script is 'locked', amendments can only be made by issuing coloured pages.

Locked: edit

The final cut of the film. Once the offline edit is complete and signed off, all other elements such as audio and VFX will complete the picture.

Locking off

Location term used when the camera is turning. Locking-off means stopping anyone from walking into the scene, and is often the job of a location marshall or runner.

Low loader

This is a specially modified truck with a flat-bed trailer used for filming cars. The bed of the trailer is just off the ground and gives the impression that the car is actually driving along the road, without it actually moving.

In front of the car and behind the truck cabin is a deck where crew can operate and film the characters in the car. The sides of the flat-bed trailer and deck will have rigging in order to secure the crew and gear within. The route of the low loader must always be worked out in advance.

LUT

Look-up table. A device used on set to alter the colour, contrast and grade of images acquired, manipulating the picture.

Magliner

A heavy duty trolley for storing and transporting camera equipment.

MCR

Machine Room. Room or rooms in post-production houses where multiple playback and recording devices are interconnected for the purposes of authoring and transferring. For example, converting an old VHS or Digi Beta tape to a HD download or to perform DVD authoring. Many post-production houses who offer these services look for technically minded new entrants to operate the machines.

Media Composer

Offline editing system by AVID.

MoS

An acronym used on a clapperboard, standing for mute of sound, it denotes a mute take

Motion capture
An actor dons a tight fitting Lycra suit with markers on each of the joints, and likely additional points over the body. The performer will then enact movement against a green screen, and is filmed by a series of cameras, which will identify the markers and track the movement. The movement map is then overlaid with animation of a character that replicates the action.

Motion control
A motion control rig allows very precise camera movements that can be repeated exactly. The camera is normally fixed on a three-axis head, which is attached to a mechanised arm; the whole unit can be programmed to move forward, back, up down, around, pan and tilt at variable speed. Commercial productions use the system frequently to showcase electrical items and, because of the precision detail of the move, effects-heavy feature films also utilise the technology.

Movement order
A map and detailed travel instructions from one point to another, ensuring that all crew can easily find a unit base or location that may not be reachable by sat nav alone.

Movie Magic
Scheduling software for long format fiction, licensed by Entertainment Partners (Sargent Disc in the UK).

The first AD (with help from second) will use the software to input all the information from the script into an individual scene breakdown including characters, props and hair and make-up requirements. Once entered into the software, the first can arrange the strips of individual scenes into a workable order, spread out a determined period of time.

Moy
A type of grip fitting, where the camera rests on the tripod.

MSR
A medium source rare-earth lamp, Phillips' version of the HMI. Efficient, reliable and gives a warm colour temperature and, like the HMI, requires ballast.

NDA
A non-disclosure agreement is a contract commonly found with larger films, where the signee is legally bound not to reveal any detail of the film or film-making process. This is to protect the story from 'leaking', to protect the privacy of above-the-line talent and ensure that the 'making of' DVD is a marketable commodity.

Neg check
A forensic scan of a film or drama script by an experienced researcher. The researcher will identify any areas of legal concern and potential risk – usually focused around copyright of character and company names – and due action is then taken. The researchers are specialised and experienced, and are also able to help find resolutions and advise on possible outcomes.

'Nervous'
A slang term used when searching for any equipment that might have been left behind: having a 'nervous wreck', 'check', e.g. 'have a quick nervous before we move to the next location'.

Offline
The process of film editing and assembly. The offline edit, using a lower-sized film version of the rushes, is the most crucial part of the editing construction, creating the structure and tempo of a project. An editor cannot implement visual effects, but can mark visual references for the online into the screen.

On board monitor
A small LCD monitor that can be attached to side of the camera to relay the image through the viewfinder. The camera operator operates via the viewfinder and the focus puller can get a feed of the same view.

Online
Once the offline (structure) of the film has been created, the online then consists of any additional visual elements in terms of effects, lighting, shading, graphics and titles.

On-the-day
Term used while preparing or rehearsing a shot. To describe a particular element of the shot that is not required in rehearsal but will be employed or enacted when the camera rolls for a take 'on-the-day'.

Pack shot
A pack shot, or product shot, is a close up of finished product that concludes almost every commercial. There is much fretting over the pack shot and, generally speaking, it's the most involved and engaged in a production, the advertising agency will tend to be during a filming day. The Advertising Standards Agency (ASA) have regulations about the minimum and maximum amount of time any commercial can feature a pack shot.

Pags
Paganini are small wooden panels used by the grip department, chiefly for levelling out track on uneven surfaces. Part of the accessories kit and usually ordered along with wedges.

Par
A lamp that emits a standard oval of flat light. Par-cans are often used in theatre for providing a standard beam of light.

PAYE
Pay as you earn is a HMRC definition for when you will pay tax on your income. If you are PAYE, you will have your tax contribution deducted at the point of payment, while a freelancer is liable to pay their own tax on an annual basis. The HMRC also define which jobs in the film and TV industry can be classed as freelance and which are PAYE. As new entrants, you are likely to be classed as PAYE and there is a lower-limit earning before having to pay tax on your earnings. Visit HMRC website for more information.

Pee-wee
A type of dolly with an extendable, hydraulic arm.

Pencil
When booking crew, a production will contact crew members to 'pencil' them, i.e. reserve a date in their diary for work. It's not a commitment to ensure work, rather reserving the dates and getting first refusal on key talent. Once the job is definitely going ahead, that crew member can be 'confirmed' and the verbal commitment is made between the production and crew member.

Per Diem
Latin for 'per day'. A daily amount of money given to crew when filming away from home to cover food and drink outside of filming hours, where catering is not provided by the production. Normally distributed daily or weekly in tiny brown envelopes, all crew must sign to prove they have received their funds.

Photosonic
High-speed camera that can run at up to 1000 frames per second, so creating incredibly detailed images.

PIBS
A Production Insurance Briefing Specification is a contract drawn up between an advertising agency and commercials production company when commissioning a commercial.

Pick-ups
Pick-ups of scenes that couldn't be fitted in to the original schedule can be caught up at another point in the schedule, if time, space and location can be found. Sometimes, pick-ups are left until after the main unit is wrapped. New and replacement scenes are generally shot after principle photography, as the director might not know what they have until they see a rough cut of the edit.

Plates
Filming plain backgrounds and backdrops for the purpose of overlaying the footage with VFX, usually undertaken by specialist second unit under advice of the main unit DoP and VFX supervisor.

PL mount
PL stands for 'positive lock' and refers to the type of fitting or interface between the lens and the body of the camera. It's like screwing in a very expensive bayonet light bulb, but with more parts that lock in, and creates a very secure link between lens and camera. If a lens doesn't have a PL mount, an adaptor can connect the two.

Playback (i)
The recording equipment on set that uses a hard drive to record every take. Directors can review footage, and script supervisors can use as instant reference.

Playback (ii)
Archive or stock footage played on a TV or monitor within the shot. For film and TV drama, this footage should be cleared for use with the following rights: all media, worldwide (all territories); and in perpetuity (forever).

Post House
Company specialising in various aspects of post production including picture, sound, colour grading and, in some cases, VFX, all under one roof from offline edit to end delivery, depending on the company. Most UK post houses are based in Soho, London. Although most delivery is now tapeless, these companies were founded in the film age, in which physical film needed to be moved from one post house to another, so were grouped close together.

PPM
Pre-production meeting. A commercials PPM is a meeting between client, agency and production company prior to filming. Meetings usually take place at the agency and are used to confirm the director's vision, along with casting, locations and costume.

A film and TV drama PPM is a long meeting consisting of every HoD, held at least two days prior to filming. The first AD leads the meeting and walks through every day of the schedule, giving each HoD the opportunity to discuss the needs and requirements of their own department. Issues can then be addressed directly and, if required, the schedule can then be changed and re-issued prior to filming.

Practical lamp
A light that appears in shot, for example, a bedside table lamp that a character switches off as they get into bed. The bulb and the power source to the lamp will be part of the Gaffer's responsibility, ensuring that it illuminates to the level required for the overall lighting set up of the scene.

Pre Light/Pre Rig
A pre rig is the rigging of lights at least a day prior to filming, and usually occurs in studios rather than on locations. Electricians need to access the overhead rig to place lights, and it is a health and safety hazard for other crew to be underneath the rig at that time.

Primes
Range of lenses with a fixed focal length, as opposed to a zoom lens, which   has a variable focal length. Prime lenses are not as versatile as zoom lenses, but are often of better quality and lower cost. The designs are simpler, with fewer moving parts, and can be optimised for one particular focal length, whereas zoom lenses must function at a variety of focal lengths.

Producers Indemnity
Insurance cover for any extra expense incurred in order to complete a production following an interruption, postponement or cancellation due to such things as cast sickness, equipment damage, etc.

PSP
Devised by the Joint Industry Grading Scheme, the Production Safety Passport is an online document for technicians who require the latest health and safety training. A crew member's PSP can be updated to create a log of all their relevant training and courses, making it easy for employers to ensure they are hiring someone trained and qualified.

Public Liability Insurance
Cover for any claim made following injury caused to a third party individual or damage to third party property by the production company or its staff.

Rainbar
A device used to create the effect of rain on set. Water is pumped into one long pipe, which is raised into the air and which has several heads to disperse the water across a large area. A bowser will be required to store the water, and a pump to push it through the pipe and rainbar.

Release
When an actor has completed all of their scenes and is no longer required for the day, they are released. Actors must be released by the assistant directors, when they are sure they do not need them again later in the filming day.

Recce

Short for reconnaissance, this is a vital part of the filming process. The director, producer, PM and selected HoDs will visit a location, and the director can discuss his concept and vision. Typically, via the recce the DoP will be able to formalise a camera list, the Gaffer a lighting list and the production designer will be able to assess what is required in terms of design, construction and sets.

REH

Short for rehearsal, and used on call sheets and pre-production diaries to denote when the actors and director will be rehearsing scenes and unavailable for other departments.

Repeats

Back-up props or costume items that can be substituted in for subsequent takes. For example, if a character is required to smash a plate in a scene, multiple identical plates will be required for the possibility of several takes.

Risk assessment

A methodical and ordered assessment of any risk at a location that might jeopardise the safety and well-being of the cast, crew or general public, and must be completed for each new filming location. The RA will identify each risk, and will indicate suitable steps to minimise it. Many set-ups require simple instructions, but low loaders, stunts, armourers and SFX require their own additional sets of risk assessments.

Rolling

Term called by the first assistant director when the camera is running for a take. This alerts the rest of the crew to suspend activities until 'cut' is called. If you are working as a floor runner, you may be required to also call out 'Rolling' too, to echo the alert to the rest of the crew. Not all crew members will be on radio or close enough to the set to hear the first assistant director.

Rotoscope

An animation technique, rotoscoping is pretty much painting over the film. In the days before motion capture, animators could use rotoscopting to draw or trace over the live action frame by frame.

Rushes

The collected files, or film, shot on a given day. At the end of the filming day, all of the data is assembled, backed up and then sent to the editing department without delay. The title of the project and the post-production instructions are marked clearly on the storage blocks by the DIT; on larger productions, false names are used for safety and security reasons.

Rushes runner

A dedicated runner, charged with transporting the rushes from the hands of the DIT straight to the post-production facility.

Russian arm

Designed and built by Ukranian film engineer Anatoliy Kokush, a Russian arm is a crane mounted securely to the top of a 4x4 vehicle, allowing for dynamic shots at speed. The motion of the arm is manipulated via a specially rigged control unit in the rear of the vehicle.

Schedule

The order of filming, this is intrinsic to everything that happens on a production . It will be created by the first AD, with input from all heads of department, and is dependent on locations and artist availability.

Scrim

A scrim acts as a diffuser for lights. Instead of dimming bulbs, which can result inconsistent light, scrim sets can be placed over the front of a lamp to dampen the strength of the beam. Scrim sets come in four different grades of gauze and cover; two of the four will cover only half the lamp.

Second unit

An additional unit of crew tasked with shooting specific material for a film or TV drama. A second unit tend to shoot without the key cast, filming shots, cutaways, inserts or stunts that the main unit are not able to include in the schedule. As they generally shoot at the same time as the main unit, a second unit director will be employed. Heads of department from the main unit will be required to oversee and staff the second unit team.

Self-employed

Only specified industry roles are allowed to be registered as self-employed, and a list of those can be found on HMRC website. At the time of writing, runners are not on that list and are therefore classed as PAYE. When you do reach a grade that is considered self-employed, you must inform the HMRC and apply for an LP10 form (known as a Lorimer letter) which will declare you as having this status.

Set box

If a production office is not at unit base, a unit box is often used to transport items that need to travel between set and production. Runners are despatched to collect and drop these boxes, which can contain anything from call sheets to spare walkie-talkie batteries. The second AD receives the unit box at base and then distributes its contents accordingly.

Sharp

Camera term, relating to the sharpness (focus) of the frame.

Shooting ratio
The shooting ratio is the amount of footage shot in comparison with how much will end up on screen. As film is expensive, shooting ratio requires close scrutiny for cost purposes; with digital cameras the cost is much lower, which results in an increased shooting ratio.

Sides
The selected A5 script pages for scenes shooting on a given day which are attached to the call sheets.

Skin man/woman
Physical actor who inhabits the full body suit of a character.

Slate: scene
Slate is both another name for the clapperboard used at the beginning (or occasionally end) of a scene and the term for a camera set up. So if you have 100 different set ups to shoot, the first set up will be 'slate one' and the take number of that 'slate' will be written in a separate box on the clapperboard.

Slate: development
Producers will usually have more than one project in development at any given time, and a slate of productions is the collective noun for those projects.

Smoke
Post-production visual effects and finishing system from Autodesk.

SMPTE time code
A time code defined by the Society of Motion Picture and Television Engineers, which label individual frames of video or film.

Time codes are a form of media metadata, and are added to film, video or audio material, and provide a time reference for editing, synchronisation and identification. The invention of time code allowed modern videotape editing possible, and led eventually to the creation of non-linear editing systems.

Speed
Sometimes called 'sound at speed'; this is relayed by the sound mixer to the unit when preparing for a take, to indicate that they are ready for the take. The term 'speed' originates from the days of celluloid film-making, when the spools of the sound tape recording was synchronised with the camera.

Spotting
A process used in post-production sound to identify (or 'spot') where the sound cues are required for music, ADR, sound effects, etc. The director will sit with the sound editor and watch the locked picture, making extensive notes on the cues required.

Squib
A small explosive containing fake blood which will erupt on contact to represent bullet impacts on objects and individuals. The squib is controlled remotely and is explosive enough to rip through clothes. Object squibs can be built into sets, props or false walls.

Stage
Studio.

Stand in
A body double who helps camera and lighting prepare for a shot without needing to call on the actors. They literally 'stand in' the actor's mark to help with blocking, focus and camera movement.

Stand-by (i)
Dedicated individuals from various departments, but is most usually a stand-by art director. Stand-bys are on constant call for the needs of the set, managing props, continuity and practical equipment. Vigilance and anticipation is required, as is keeping cool under pressure.

Stand-by (ii)
A common term while using a walkie-talkie. Usually a response to a call for an update; you request the caller to 'stand-by' while you ask or clarify something before giving them a response.

Strike
To remove items from a set, or remove a set completely.

Symphony
Online editing software by AVID.

Talent
Actors

Tank
Specifically designed tanks for underwater or on-water filming; larger tanks will also have a blue-screen backdrop.

Ten-One
Covert AD speak for going to the toilet to spare blushes.

Ten-Two
Covert AD speak for a longer visit to the bathroom.

Three-axis head
A camera mount that will attach to the end of a crane or arm. The axis of a head refers to the direction it can move in: a one-axis head will move side to side; a two-axis head will be able to move side to side and up to down; and a three-axis head can spin around in all directions.

Three-phase
The description given to a type of power output. Three-phase power from a genny produces an even and balanced type of electricity, meaning that you can charge a mobile phone and power a 12k lamp from the same genny.

Three-way
One trailer split into three sections to house supporting leads.

Time lapse
A camera technique where film is caught at a very slow rate over a long period of time, to be played back at a faster rate.

Timeline
When piecing the film together, the editor will arrange all of their shots in order using post production software. The timeline is where the edit takes shape.

Time off the clock
The rest period between two consecutive days working on the same production must be 11 hours, the minimum required by the European Working Time Directive, and this is referred to as 'time off the clock'. A production should be charged if they don't adhere to the directive.

Time Slice
A unique special effect that appears to slow down time, as famously used in the Matrix films. The Time Slice effect is created by positioning a long line of cameras an equal distance apart, each one capturing an image either at the same time or sequentially in just milliseconds. Once the images are assembled they give the impression of super-slow motion, and it looks like the camera is swooping around the action at a normal or fast rate.

Travel day

When crew are required to travel a long distance for filming they are paid for the day of travel, usually at their daily rate.

Travelling

A term used on the walkie-talkie to indicate that you are on the move, usually towards the set. It's an update to let the AD department know you are en route.

Travel itinerary

A detailed series of instructions for an individual crew member's travel. It will contain all relevant details including unit driver; taxi, flight or train information; car service or collection at destination; and hotel details. The document is created by the travel coordinator, APC or production coordinator and distributed to the necessary people.

Turn-over

When the camera has begun to record or film the action. When preparing for a take, each department will declare their readiness for the action by calling out their status. 'Turn-over' will be called out by a member of the camera team to indicate that camera is recording, and the first AD may then call 'action'.

Turnaround: script

When a project in development moves from the ownership of one organisation to another. Usually, productions are developed with a studio or production company and if, for whatever reason, that relationship stops, the project is deemed to be 'in turnaround' until it finds a new home for development and production.

Turnaround: schedule

Each member of crew should have at least 11 hours off before returning to filming, and should not be asked to break this 'turnaround' period. For example, if filming wraps at 7pm, the production company are not legally allowed to ask you to work again before at least 6am the following day.

TX

Transmission: the actual broadcast time of a programme

Unit base

A secure area of assembled location vehicles, from which cast and crew travel out short distances to locations. Vehicles will often be aligned to create a perimeter, with all doors opening inwards, so creating a temporary compound.

Unit sign
Fluorescent arrow sign pointing towards your unit base/location, usually fixed around lamp-posts. Each production has its own short-name version printed on it to avoid confusion with other productions. Some London boroughs do not permit unit signs as too many are left *in situ* after filming.

Use fee
The total fee for an on-screen performer, including repeats, volume of TXs.

Video village
A designated area of the set where playback monitors and recorders are placed. In commercials, a separate video village is often created for the agency representatives.

Viewfinder
A director and DoP's tool, the viewfinder is a hand-held 'looking glass' used to easily determine at what angle the camera should be. Lenses can be attached to the handle if required.

Vignette: grade
A technique used in the grade to draw the focus and light to a specified area of the frame. The effect creates a darker border around the edge of the frame.

Vignette: story
Essentially a small detail, exchange or moment, created by writer, director, actor or all three, which is a story within the story. A vignette usually reveals much about the characters.

VISA
A VISA is an authority issued by the embassy/consulate of a country that permits a traveller to visit that particular country. The majority of visas are stamped inside your passport, while some are either separate documents or issued electronically. Visas are issued with specific limitations regarding purpose of visit and length of stay, and it is the traveller's responsibility to obtain necessary visas for their travel itinerary.

Walkie-Talkies
Good communication is the most essential part of the film-maker's kit, and walkie-talkies are central. 'Walkies' can have up to 15 channels and, with covert kits fitted, enable a film crew to talk from department to department without interruption. On long-format productions, channels are allocated to each department, for example, channels one and two for assistant directors, three for electrical department, four for camera, etc.

Wedges
Door stops used by grips in conjunction with pagannini's (pags) to level out dolly track.

Wetdown
Hosing an area down with water to give the appearance of recent rainfall.

Wild tracks
Sound recording when there is no camera filming. Often used for atmosphere and additional dialogue *in situ*.

Winnie
Winnebago: a travelling motor home. Usually reserved for the actors, directors and assorted head honcho's; winnies range in size and facilities.

Wrap
The end of the working day. The unit will wrap within the normal deadlines, but individuals may be wrapped throughout the working day. Actors or crew who are not required for other scenes or those who charge by the hour, such as vets, can be let go early. Production companies and assistant directors should ensure they are fully informed of the start time and wrap time of everyone on set, as the official leaving time is used to cross-check against invoices. A second AD will usually compile a report and submit it at the end of the working day.

Associations, Guilds and Organisations

All details correct at the time of going to press

ACTA
Animal Consultants and Trainers Association
01753 683 773
info@acta4animals.com
www.acta4animals.info

Advertising Association
7th Floor North Artillery House
11-19 Artillery Row
London SW1P 1RT
020 7340 2651
aa@adassoc.org.uk
www.adassoc.org.uk

Advertising Producers Association
47 Beak Street
London W1F 9SE
020 7434 2651
info@a-p-a.net
www.a-p-a.net

Assistant Directors Association
admin@adauk.org
www.adauk.org

AMPAS (Association of Motion Picture Arts & Sciences)
21 Stephen Street
London W1T 1LN
events.london@oscars.org
www.oscars.org

Association of Motion Picture Sound
27 Old Gloucester Street
London WC1N 3AX
01753 669 111
admin@amps.net
www.amps.net

Arts Council England
London office: 21 Bloomsbury Street
London WC1B 3HF
London
SW1P 3NQ
0845 300 6200
chiefexecutive@artscouncil.org.uk   www.artscouncil.org.uk

Association of Camera Operators
020 3397 0775
president@theACO.net
www.theaco.net

BAFTA
195 Piccadilly
London W1J 9LN
020 7734 0022
info@bafta.org
www.bafta.org

BECTU
373-377 Clapham Road
London SW9 9BT
020 7346 0900
info@bectu.org.uk
www.bectu.org.uk

British Kinematograph Sound & Television Society
Pinewood Studios
Pinewood Road
Iver Heath
Bucks SL0 0NH
01753 656656
info@bskts.com
www.bksts.com

British Board Of Film Classification
020 7440 1570
feedback@bbfc.co.uk
www.bbfc.co.uk

British Council Film Department
10 Spring Gardens
London SW1A 2BN
020 7389 4385
arts@britishcouncil.org
www.britishcouncil.org/

British Film Commission
The Arts Building
Morris Place
London N4 3JG
020 7613 7675
enquiries@britishfilmcommission.org.uk
www.britishfilmcommission.org.uk

British Film Designers Guild
Pinewood Studios
Pinewood Road
Iver Heath SL0 0NH
07823 348 431
info@filmdesigners.co.uk
www.filmdesigners.co.uk

British Society Of Cinematographers
North Lodge
Pinewood Studios
Pinewood Road
Iver Heath SL0 0NH
01753 888 052
office@bscine.com
www.bscine.com/

Casting Directors Guild
www.thecdg.co.uk

Cinema & Television Benevolent Fund
22 Golden Square
London W1F 9AD
020 7437 6567
info@ctbf.co.uk
www.ctbf.co.uk

Creative Diversity Network
officeadmin@creativediversitynetwork.com
www.creativediversitynetwork.org

Creative England
0844 824 6042

info@creativeengland.co.uk   www.creativeengland.co.uk

Creative England: Regional Offices

Bristol
1st Floor College House, 32-36 College Green
Bristol, BS1 5SP

Elstree Studios
Shenley Road, Borehamwood
Hertfordshire, WD6 1JG

Salford
Pod 52, The Greenhouse
Media City UK
Salford, M50 2EQ

Sheffield
The Electric Works
Sheffield, S1 2BJ

Creative Industries Federation
90 Long Acre
Covent Garden
London WC2E 9RZ
info@creativeindustriesfederation.com
http://www.creativeindustriesfederation.com

Creative Scotland
Waverley Gate, 2-4 Waterloo Place
Edinburgh EH1 3EG
0330 333 2000
enquiries@creativescotland.com
www.creativescotland.com

Department for Culture, Media and Sport
100 Parliament Street
London SW1A 2BQ
020 7211 6000
enquiries@culture.gov.uk
www.culture.gov.uk

Directors Guild Of Great Britain
Studio 24
Royal Victoria Patriotic Building
John Archer Way
London SW18 3SX
020 7240 0009
info@dggb.org
www.dggb.org

Directors UK
8-10 Dryden Street
London WC2E 9NA
020 7240 0009
info@directorsuk.com
https://www.directors.uk.com/

Documentary Filmmakers Group (Now part of the European Documentary Network)
edn@edn.dk
http://www.edn.dk/

Equity
Guild House
Upper St. Martins Lane
London WC2H 9EG
020 7379 6000
info@equity.org.uk
www.equity.org.uk
Check website for regional offices

Film Distributors' Association
22 Golden Square
London W1F 9JW
020 7437 4383
www.launchingfilms.com

Federation of Commercial Audiovisual Libraries (FOCAL)
79 College Road
Harrow HA1 1BD
020 3178 3535
info@focalint.org
www.focalint.org

Guild Of British Camera Technicians
020 8813 1999
admin@gbct.org
www.gbct.org

Guild Of British Film & Television Editors
72 Pembroke Road
London W8 6NX
01531 636 318
secretary@gbfte.org
http://www.gbfte.org/

Guild of Stunt & Action Coordinators
72 Pembroke Road
London W8 6NX
01531 636 318
stunts.uk@btinternet.com   http://www.stuntguild.org.uk/

Guild Of Television Cameramen
Briar Cottage
Holyhead Road
Llanfairpwll
Gwynedd LL61 5YX
0300 111 4123
administration@gtc.org.uk
www.gtc.org.uk

Institute Of Professional Sound
PO Box 208
Havant PO9 9BQ
0300 4008 427
secretariat@ibs.org.uk
www.ips.org.uk

Joint Industries Grading Scheme
http://jigs.org.uk

National Association of Screen Make-up and Hairdressers
91 Carlton Road
Walton-on-Thames
Surrey KT12 2DQ
01932 660 935
info@nasmah.co.uk   www.nasmah.co.uk

Producers Alliance for Cinema and Television
3rd Floor, Fitzrovia House
153-157 Cleveland St
London W1T 6QW
020 7380 8230
info@pact.co.uk   http://www.pact.co.uk

Production Managers Association
Ealing Studios
Ealing Green
London W5 5EP
020 8758 8699
pma@pma.org.uk   www.pma.org.uk

PRS for Music
2 Pancras Square
London N1C 4AG
020 7580 5544
www.prsformusic.com

Royal Television Society
3 Dorset Rise
London EC4Y 8EN
020 7822 2810
info@rts.org.uk
www.rts.org.uk

Creative Skillset
020 7713 9800
info@creativeskillset.org
http://creativeskillset.org/

Steadicam Guild
www.steadicamoperators.org

The Production Guild
Room 329, Main Admin Building
Pinewood Studios
Iver Heath SL0 0NH
01753 651 767
pg@productionguild.com
www.productionguild.com

The Writers' Guild Of Great Britain
134 Tooley Street
London SE1 2TU
020 7833 0777
adminwritersguild.org.uk   www.writersguild.org.uk

UK Screen Association
2nd Floor
Waverley House
7-12 Noel Steet
London W1F 8GQ
020 7734 6060
www.ukscreenassociation.co.uk

Vision Mixers Guild
PO Box 15678
Bromsgrove B60 9GN
www.visionmixers.tv

Women In Film And Television
92/93 Great Russell Street
London WC1B 3PS
020 7287 1400
info@wftv.org.uk
www.wftv.org.uk

Apps, Articles, Blogs, Podcasts & Publications

Publication / Websites

American Cinematographer	www.theasc.com
British Cinematographer	www.britishcinematographer.co.uk
Broadcast Magazine	www.broadcastnow.co.uk
Campaign Magazine (Advertising)	www.campaignlive.co.uk
Cineuropa	www.cineuropa.org
Cinema Blend	www.cinemablend.com
Creative Review (Advertising)	www.creativereview.co.uk
Deadline (US and International)	www.deadline.com
Empire	www.empireonline.com
IndieWire	www.indiewire.com
Little Black Book (Advertising)	www.lbbonline.com
Make Up Artist Magazine	https://makeupmag.com/
Moviescope Magazine	www.moviescopemag.com
No Film School	http://nofilmschool.com
Prolific North	www.prolificnorth.co.uk/category/news/broadcasting
Screen	www.screendaily.com
Shots Magazine (Advertising)	www.shots.net
Sight & Sound Magazine	www.bfi.org.uk/news-opinion/sight-sound-magazine
Stage Screen and Radio	Available to BECTU members
Televisual Magazine	www.televisual.com
The Drum	www.thedrum.com
The Guardian (media section)	www.theguardian.com/uk/media
The Hollywood Reporter (US)	www.hollywoodreporter.com
The Verge (Tech)	www.theverge.com
The Wrap	www.thewrap.com
Variety (US)	www.variety.com
TV Wise	www.TVwise.co.uk
4RFV News	www.4rfv.co.uk

Blogs And Websites

Academy Originals www.youtube.com/user/AcademyOriginals
Video archive from AMPAS

American Film Institute www.youtube.com/user/afi
YouTube channel from the AFI archive

ArtDepartmental www.artdepartmental.com

AVID blogs www.avidblogs.com
Interviews and articles with the world's leading editors and sound editors

BAFTA Guru www.youtube.com/user/BAFTAGuru
Talks and interviews from BAFTA

The Black and Blue www.theblackandblue.com
Blog and resources from California-based camera assistant

The Black List www.blcklst.com
Screenwriting treasure trove

BSC Vimeo Channel https://vimeo.com/bscine
British Society of Cinematographers member interviews

Clothes on Film www.clothesonfilm.com

Cinephilia and Beyond www.cinephiliabeyond.org/
Articles and interviews about the art of cinema

Cinesummit www.cinesummit.com

Craft Truck www.crafttruck.com
Conversations and interviews with leading US pro film-makers

David Thomas www.davidthomasmedia.com/index.aspx
Business and career advice for freelancers

Delamar Academy (Make-up) www.delamaracademy.co.uk/blog

DP/30 www.youtube.com/user/TheHotButton
Archive of interviews

Dollygrippery www.dollygrippery.net

Done Deal Pro www.donedealpro.com
Film deals and screenwriting

Emtacs http://www.emtacs.co.uk/forms-links-deadlines/
Newsletters, including Information on tax, VAT, NI and more from a specialist accountancy firm

FilmSound.org www.filmsound.org

Doug Richardson www.dougrichardson.com
Scriptwriting advice and resources

Editors Guild (US) www.editorsguild.com/FromTheGuild.cfm
Archive of news, interviews and articles; mostly US-based

Filmmaker IQ www.filmmakeriq.com

Filmmaker Magazine www.filmmakermagazine.com

Frocktalk http://frocktalk.com/
Blog: Celebrating the art of costume design in motion pictures

Get into Film www.youtube.com/user/getintofilm
Companion YouTube channel for Into Film

Into Film www.intofilm.org
Educational charity for young film-makers

It's a First AD Thing www.goingforpicture.tumblr.com
US based AD blog

John August www.johnaugust.com
Scriptwriting advice and resources

Johnny Elwyn www.jonnyelwyn.co.uk
Post-production blog

Mentorless http://www.mentorless.com
Indie Filmmaking blog

Philip Shelley www.script-consultant.co.uk

Set Lighting Blog (US) *http://setlighting.tumblr.com/*
Hollywood Gaffer blogs about lighting techniques and working on set

Simon Wright www.youdbetterwork.com
Advice for working in TV, but many salient points that apply to film and drama

So You Want to Work in Movies? (US) www.cineman.co.uk

Stephen Follows www.stephenfollows.com
Producer and blogger

Straight Cut Blog www.manhattaneditworkshop.blogspot.co.uk
New York-based edit blog

Terry Rossio www.wordplayer.com/company
Scriptwriting advice and resources

Yvonne Grace www.scriptadvice.wordpress.com
Screenwriter and script consultant

Books

Will Judge, *Film Runner* (2010).
Mike Goodridge & Tim Grierson, *FilmCraft: Cinematography* (Ilex Press, 2012).
Deborah Nadoolman Landis, *FilmCraft: Costume Design* (Ilex Press, 2012).
Mike Goodridge, *FilmCraft: Directing* (Ilex Press, 2012.)
Justin Chang, *FilmCraft: Editing* (Ilex Press, 2012).
Geoffrey McNab & Sharon Stewart, *FilmCraft: Producing* (Ilex Press, 2012).
Fionnuala Halligan, *FilmCraft: Production Design* (Ilex Press, 2012).
Tim Grierson, *FilmCraft: Screenwriting* (Ilex Press, 2012).
Walter Murch, *In the Blink of an Eye: A perspective on Film Editing* (Silman-James Press, 2001).
John Yorke, *Into the Woods* (Penguin Books, 2014).
Liz Gill, *Running the Show: The Essential Guide to being a First Assistant Director* (Focal Press, 2012).
Penny Delamar, *The Complete Make Up Artist* (Cengage Learning, 2015).
Gerald Millerson, *Lighting for Film and TV* (FOCAL Press, 1999).
Robert Evans, *The Kid Stays in the Picture* (Hyperion, 1994).
William Goldman, *Adventures in the Screen Trade: A personal view of Hollywood* (Abacus, 1996).
William Goldman, *Which Lie Did I Tell?* (Bloomsbury, 2001).
Robert McKee, *Story* (Harper Collins, 2010)

Apps

Search and download via the app store online.

Continuity Board Pro
Mood Board
iAnnotate
Map-A-Pic

Software

NOTE: you do NOT need to purchase this software, but you can research them online. Most of software and companies listed below are used industry-wide

Final Draft www.finaldraft.com
Screenwriting software

Media Composer www.avid.com/UK/products/media-composer
Editing software

MovieMagic www.ep.com/scheduling
Scheduling software

Pro Tools www.avid.com/UK/products/family/Pro-Tools
Post-production audio software

Scenechronize www.ease.com/scenechronize
Secure file-sharing software specifically used by film production (currently used by Netflix productions)

Spotting Notes www.spottingnotes.com
Post-production sound software

Microsoft Office Suite
Word and Excel to write and log invoices.

Open Office
Open source alternative to Microsoft Word

Dropbox https://www.dropbox.com/
Cloud based storage

WeTransfer https://www.wetransfer.com/
For sending large files such as video or images

Radio Shows

The Film Show, BBC Radio 4
The Media Show, BBC Radio 4
The Business of Film with Mark Kermode, Radio 4 (3-part series on BBC iPlayer)

Podcasts

Most of these podcasts are US-based, but do talk about universal themes

BBC Academy Podcast
The Guru by BAFTA
Writers' Guild of GB
Broadcast: Talking TV
Sound of Cinema

The Barbican Film Podcast
The Media Show (BBC)
That Studio Show (formerly That Post Show)
Going POSTal
The Edit Bay
Digital Production BuZZ
The Cutting Room
Fitness in Post
Go Creative

Training Organisations and Job Opportunities

New entrants to the business should NOT pay online companies for access to jobs boards. Most opportunities are posted online for free.

01zero-one www.01zero-one.co.uk
Various training courses and talks

1st Option Training www.1stoptiontraining.com
Health and safety

4Talent http://4talent.channel4.com/
Channel 4 production training scheme

Amersham & Wycombe College www.amersham.ac.uk
Short courses in professional film-making with close ties to the industry

APA www.a-p-a.net/jobs
Advertising Producers Association jobs board

APATS http://www.productionguild.com/training/assistant-production-accounting-training
Assistant Production Accountant Scheme

Angels The Costumiers http://www.angels.uk.com/apprenticeships.php
Apprenticeship scheme

BAFTA Crew www.bafta.org/initiatives/supporting-talent/bafta-crew

BAFTA Guru http://guru.bafta.org/

BBC Academy www.bbc.co.uk/academy

BBC Health & Safety www.bbc.co.uk/academy/work-in-broadcast/health-and-safety/a-z
Online course

BECTU www.bectu.org.uk

BFI Film Academy www.bfi.org.uk/education-research/5-19-film-education-scheme-2013-2017/bfi-film-academy-scheme
Aimed at 16-19 year olds

BFI NET.WORK http://network.bfi.org.uk
Development fund for emerging filmmakers

BKSTS www.bksts.com/secure/training.asp

CallTime Company www.calltimecompany.com
(See Pearls of Wisdom section)

City & Guilds www.cityandguilds.com
Electrician qualification

Creative Access www.creativeaccess.org.uk

Creative England www.creativeengland.co.uk

Creative Skillset www.creativeskillset.org

Creative Sparkworks http://www.creative-sparkworks.org/
Lambeth based arts charity

Cyfle www.cyfle.co.uk
Welsh training organisation

Develop Talent www.wedeveloptalent.co.uk

Escape Studios www.escapestudios.com
Visual effects based at Pearson College, London

Explore Filmmaking www.futurelearn.com/courses/explore-filmmaking
Free online course from BFI Film Academy and NFTS (runs once a year)

Federation of Commercial Audiovisual Libraries www.focalint.org/footage-skills-and-services/training
Training in archive research and management

Floor Runners Boot Camp *www.floorrunnersbootcamp.com*

Four Corners www.fourcornersfilm.co.uk/training
Training providers in film and photography

Guild of British Camera Technicians www.gbct.org/training.html

Grand Scheme Media www.grandscheme.tv
Skillset-approved training providers and consultants

Grapevine Jobs www.grapevinejobs.com

Hiive https://app.hiive.co.uk/
Skillset backed network

Indie Training Fund www.indietralnlngfund.com

Industrial Scripts http://screenplayscripts.com

Into the Woods www.johnyorkestory.com
Run by John Yorke, founder of Company Pictures and ex-BBC Drama chief; now Managing Director of Angel Station TV and Drama Consultant to King Bert Productions

ITV Traineeships www.itvjobs.com/working-here/broadcast-and-online/news/trainees

King Rollo Films www.kingrollofilms.co.uk/training.html
Animation

MAMA Youth Project http://www.mamayouthproject.org.uk/
Industry training aimed at 18-25 year olds from diverse backgrounds

Creative Europe Desk UK http://www.creativeeuropeuk.eu/what-we-do

National Association of Screen Make-up Artists and Hairdressers www.nasmah.co.uk

National Film and Television School www.nfts.co.uk
Look for short courses

Neil Gorton School www.gortonstudio.co.uk
Prosthetics

PAM www.preciousaboutmakeup.com

People looking for TV work: Runners https://www.facebook.com/groups/tv.runners/
Facebook group. Mostly TV opportunities direct from employers, peer to peer CV review and general running advice. Read the pinned posts before you write and obey the admin rules, they are very experienced people who run it for free.

Production Design Training Course www.productiondesign.co.uk/training.php

The Production Guild www.productionguild.com
Various training courses for runners, accountants, locations and production

Production Managers Association www.pma.org.uk/other_training
Regular training courses for production

Ravensbourne College www.ravensbourne.ac.uk
Short courses

Regional Theatre, Young Directors Scheme www.rtyds.co.uk/rtyds-for-directors.php
Paid training programmes for young directors

RTS Futures www.rts.org.uk/rts-futures

Sargent-Disc http://www.sargent-disc.com/sargent-disc-uk/training.aspx
Accountancy training

Scenic Painting Course www.scenicpainters.com

Shaune Harrison Make Up Artist Academy www.shauneharrisonacademy.com

Soho Editors Training www.sohoeditors.com/uk/training

SSR www.s-s-r.com/courses.php
Digital, post-production and post-sound courses

Talking Point www.talkingpoint.uk.net

Terry Ackland-Snow www.filmdi.com
Production designer courses

thecallsheet *www.thecallsheet.co.uk*

The Unit List www.theunitlist.com/
Jobs website run by Jude Winstanley

VET Hoxton www.vet.co.uk/
Film and editing training, now owned by Molinare Post Production

Visual Impact www.visuals.co.uk/events/events.php
National hands-on camera events

Warner Bros. Creative Talent www.warnerbroscreativetalent.co.uk/Home/Opportunities

Useful Links

4RFV www.4rfv.co.uk
Online directory

Albert http://wearealbert.org
Environmental sustainability for Film and TV

BBC Academy www.bbc.co.uk/academy

BECTU (Rates) www.bectu.org.uk/advice-resources/rates
Up-to-date guidelines for individuals pay rates

BECTU's Ask First List www.bectu.org.uk/news/ssr
Trade union for Film and TV, can act on behalf of members in claims against companies and offer advice. This list highlights companies that are currently under suspicion of improper employment practises.

Behance www.behance.com
If you work in a visual department such as costume, make-up or production design, you might find it useful to present your portfolio and work on these networks. You should get in the habit of cross-promoting them, by linking from Facebook, Twitter and Linkedin.

Call Time Company www.calltimecompany.com

Channel 4 Talent http://4talent.channel4.com/

Citizens Advice Bureau www.citizensadvice.org.uk

Claim for Money www.gov.uk/make-court-claim-for-money/overview
Government guide to taking a company to a small claims court (for under £10k)

Creative Access www.creativeaccess.org.uk
Opportunities for BAME job seekers

Creative Skillset www.creativeskillset.org

Creative Toolkit www.creativetoolkit.org.uk/home

Facebook www.facebook.com
There are many informal groups on Facebook, set up to help runners get started in their careers.

Freeagent www.freeagent.com
Cloud-based accounts software for sole traders

Health and Safety Executive
www.hse.gov.uk/firstaid/first-aid-training.htm
HSE website with links to training providers in the UK. It's worth noting that first aid certificates only last three years; after the certificate expires, you are no longer viewed as qualified.
www.hse.gov.uk/entertainment/theatre-tv
Specific advice for those working in film, theatre and TV

HMRC http://webarchive.nationalarchives.gov.uk/20140109143644/http://www.hmrc.gov.uk/specialist/fi-notes-2012.pdf
Film and TV tax guidelines

Instagram www.instagram.com
Useful for presenting design and artwork, cross promote with other social networks.

ITV Apprenticeships www.itvjobs.com/working-here/apprenticeships

Kays Directory www.kays.co.uk
Online directory

The Knowledge Online www.theknowledgeonline.com
Online directory

Linkedin www.linkedin.com
There are many groups on Linkedin and it's very useful for connecting with colleagues on a more professional basis.

The Location Guide http://www.thelocationguide.com
International filming destinations and services

Metcheck www.metcheck.com
Weather report by location and hourly breakdown.

Minimum Wage Checker www.gov.uk/am-i-getting-minimum-wage
Online tool to check if you are being paid the minimum wage

Pay On Time www.payontime.co.uk/late-payment-legislation-interest-calculators
A guide to charging interest on invoices

Pinterest www.uk.pinterest.com
Useful for design departments to find reference material and present their own portfolio

Raising Films http://www.raisingfilms.com/
Blog and activist group for parents working in film and television.

Samaritans www.samaritans.org Tel: 08457 90 90 90
Never be afraid to ask someone for help.

Sky Academy https://www.skyacademy.com/whats-sky-academy

Studio Map http://www.thecallsheet.co.uk/filming-uk
Comprehensive map of the UK's leading studio facilities.

TV Watercooler www.tvwatercooler.org
Lots of useful resources, aimed primarily for those interested in working in television.
Also contains a list of companies that offer work experience placements, compiled by Lizzie Evans

Twitter www.twitter.com
Follow industry people and publications: look for #tvjobs and #filmjobs

Networking and Events:

You may need to become a member of these organisations in order to attend some of these events.

Festivals, conferences, exhibitions, events

BAFTA	www.bafta.org/whats-on
BFI Media Conference	http://www.bfi.org.uk/education-research/teaching-film-tv-media-studies/bfi-media-conference
BSC Expo	http://www.bscexpo.com
BVE	www.bvexpo.com
Cinemajam	cinemajam.com
Creative England	www.creativeengland.co.uk/events
Edinburgh International TV Festival	www.thetvfestival.com
Editfest London	americancinemaeditors.org/editfest-london
Film London	filmlondon.org.uk/industry
IBC (Holland)	www.ibc.org
IMATS	www.imats.net

(Make up trade show)

London Screenwriters Festival	www.londonscreenwritersfestival.com
Media Production Show	mediaproductionshow.com
Meetup.com -	www.meetup.com

(There are several groups currently listed for informal meet ups on an ad hoc basis. Search for groups near you and make sure you research them thoroughly.)

Open Doors	https://app.hiive.co.uk/swarms/tech-connect-london/68/#/

(Series of events for 16-30 year olds, with creative companies and freelancers)

Salford Media Festival	www.salfordmediafestival.co.uk
Screen Summit	www.screenfilmsummit.com/home
Soho Create Festival	www.sohocreate.co.uk
Sprocket Rocket Soho	www.sprocketrocketsoho.com
SIGGRAPH	https://london.siggraph.org/

(CGI festival based in LA with satellite events around the world)

Televisual Factual Festival	http://www.televisual.com/festival/
Total Focus Expo	www.totalfocusexpo.com
VFX Festival	www.thevfxfestival.com
Victoria & Albert Museum	https://shop.vam.ac.uk/whatson

(Talks and exhibitions about fashion, costume, design and art)

WFTV	www.wftv.org.uk/news-and-events/calendar

Acknowledgements

My most sincere thanks to Nikki Baughan, copy editor extraordinaire, Samantha Chiles for proofreading and Maggie Roxburgh for formatting

Thanks to everyone involved in this book for their wisdom, support and advice, including:

Catherine, Martha and Joe Gallagher; Carol & Eugene Gallagher; Douglas Cameron (DCMS); Nick Maine (BFI); Simon Fathers, Creative Skillset; BFI; Sally Lock; Catherine Hall; Entertainment Partners; Michael K. Wofford; Patrick James Stephens; John Yorke; Professional Writing Academy; Stephen Follows; Dr Kion Ahadi; Ian Palmer; Frankie Ferrari; Ian & Bethan Pearce; Iain Macintosh; Ian Sharples; Nadiya Luthra; Nick Ferguson; Shaun Nickless, Adam Birley, Miguel Zenha; Will Judge; Charlie Phillips; Matt Rothwell; Kenneth O'Toole; Dr Jago Ridout; James Mackie; James Johnson; Jess Lenton; Susie Gordon; Eugene Costello; Alison Williams; Josh Llewellyn; Carola Ash; Tom Swayne; Mick Audsley; Phil Brown; Jonathan Lewsley; Carly Gilbert; Lizzie Evans Stephen Follows; Jacqui Taunton Fenton; Rinaldo Quacquarini; Vicki Allen; Tamana Bleasdale; Ole Mienert; Stephen Haren; Dan Bourke; Charlie Freemantle; Yuen-Wai Liu; Nicky Ball; Pip Day; Sian Fever; Duncan Burbridge: Ian Differ; Justin Summers; Amy Johnson; everyone at The Third Floor: Alex Deller; Brashna Agha; Tom Avison; Abigail Berry; Bridget Hayes of Audiosend; Mark Watson; Caroline Fleming; Vicky Winter; Allison Dowzell; Steve Hetherington; Tony Carter; everyone at *thecallsheet.co.uk* and all the members of *thecallsheet.co.uk* for teaching me things whether you knew it or not.

Thanks to LCD Soundsystem, Philip Glass, The National and The Craig Charles Funk & Soul Show for providing the soundtrack to most of the writing, rewriting and editing of this book.

And a huge thanks to all of our interviewees and contributors to the Pearls of Wisdom.

Thanks to AVID for providing feedback for this book. A particular thank you to Stephanie Genin and Keri Middleton, for their support.

Avid Media Composer is the ubiquitous editing software used in the film and TV drama industry; indeed, it is easier to count the productions that do not use Avid products than those that do. Their intuitive software and workflow compatibility has been shaped using feedback from users. If you aim to work in post-production, it is certain that you will come into contact with Avid Media Composer and Pro Tools; take a look at the Avid UK website to find out more about the software (**www.avid.com/uk**)

Avid, Media Composer and Pro Tools are trademarks or registered trademarks of Avid Technology, Inc. or its subsidiaries in the United States and/or other countries.

Bibliography

BECTU Tax guide for Freelancers, 2012
https://www.bectu.org.uk/advice-resources/tax-guide

BECTU
https://www.bectu.org.uk/home

BFI Statistical Yearbook 2014
http://www.bfi.org.uk/sites/bfi.org.uk/files/downloads/bfi-statistical-yearbook-2014.pdf

The British Film and Televsion Industries – Decline or Opportunity? House of Lords Select Committee (Vol. 1, 2010)
http://www.publications.parliament.uk/pa/ld200910/ldselect/ldcomuni/37/37i.pdf

The British Film and Television Industries, Communications Committee – House of Lords Communications Act 2003
http://www.publications.parliament.uk/pa/ld200910/ldselect/ldcomuni/37/3702.htm

Cut Out of the Picture: A study of gender inequality among directors within the UK film industry by Stephen Follows and Alexis Kreager
https://www.directors.uk.com/news/cut-out-of-the-picture

Succès de plume? Female Screenwriters and Directors of UK Films, 2010-2012 by David Steele (BFI)
http://www.bfi.org.uk/sites/bfi.org.uk/files/downloads/bfi-report-on-female-writers-and-directors-of-uk-films-2013-11.pdf

Douglas Cameron, DCMS**,** *Creative Industries – Focus on Employment* (June 2014).
https://www.gov.uk/government/uploads/system/uploads/attachment_data/file/324530/Creative_Industries_-_Focus_on_Employment.pdf

Film, Television and Production Industry Guidance Notes published by HMRC
http://webarchive.nationalarchives.gov.uk/20140109143644/http://www.hmrc.gov.uk/specialist/fi-notes-2012.pdf

Film London
http://filmlondon.org.uk

Higher Education Statistics Agency
https://www.hesa.ac.uk/

History of public service broadcasting in the UK – Parliament
http://www.publications.parliament.uk/pa/ld200910/ldselect/ldcomuni/37/3707.htm

Jean-Claude Marquie, Philip Tucker, Simon Folkard, Catherine Gentil and David Ansiau, *Chronic effects of shift work on cognition: findings from the VISAT longitudinal study* by (Université Toulouse, 2014).
http://oem.bmj.com/content/early/2014/10/08/oemed-2013-101993.abstract

Mediateque, *From the Cottage to the City: the Evolution of the UK Independent Production Sector.* (Report commissioned by the BBC, 2005).
http://downloads.bbc.co.uk/aboutthebbc/insidethebbc/howwework/reports/pdf/independent_production.pdf

ONS – Office for National Statistics
http://www.ons.gov.uk

Richard Tait, *Margaret Thatcher and Media Policy* (Cardiff University, School of Journalism, Media and Cultural Studios).
http://www.cardiff.ac.uk/jomec/jomecjournal/3-june2013/Tait_Thatcher.pdf

Sector insights: skills and performance challenges in the digital and creative sector from the UK Commission for Employment and Skills (June 2015)
https://www.gov.uk/government/uploads/system/uploads/attachment_data/file/433755/Skills_challenges_in_the_digital_and_creative_sector.pdf

Skillset 2012 & 2016 Employment Census
http://creativeskillset.org/assets/0000/5070/2012_Employment_Census_of_the_Creative_Media_Industries.pdf
http://creativeskillset.org/assets/0002/0952/2015_Creative_Skillset_Employment_Survey_-_March_2016_Summary.pdf

Skillset Workforce Survey
http://creativeskillset.org/assets/0001/0465/Creative_Skillset_Creative_Media_Workforce_Survey_2014.pdf

We Are UK Film
http://www.weareukfilm.com

Warc
http://www.warc.com

Ed Catmull with Amy Wallace, *Creativity, Inc: Overcoming the unseen forces that stand in the way of true inspiration* (Random House, 2014.)

Jack Cardiff, *The Magic Hour* (Faber & Faber, 1997).

James Mackie, *Living on the Edge? A study of freelance workers in UK Film and TV – How do they survive and why do they carry on?* (University of Leicester, 2015).

Laszlo Bock, *Work Rules* (Twelve, 2015).

Malcolm Gladwell, *Outliers* (Penguin Books, 2009).

Nick Davies, *Hack Attack: How the truth caught up with Rupert Murdoch* (Random House, 2014).

Oliver & Ohlbaum Associates Ltd. (prepared by), *Estimating the economic contribution of independent production outside London. A report for PACT* (May 9, 2013).

Stephen Follows
https://stephenfollows.com/

The Economic History of the International Film Industry
Gerben Bakker, University of Essex
http://eh.net/encyclopedia/the-economic-history-of-the-international-film-industry/

A Brief History of the Rank Organisation
https://vciclassicfilms.wordpress.com/rank/

Historical Dictionary of British Cinema by Alan Burton, Steve Chibnall
(The Scarecrow Press, 2013).

92669338R00176

Made in the USA
Columbia, SC
29 March 2018